MANAGING
INTERCULTURAL
CONFLICT
EFFECTIVELY

Communicating Effectively
in Multicultural Contexts

Series Editors: William B. Gudykunst and Stella Ting-Toomey

Department of Speech Communication
California State University, Fullerton

The books in this series are designed to help readers communicate effectively in various multicultural contexts. Authors of the volumes in the series translate relevant communication theories to provide readable and comprehensive descriptions of the various multicultural contexts. Each volume contains specific suggestions for how readers can communicate effectively with members of different cultures and/or ethnic groups in the specific contexts covered in the volume. The volumes should appeal to people interested in developing multicultural awareness or improving their communication skills, as well as anyone who works in a multicultural setting.

Volumes in this series

1. **BRIDGING JAPANESE/NORTH AMERICAN DIFFERENCES**
   William B. Gudykunst and Tsukasa Nishida

2. **INTERCULTURAL COMMUNICATION TRAINING:**
   An Introduction
   Richard W. Brislin and Tomoko Yoshida

3. **EFFECTIVE COMMUNICATION IN MULTICULTURAL
   HEALTH CARE SETTINGS**
   Gary L. Kreps and Elizabeth N. Kunimoto

4. **MULTICULTURAL PUBLIC RELATIONS:**
   A Social-Interpretive Approach
   Stephen P. Banks

5. **COMMUNICATING EFFECTIVELY WITH THE CHINESE**
   Ge Gao and Stella Ting-Toomey

6. **MANAGING INTERCULTURAL CONFLICT EFFECTIVELY**
   Stella Ting-Toomey and John G. Oetzel

MANAGING INTERCULTURAL CONFLICT EFFECTIVELY

Stella Ting-Toomey • John G. Oetzel

Sage Publications
International Educational and Professional Publisher
Thousand Oaks ▪ London ▪ New Delhi

For information:

Sage Publications, Inc.
2455 Teller Road
Thousand Oaks, California 91320
E-mail: order@sagepub.com

Sage Publications Ltd.
6 Bonhill Street
London EC2A 4PU
United Kingdom

Sage Publications India Pvt. Ltd.
M-32 Market
Greater Kailash I
New Delhi 110 048 India

Printed in the United States of America

Library of Congress Cataloging-in-Publication Data

Ting-Toomey, Stella.
 Managing intercultural conflict effectively / by Stella Ting-Toomey
and John G. Oetzel.
     p. cm. — (Communicating effectively in multicultural contexts ; v. 6)
 Includes bibliographical references and index.
   ISBN 0-8039-4842-5 (cloth : acid-freee paper) — ISBN 0-8039-4843-3
 (pbk. : acid-free paper)
   1. Culture conflict. 2. Intercultural communication. 3. Social
 conflict. 4. Ethnic conflict. 5. Interpersonal conflict. I. Oetzel,
 John G. II. Title. III. Series.
   HM1121 .T56 2001
   303.48′2—dc21   2001000351

01 02   03   04   05   06   10 9 8 7 6 5 4 3 2 1

Acquiring Editor: Margaret H. Seawell
Editorial Assistant: Alicia Carter
Production Editor: Claudia A. Hoffman
Editorial Assistant: Kathryn Journey
Copy Editor: Amy Kazilsky
Typesetter: Rebecca Evans
Indexer: Molly Hall
Cover Designer: Jane M. Quaney

CONTENTS

LIST OF FIGURES
AND TABLES

List of Figures

List of Tables

PREFACE

This book grew out of our own search for a culture-sensitive text to teach intercultural conflict at the undergraduate level. Although there exist several excellent conflict texts on interpersonal conflict, there is a scarcity of texts that deal directly with the theme of intercultural conflict process. Intercultural conflict process often starts with different culture-based expectations of how a misunderstanding should be handled. If the different cultural parties continue to engage in ethnocentric ways of approaching the disagreement or misunderstanding, the initial cultural collusion can easily spiral into a complex, polarized conflict situation. Conflict is indeed a cultural challenge and, simultaneously, an opportunity for us to learn about diverse approaches in framing a conflict situation and in honing our constructive conflict management skills.

Unfortunately, as we searched for a sound conflict text that includes a strong cultural perspective in examining a variety of conflict issues and contexts, we came up short. This void led us to work on this book project for the past several years. Based on our combined research interest in intercultural-intimate conflict and small-group/organizational conflict, we were able to work collaboratively to distill the best ideas in our own thinking and present them to you.

We have written this book for individuals who would like to better understand the intercultural conflict process. We believe in the importance of incorporating theoretically based research work in the text. We intend the text to be used in conflict management classes at the undergraduate (or beginning graduate) level or as a supplemental text to existing intercultural or interpersonal communication classes. Thus, we have attempted to write in a straightforward, accessible style. We believe that in a good undergraduate conflict text, the theoretical and practical aspects of intercultural conflict management should blend nicely together. Without a coherent theory, the book may consist of scattered ideas in different chapters. Without practice, the theory may stay on a highly abstract level with no concrete guidance or direction to reinforce the theoretical ideas. In writing this book, we worked toward a balanced approach in synthesizing theories and research-based studies with recommended conflict skills and practice. The book should serve as a useful resource for intercultural professionals and conflict practitioners who are interested in understanding the intercultural conflict process in more depth.

This book is organized into six chapters. Chapter 1 presents four practical reasons for why we should pay special attention to intercultural conflict. Terms such as *culture* and *intercultural conflict* are defined. The chapter ends with seven key assumptions about the study of intercultural conflict and highlights the importance of developing systems consciousness in mindfully managing intercultural conflict. Chapter 2 maps out a new model, the culture-based situational conflict model, which consists of four components: culture-based primary orientation factors, situational features, conflict process factors, and conflict competence criteria and outcomes. The model emphasizes the importance of understanding conflict from a cultural variability perspective. Cultural values such as individualism-collectivism and power distance shape our initial expectations, attitudes, emotional reactions, face concerns, and behaviors toward approaching or avoiding a conflict. Concurrently, situational features such as perceived ingroup-outgroup boundaries (e.g., ethnocentrism and prejudice), relationship parameters, conflict goal assessments, and conflict intensity serve as mediating variables between the primary orientation factors on one hand and the conflict process factors on the other. The chapter ends with a discussion of four conflict competence criteria: appropriateness, effectiveness, satisfaction, and productivity. Chapter 3 extends the culture-based situational conflict model with concrete examples and critical incidents concerning intercultural-intimate conflicts. More specifically, situational features such as ethnocentric lenses and biased interpersonal attributions, prejudice and racism issues, and different intimate conflict goals are discussed. Process factors such as intimate conflict expressions and relational conflict responses are explained. The chapter ends with a set of practical guidelines for dealing with intercultural-intimate conflict effectively.

Chapter 4 addresses the complex topic of intercultural small-group conflict. The reasons for the complexity of small group conflict are probed. From a systems perspective, group input factors such as culturally diverse small-group composition, social identity and proportional representation, and cultural value patterns are explained. Ample dialogue examples are used to illustrate the various frictions and misunderstandings that can arise in small group conflict process. Finally, four practical suggestions are proposed for managing conflict constructively in a culturally diverse group. Chapter 5 underscores conflict problems between managers and employees in multinational and domestic diversity organizations. A new model, the organizational conflict management model, is used to highlight four primary approaches in framing a conflict process. The four approaches are based on combined individualism-collectivism and small/large power distance value patterns. These four approaches are impartial, status-achievement, benevolent, and communal. Rich workplace examples are used to illustrate these different organizational conflict approaches. The chapter ends with a set of practical guidelines for managing conflicts between managers and employees in diverse organizations. Finally, Chapter 6 concludes with the motif of intercultural conflict competence. Three conflict competence dimensions—knowledge, mindfulness, and constructive conflict management skills—are identified. Mindfulness is viewed as the integrative hook that links culture-based knowledge with constructive conflict management skills. Altogether, 10 constructive conflict management skills are suggested: mindful observation, mindful listening, mindful reframing, identity validation, facework management, productive power balancing, collaborative dialogue, problem-solving skills, transcendent discourse, and interaction adaptability.

With mindful commitment, we believe conflict participants can transform themselves into collaborative dialogue negotiators in managing many culture-based conflict differences. With cultural sensitivity and committed practice, we believe many intercultural conflict situations can be managed competently. The book ends with an appendix that contains a multinational research project report and factor analysis results. The factor analysis results are scales that can be used to measure face and facework-related conflict behaviors. Our intention is to make those facework scales accessible for students and researchers who are interested in furthering their work on multinational or multiethnic facework and conflict styles. For conflict students who are interested in tracking some of the original sources of our work, and other preeminent researchers' work, these sources are listed in the references.

Six features distinguish this conflict book from others. First, this book offers a new model, a culture-based situational conflict model, to serve as a map and guide to help you in understanding and explaining the culture-based and situational-based factors that enter into any intercultural conflict episode. Second, this is one of the first books that clearly emphasizes the role of culture and how culture serves as the primary imprint in our habitual conflict responses. This is also one of the first books to thread through the discussion of culture in a variety of conflict contexts (e.g., intimate conflict, small group conflict, and organizational conflict). Third, although the book is theoretically directed, it is also a down-to-earth practical book that contains ample examples, conflict dialogues, and critical incidents to illustrate the complexity of intercultural conflict interaction. Fourth, specific guidelines at the end of each chapter and the competence-based perspective in the last chapter underscore the pragmatic orientation of the entire book. Fifth, the book is a multidisciplinary text that draws from the research work of a variety of disciplines such as cross-cultural psychology, social psychology, sociology, marital and family studies, international management, and communication. As such, readers gain a broad yet integrative perspective in assessing intercultural conflict situations. Last, the book is written in a clear, easy-to-understand writing style. The various figures and tables should help readers grasp the materials because of easy-to-digest summary formats.

ACKNOWLEDGMENTS

Writing this book was an exhilarating and exhausting task. We are indebted to many individuals who encouraged and motivated us to bring this book into fruition. First and foremost, we want to thank Bill Gudykunst for his unflagging support throughout the writing of this book. His thoughtful comments and insights improve the "big picture" of the book. We also want to thank Margaret Seawell, the communication editor at Sage, who shepherded the book from its manuscript form to a beautiful, well-polished book. We appreciate her gracious support and perseverance in seeing this book through to the end. In addition, we express our appreciation to Amy Kazilsky, copy editor for Sage, for her meticulous editing of our manuscript. We also want to thank our colleagues at the California State University at Fullerton and the University of New Mexico for providing a collegial environment in which to conduct our scholarly work. We want to acknowledge the "voices" of our students whom we are privileged to teach and from whom we continue to learn. Their input and questioning helped us to refine the many ideas presented in the book. We also want to acknowledge the help of Peter Lee, who assisted in the preparation of the figures in this book. Individually, there are several people in our personal and professional lives to whom we would like to express our acknowledgments.

John: I would like first to thank my partner and wife, Keri, for providing me with love, caring, and continuous support throughout the writing of this book. I also want to thank Stella for inviting me to work on this book with her. I have learned tremendously in my collaborative work with her, and she has continued to serve as a great mentor and supportive friend to me. I would also like to thank several individuals who reviewed sections of the manuscript: Curtiss Bailey, Valerie Beaubeau, Martha Chew, Britta Limary, Tomoko Masumoto, Yoshi Miike, Frank Perez, Pratibha Shukla, and Jan Woomavoya. I would also like to extend my special thanks to C. J. Ondek and Kersti Tyson, who read an entire draft of the book. I appreciate their timely feedback and invaluable suggestions.

Stella: I would like to express my appreciation to my husband Charles and son Adrian for their good humor and warm support throughout the writing of this book. Their "lighthearted" loving spirit uplifted the long hours working on this book project. I want to thank John for his commitment and patience in collaborating and writing this book with me. His professionalism and keen intellect made the collaboration an enjoyable, give-and-take learning experience. I also want to extend my special thanks to Annette Bow, Leeva Chung, Atsuko Kurogi, Peter Lee, Ramona Rose, and Jessica Tan for their constant encouragement and good cheer throughout the development of this manuscript. Finally, I want to thank California State University at Fullerton, for granting me a one-semester sabbatical leave to complete the book.

In writing this book, we have also learned more about our own culture-based conflict approaches and conflict styles. We were also made aware of the sustained commitment and effort needed to instill change and transformation in our own conflict habits and tendencies. We hope that by reading this book, some of the conflict concepts and skills will resonate with you and that you are able to creatively translate facets of the knowledge and skills into mindful conflict practice.

1

INTERCULTURAL CONFLICT

An Introduction

When people from different cultures engage in conflict, they often have different expectations of how the conflict should be handled. The underlying values and norms of a culture often frame conflict expectations. How we define the conflict problem, how we "punctuate" the differing triggering event that leads to the conflict problem, and how we view the goals for satisfactory conflict resolution are all likely to vary across cultures, situations, and individuals.

Intercultural conflict often starts with different expectations concerning appropriate or inappropriate conflict behavior in a conflict scene. If the different cultural members continue to engage in inappropriate or ineffective conflict behaviors, the miscommunication can easily spiral into a complex, polarized conflict situation. In a polarized conflict, trust and respect are often threatened, and distorted perceptions and biased attributions are likely to emerge.

As we enter the 21st century, direct contact with culturally different people in our neighborhoods, schools, and workplaces is an inescapable part of life. With immigrants and minority group members representing nearly 30% of the present workforce in the

1

United States, an understanding of competent conflict management is especially critical in today's society. Managing intercultural conflict competently means managing conflict appropriately, effectively, satisfactorily, and productively.

Although everyday intercultural conflicts are often based on cultural ignorance or misunderstanding, it is obvious that not all intercultural conflicts are based on miscommunication. Some intercultural conflicts are based on a deep-seated hatred and a centuries-old antagonism, often arising from long-standing historical grievances (e.g., as in Northern Ireland and the Middle East). However, a majority of everyday conflicts that we encounter in the workplace or interpersonal relationships can be traced to cultural misunderstanding or ignorance.

This chapter examines the reasons why we should understand intercultural conflict from a competence-based approach. This approach is developed in three sections. First, we offer several practical reasons why we should pay special attention to competent conflict management across cultures. Second, we emphasize the central role that culture plays in destructive versus constructive conflict. Third, we discuss the basic assumptions of intercultural conflict.

PRACTICAL REASONS

With rapid changes in the global economy, technology, transportation, and immigration policies, the world is becoming a small, intersecting community. We find ourselves in increased contact with people who are culturally different. In a global workforce, people bring with them different work habits and cultural practices. For example, cultural strangers may approach teamwork and problem-solving tasks differently. They may develop friendships and romantic relationships differently. They may also have different conflict needs, wants, and expectations.

The study of intercultural conflict is about the study of conflict that evolves, at least in part, because of cultural group membership differences. It is about acquiring the necessary knowledge and skills to manage such differences constructively and creatively. There are indeed many practical reasons for studying intercultural conflict management. We offer four reasons here: interpersonal relationship satisfaction, creative problem solving, the growth of the global workforce, and domestic workplace diversity.

Interpersonal Relationship Satisfaction

Conflict provides a testing ground for the resilience of our everyday relationships. According to researchers in interpersonal conflict (e.g., Cupach & Canary, 1997), it is not the frequency of conflict that determines whether we have a satisfying or dissatisfying relationship. Rather, it is the competencies that we apply in managing our conflicts that will move the relationship along a constructive or destructive path.

Conflict, when managed competently, can bring about positive changes in a relationship. It allows the conflict partners to use the conflict opportunity to reassess the state of the relationship. It opens doors for the individuals in conflict to discuss in depth their wants and needs in a relationship. It clarifies misunderstandings and strengthens common interests and goals. It also promotes individual and relationship growth.

On the other hand, incompetent conflict management affects physical and mental health. According to recent conflict research (Gottman, 1999; Siegman, 1994), negative conflict behaviors (e.g., verbal criticisms, defensiveness, anger explosion, or suppression) in marital relationships evoke hypertension and produce ulcers. Prolonged negative conflict spirals prompt poor physical and mental health. Dysfunctional conflict patterns in our intimate relationships also affect our everyday work performance.

Thus, competent conflict management is a life skill; it helps us to be in sync with others and ourselves. Competent conflict practice brings out vulnerable feelings and at the same time creates an opening for further dialogue and mutual responsiveness. Effective conflict negotiation serves as a buffer to psychological and emotional strain. It promotes an occasion for renewed connection and a quality relationship. In intercultural conflict negotiation, both cultural and interpersonal relationship factors often come into juxtaposition. Behavioral flexibility and adaptability are needed to resolve conflicts that occur, in part, because of cultural differences.

Creative Problem Solving

Competent intercultural conflict management enriches our creative problem-solving abilities. Whether we are involved in solving a multiethnic community problem, a school-based intergroup problem, or an international workplace problem, no single individual possesses the breadth and depth of knowledge to resolve an entangled conflict issue. Our ability to value different approaches to problem solving and mindfully move away from traditional either/or thinking can create and expand diverse options in managing a conflict dilemma.

According to creativity research (Sternberg, 1999; Sternberg & Lubart, 1995), we learn more from people who are different from us than from those who are similar to us. At the individual level, creativity involves a process of taking in new ideas and of being thrown into uncertainty. If the chaos or crisis is managed productively, members are often able to come up with a synergistic perspective that involves the best of all viewpoints. The word *crisis* in Chinese connotes danger and opportunity. Although a crisis creates a dangerous situation, it also develops an opportunity for reassessment and innovative planning.

At the small group research level, results indicate that although the quantity of ideas has remained the same in homogeneous and ethnically heterogeneous groups (e.g., in brainstorming solutions to a creative task), the quality of ideas has been evaluated differently. Ideas produced by ethnically diverse teams, for example, have been rated an average of 11% higher than those of homogeneous teams (McLeod, Lobel, & Cox, 1996). Furthermore, findings also indicate that highly innovative companies in the United States have taken "deliberate steps to create heterogeneous work teams with the objective of bringing different points of view to bear on problems" (Cox & Beale, 1997, p. 38). Culturally and ethnically diverse teams have the potential to solve problems creatively because of several factors. Some of these factors include a greater variety of viewpoints brought to bear on the issue, a higher level of critical analysis of alternatives, and a lower probability of groupthink due to the heterogeneous composition of the group.

Multicultural teams often benefit from different cultural responses to questions such as "What is the context that frames the conflict?" "What is the nature of the problem?" "How can we address the problem from the local culture standpoint and from the global culture framework?" "What are the viable goals and strategies in resolving this conflict from multiple cultural perspectives?" Using divergent problem-solving approaches, often, collaborative multicultural teams, with sustained commitment, can develop synergistic approaches to resolve their problems.

A cultural synergistic approach is about managing the dialectic of change and stability in a system. The synergistic approach to problem solving involves three steps: cross-cultural description, cultural interpretation, and cultural creativity. Adler (1997) explains:

> Global managers first define problems from the perspectives of all cultures involved. Second, they analyze the patterns that make each culture's behavior logical from within its own perspective. Third, they create solutions that foster the organization's effectiveness and productivity without violating the norms of any culture involved. (p. 118)

A cultural synergistic approach requires a fresh mind-set to build on commonalities and fuse differences resulting in more effective and more satisfactory outcomes. Through combined creativity and collaborative problem-solving processes, individuals expand their outlook and options in generating solutions to a conflict problem. Local product development teams, customer service groups, marketing and sales teams, human resource groups, nonprofit organizations, and global managers and employees can all benefit from using diversity as a creative resource in solving problems.

A cultural synergistic approach, however, takes time, patience, training, and commitment to implement and develop. It involves a systematic yet creative approach to deal with hidden cultural assumptions, values, and expectations. It demands a systematic discovery of comparative perceptions and comparative intentions that underlie the problematic conflict issue (Clarke & Lipp, 1998). It is also one of many approaches that deals with diverse culture-based conflict situations. By learning about the recent advances in intercultural conflict management research, individuals can incorporate new scripts and synergistic thinking in dealing with culturally dissimilar others. Knowledge, together with competent practice on a daily basis, can help individuals in diverse groups and relationships to become constructive conflict bridge-builders across cultures.

Global Workplace

Workplace diversity on the global level represents both opportunities and challenges to individuals and organizations. Individuals in the forefront of workplace diversity must rise to the challenge of serving as global leaders to manage diversity with skill and cultural sensitivity. According to a recent Training and Development trend report (Training and Development, 1999), three competencies critical in the global workplace are communication skills, problem solving, and global leadership.

Factors that contribute to the diversity of the workforce on the global level include but are not limited to the development of communication technology (e.g., fax, e-mail, the Internet), regional trading blocs (e.g., the European Union, the North American Free Trade Agreement [NAFTA]), and immigrant worker and guest worker policies (e.g., Turkish migrant workers in Germany). A recent Office Team survey of 1,400 chief information officers indicates that 77% of respondents think that increased use of technology will require workers to communicate more effectively and articulately on the global level (Training and Development, 1999).

In this era of global economy, it is inevitable that employees and customers from dissimilar cultures are in constant contact with one another, whether it is through face-to-face or mediated contacts. Thus, intercultural communication skills remain vitally important to success in the global work environment.

In addition, a recent Workforce 2020 trend report shows that four of every five new jobs in the United States are generated as a direct result of international business. Furthermore, 33% of U.S. corporate profits are derived via import-export trade (Judy & D'Amico, 1997). Even if we do not venture out of our national borders, global economy and, hence, global contact become crucial parts of our everyday work lives. Beyond global business, increased numbers of individuals are working in overseas assignments, such as government service, humanitarian service, and international education. At home and abroad, acquiring the competencies of intercultural conflict management is a necessary first step in becoming a global citizen of the 21st century.

After surveying 75 CEOs in 28 countries in a landmark 4-year study, Rosen et al. (Rosen, Digh, Singer, & Phillips, 2000) summarize that the following four global literacies are critical in the making of an effective global leader: (a) personal literacy: understanding and valuing yourself; (b) social literacy: engaging and challenging others; (c) business literacy: focusing and mobilizing your organization; and (d) cultural literacy: valuing and leveraging cultural difference. Accurate, culture-based conflict knowledge, mindfulness, and constructive conflict management skills (see Chapter 6) are three key dimensions that we believe enhance the profile of a global-minded conflict manager. Global literacies and domestic diversity literacies are increasingly affecting one another in the workplace environment.

Domestic Workplace Diversity

The study of intercultural conflict management in the United States is especially critical for several reasons. First, immigrants (many are non-native English speakers) and minority group members will account for a third of the *new entrants* into the U.S.

workforce in the 21st century. Second, and more specifically, by 2006, African, Asian, and Latin Americans will together compose more than 30% of the general U.S. workforce. Third, skilled and highly educated immigrants (especially in the areas of computer and engineering service industries) play a critical role in U.S. advanced-technology industries.

The payrolls of leading information technology (IT) companies such as Intel and Microsoft include "many highly skilled, foreign-born employees. In their absence it would be difficult for America to regain its global lead in IT" (Judy & D'Amico, 1997, p. 21). Many U.S. immigrants have contributed positively (historically and presently) to the social and economic development of the nation. The richness of cultural diversity in U.S. society has led to many dramatic innovative breakthroughs in the fields of physics, medicine, and technology.

Inattention to diversity issues in the workplace can lead to the following costs: (a) low morale because of culture clash, (b) high absenteeism because of psychological stress, (c) substantial dollars that must be spent to retrain individuals because of high employee turnover, (d) much time wasted because of miscommunication between diverse employees, and (e) the enormous amount of personal energy expended in defensive resistance to inevitable change (Loden & Rosener, 1991). The long-term advantages of managing diversity effectively at the organizational level are (a) full use of the organization's human capital, (b) increased knowledge and enhanced mutual respect among diverse employees, (c) increased commitment among diverse employees at all organizational levels and across all functions, (d) greater innovation and flexibility as others participate more constructively in problem-solving teams, and (e) improved productivity as more employee effort is directed at achieving the system's goals and less energy is expended in dealing with cultural miscommunication issues (Loden, 1996; Loden & Rosener, 1991).

At the dawning of the 21st century, it is inevitable that we will encounter people from diverse cultures and ethnicities in our own backyards. Learning to understand such cultural differences and dealing with these differences proactively will serve as a major step toward building a more harmonious multicultural society. We have reviewed four practical reasons why the study of intercultural conflict management is an important topic. We now turn to a discussion of the critical role of culture in the conflict negotiation process.

CULTURE: A LEARNED MEANING SYSTEM

What is culture? Culture is a learned system of meanings that fosters a particular sense of shared identity and community among its group members. Members of a culture learn the meanings of right and wrong that produce particular consequences in a community. They learn the meanings or interpretations of what constitute proper and improper conflict behaviors by adhering to or deviating from such behaviors in a particular community. In sum, *culture* is defined in this book as "a learned meaning system that consists of patterns of traditions, beliefs, values, norms, and symbols that are passed on from one generation to the next and are shared to varying degrees by interacting members of a community" (Ting-Toomey, 1999, p. 10). We explore some of the key elements of culture—traditions, beliefs, values, norms, symbols, and meanings—in the following sections.

Culture: Traditions, Beliefs, and Values

Culture is like an iceberg: the deeper layers (e.g., traditions, beliefs, and values) are hidden from our view; usually, we see and hear only the uppermost layers of cultural artifacts (e.g., fashion, trends, popular music) and of verbal and nonverbal symbols. Based on observed surface-level similarities, we may hear travelers in foreign countries comment, "People in all these cultures are basically the same: They eat like us, they dress like us, they must think like us." This ethnocentric observation, unfortunately, is profoundly misleading because "underneath," people are not the same. The underlying set of beliefs and values that we learn within a culture and the meanings that we attach to them create fascinating cross-cultural variations.

Culturally shared traditions can include myths, legends, ceremonies, and rituals (e.g., celebrating Kwanzaa, Ramadan, or Thanksgiving) passed on from one generation to the next via an oral or written medium. *Culturally shared beliefs* refer to a set of fundamental assumptions that people hold dearly without question. These beliefs can revolve around questions as to the origins of human beings, the concept of time, space, reality, the existence of a supernatural being(s), and the meaning of life, death, and the afterlife. Proposed answers to many of these questions can be found in the major religions of the world, such as Christianity, Islam, Hinduism, and Buddhism. Typically, people who subscribe to religious philosophies maintain their beliefs on faith, often accepting the fundamental religious precepts without question.

People also differ in what they value as important in their cultures. *Cultural values* refer to a set of priorities that guide desirable or undesirable behaviors or fair or unfair actions. Cultural values (e.g., group harmony vs. individual competitiveness) can serve as the motivational bases for desired goals in a conflict. They can serve as the explanatory logic for why people behave the way they behave in a particular conflict scene. They can also serve as the cultural wisdom in which competent versus incompetent conflict actions are judged. To understand various conflict patterns in a culture, we have to understand the deeply rooted cultural values that give meanings to such patterns.

It does not make any sense if we claim that "Atsuko likes to avoid conflict because she is Japanese" or that "Angela likes to deal with conflict assertively because she is from the United States" without understanding the logic of why people behave the way they behave. Cultural values such as collectivism and individualism (Triandis, 1995a) help to explain partially such cross-cultural conflict style differences. Collectivistic values basically emphasize the importance of group harmony, fitting in, and relational interdependence. Individualistic values, on the other hand, stress the importance of pursuing personal goals, autonomy, and independence (for a detailed discussion, see Chapter 2).

Understanding cultural values such as the Japanese preference for group harmony and the American preference for individualism may help to guide us initially to explain why different cultural group members respond differently to a conflict episode. Hence, Atsuko prefers an avoidance conflict style because she wants to preserve relational and group harmony during an antagonistic dispute session. Meanwhile, Angela prefers an assertive conflict style because she subscribes to an individualistic ownership outlook in conflict management. If someone disagrees with her opinion, she expects that he or she will rebut and counterargue her positional statement.

Cultural values, together with individual attributes and situational factors, shape and mold conflict attitudes and behaviors. Cultural values drive the core meanings and metaphors that we hold toward conflict. How we define the conflict situation, how we frame our attitudes and outlooks on a particular conflict episode are strongly influenced by the imprint of our cultural values. Cultural values influence the norms, symbols, and meanings we use to deal with a conflict scene.

Culture: Norms, Symbols, and Meanings

Cultural *norms* refer to the collective expectations of what constitutes proper or improper behavior in a given situation (Olsen, 1978). They serve as the standards or a set of rules for what we should or should not do in a conflict scene. They also serve as guidelines for how we should carry out a coherent conflict script in a particular conflict episode. A *conflict script* describes the interaction placement and appropriate sequence of verbal and nonverbal message exchanges. For example, a conflict script can indicate who should be the spokesperson for the team during conflict, who should sit where, who should have the authority to negotiate obstacles, the role of the translator, and negotiation agenda. Whereas cultural beliefs and values are deep-seated and invisible, norms can be readily inferred and observed through behaviors that unfold in a conflict script.

Cultural traditions, beliefs, and values intersect to influence the development of collective norms in a culture or ethnic community. Oftentimes, our ignorance of a different culture's norms and rules can produce unintentional clashes between us and people of that culture. We may not even notice that we have violated another culture's norms in a particular conflict scene (e.g., by addressing our opening remark to the wrong person without a mindful recognition for the status dynamics in the other team). The result may be an exacerbation of the conflict.

A *symbol* is a sign, artifact, word(s), gesture, placement, or nonverbal behavior that stands for or reflects something meaningful. We use language as a symbolic system (with words, idioms, and phrases) that contains rich culture-based categories to organize and dissect the fluctuating world around us. Language is a prism through which we interpret the conflict world around us. Naming particular conflict events (e.g., uphill struggle or a battlefield) via language usage is part of this symbolic system. Intercultural frictions often arise because of the ways we name or catalog the different groups of individuals or conflict behaviors around us. The *meanings* or interpretations that we attach to the symbol (e.g., a national flag or a word such as *power*) can have both objective and subjective levels. People globally can recognize a particular country by its national flag because of its design and color. However, people (e.g., of different ethnic backgrounds) can also hold subjective evaluations of what the flag means to them, such as a sense of pride or oppression.

Another such example involves the linguistic symbol of the word *conflict*. For example, in the French culture, conflict is likened to a "war—an encounter between contrary elements that oppose each other and 'to oppose' is a strong term, conveying powerful antagonism" (Faure, 1995, pp. 41-42). Although the French like a debate, they do not like to engage in a conflict. For the Chinese, the word conflict is equated with intense fighting and contradictory struggle. To engage in a conflict with someone is, in the Chinese mind-set, disruptive to the harmonious fabric of a personal relationship. In Chinese culture, any type of dispute or antagonistic conflict is seen as inviting chaos or *luan*. Most Chinese nurture the belief that conflict should be approached with self-discipline and self-restraint. Although they prefer to discuss or *tao lun* differences (which implies nonjudgmental exploration), they do not like to critically evaluate or *tan pan* differences (which implies that a judgment will be rendered via verbal exchange). Thus, understanding the core linguistic symbols and the culture-laden meanings behind these symbols may be critical to the initiation, negotiation, and resolution phases of any intercultural conflict episode.

In comparison with many of these definitions, the Anglo-Saxon definitions for conflict connote a broader package of meaning, such as perceived incompatible goals or perceived interference of the other in achieving the desired outcomes (Folger, Poole, & Stutman, 2000; Lulofs & Cahn, 2000). Thus, from this outcome-based definition, the word conflict reflects a wider range of problematic interaction phenomena.

On a broad level of analysis, the common metaphors that reflect a Western approach to conflict include, for example, conflict is like a war zone (e.g., "I wait for an opening, and then I attack"), conflict is like a trial (e.g., "You're accusing me of something I didn't do"), conflict is explosive (e.g., "I just needed to let off steam"), and conflict is a mess ("Let's not open that can of worms"). Wilmot and Hocker (1998) observe that the core metaphor of conflict in the United States and Western Europe is to view conflict as "warlike and violent." As they comment,

> The *scene* is that of a battlefield; the *actors* are people of warring groups who are committed to wiping each other out since the other is perceived as threatening. . . . The war metaphor influences the entire perception of the conflict. Both winning and losing sides feel incomplete; victors desire more power, and losers shore up their defenses for the next attack. (p. 13)

With a warlike mentality, it will take extraordinary hard work and effort to reach a peaceful conflict resolution stage.

Also interesting, whereas the word *peace* means absence of conflict in many Western cultures, peace in Chinese means harmony and a balanced relational system within and beyond the actual conflict relationship. Peace is thus viewed from a long-term relational perspective more so than a one-shot episodic accomplishment. For many collectivists, healing and mending the hurts and disappointments in the conflict relationship is as important (if not more important) than solution-closure on the content issue. On a global level, Lederach (1997) uses the term *reconciliation* in underscoring the importance of mending a broken relationship between antagonists. For him, a conflict reconciliation process represents a space or a location for encounter, where parties to a conflict meet face-to-face with one another in a nonthreatening, neutral zone. The reconciliation process must be "proactive in seeking to create an encounter where people can focus on their relationship and share their perceptions, feelings, and experiences with one another, with the goal of creating new perceptions and a new shared experience" (Lederach, 1997, p. 30).

In sum, the metaphors, phrases, or symbols that we use to formulate conflict approaches and behaviors—conflict is an uphill battle, she really pushed my button, power, authority, compromise, concessions—often present the following intercultural problems. First, the conflict metaphors or symbolic words that negotiators use often do not reflect equivalent conceptual meanings across different cultures. Second, the conflict phrases that different disputants use may conjure different emotionally laden meanings than were originally intended. Third, the attitudinal tone (especially if the speaker is using English as a second language) behind such language usage may provoke different evaluative reactions. Last, the nonverbal gestures, the facial expressions, and the body postures that accompany the verbal dispute process may be entirely misconstrued, thus provoking further conflict spirals in the intercultural communication process. Intercultural communication is often referred to as a symbolic exchange process between persons of different cultures (see Ting-Toomey, 1999). In the symbolic exchange process, conflict intentions are inferred and perceptions and cultural-based interpretations are formed. We use culturally conditioned language and nonverbal movements to communicate, to manage impressions, to persuade, to develop relationships, to negotiate, to compete, and to collaborate. Verbal and nonverbal cues are the emblems of our cultural and personal identities. To increase the likelihood of satisfactory outcomes in conflict, we must become mindful of our symbolic exchange process—on both the verbal and nonverbal levels—with cultural and personal sensitivity.

Based on the above discussion, the premise of this book emphasizes how different culture-based, individual-based, and situation-based factors shape an intercultural conflict episode (for a detailed discussion, see Chapter 2). We also believe that communication patterns are culturally encoded on an unconscious level: learned at an early age through our primary family socialization system, religious institutions, political and economic systems, schools, mass media, peer groups, and personal experiences.

INTERCULTURAL CONFLICT: BASIC ASSUMPTIONS

A Conflict Critical Incident

Let us begin with a critical incident to illustrate some basic assumptions of intercultural conflict:

Felipe Cordova is a senior official in the Philippines Ministry of Communication. He is proud of the fact that he has been invited to the United States to attend an international conference and is excited at the prospect of his first trip there. Upon entering the United States, he has to pass through immigration and customs. The immigration officer, Paul Smith, subjects him to a long series of questions concerning how long he intends to stay, how much money he has, whether he intends to visit relatives, whether he understands the visa regulations, and so on. Felipe grows increasingly irritated and finally refuses to answer any more questions. He suffers all this with repressed indignation, but swears to himself that he will never return to this uncivilized country again.

(Cushner & Brislin, 1996, pp. 137-138)

How would you explain Felipe's obstinate and uncooperative attitude toward the immigration authorities? (a) He is fatigued and irritable because of the long plane ride; (b) he feels he is being singled out as a suspicious person and is insulted; (c) he feels the officer's questioning is too personal and resents having to disclose such information; or (d) his expectations as to his status and treatment in the United States have been strongly violated. If your answer is (d), *congratulations.* A validation sample of 60 experienced cultural experts agreed that (d) was the most logical response in explaining the above critical incident. In this particular incident, a cultural clash of values paves the groundwork for the simmering frustrations and increased tensions.

Felipe, as a senior official representing the Philippines, believes that his invitation to the international conference in the United States reflects his high-status position in his country. He expects to be treated as an honored guest upon his arrival. As such, he expects his path through the bureaucracy to be smooth and unhindered. His expectations as to his high status are strongly violated when he is treated like any Filipino immigrant or common visitor. He feels both outraged and humiliated. His power distance value identity (i.e., as a high-status Ministry of Communication functionary from the Philippines) and *face* identity (i.e., his pride and social esteem) have experienced a sharp insult and severe degradation.

The Philippines, together with Malaysia, Korea, Japan, Guatemala, Panama, Mexico, and many Arab countries have been identified as large power distance cultures (Hofstede, 1991) whose members give priority treatment and asymmetrical respect to people who are in high-status positions. In comparison, in small power distance cultures such as Denmark, Norway, Australia, New Zealand, and the United States (to a moderate degree), members in either high-status or low-status positions strive to foster fairness and equality in interactions, regardless of status, rank, or position. Despite Felipe's high-status position, the U.S. immigration officer, Paul, is applying the "one size, same standard" treatment to this incoming tourist. Staying true to his Filipino high-status conflict script, Felipe "grows increasingly irritated and finally refuses to answer any more questions. He suffers all this with repressed indignation" (Cushner & Brislin, 1996). From Felipe's point of view, a conflict has occurred (albeit on a very subtle level); because of his high-status position, however, he continues to mask his anger by a "repressed indignation"—which reflects a sign of self-discipline and maturity in the Filipino conflict script.

Seven Intercultural Conflict Assumptions

Expectancy violations are a common precursor to an escalatory intercultural conflict episode. What is intercultural conflict? *Intercultural conflict* is defined in this book as the *experience of emotional frustration in conjunction with perceived incompatibility of values, norms, face orientations, goals, scarce resources, processes, and/or outcomes between a minimum of two parties from two different cultural communities in an interactive situation.* Intercultural conflict revolves around the diverse cultural approaches people bring with them in expressing their differential values, norms, face-saving orientations, goal emphasis, and conflict styles in managing a conflict episode (for a detailed discussion, see Chapter 2). The more divergent the two cultural conflict approaches, the wider the misunderstanding and conflict gap between members of the two cultures.

The following seven assumptions guide our conceptualization of the term intercultural conflict. They are presented as a preliminary picture in understanding the underlying forces that drive an intercultural conflict toward a destructive or constructive route.

Assumption 1: Intercultural conflict involves emotional frustrations or mismatched expectations that stem, in part, from cultural group membership differences. When we experience conflict, we experience emotional vulnerabilities and frustrations. Part of the emotional frustration often stems, in part, from cultural difference, mismatched expectation, or ignorance.

When individuals from two cultural groups communicate, there exist both differences and similarities between the two cultural members. Intercultural conflict takes place when our cultural group membership factors affect our conflict process on either a conscious or unconscious level. The cultural membership differences can include deep-level differences such as cultural beliefs and values. Concurrently, they can also include the mismatch of applying different norms and expectations in a particular conflict scene.

For example, in the critical incident, Felipe's frustrations grow in part because of different cultural values placed on the meaning of respect. Felipe, from a large power distance value background, expects special treatment and high-status respect from Paul, whom he views as merely a humble servant of the immigration office. Paul, from a small power distance value orientation, is also experiencing growing frustrations by Felipe's refusal to answer any further questions. He expects Felipe to behave like any incoming tourist, subject to a standardized procedure of security check questions.

In moving the conflict to a constructive path, both Felipe and the immigration officer need intercultural communication training; they must learn about each other's cultural values and norms in framing their initial encounter. Although cultural values serve many useful functions (such as identity meaning and group inclusion functions), they also serve as cultural blinders to alternative ways of thinking and acting. Different cultural values often create unintentional clashes. These well-meaning clashes basically refer to well-meaning encounters that cause frictions and conflicts because people are behaving properly and in a socially skilled manner "according to the norms of their own culture" (Brislin, 1993, p. 10). Unfortunately, the behaviors considered as proper or effective in one culture can be considered improper or ineffective in another culture. The term *well-meaning* is used because no one in the intercultural encounter intentionally behaves obnoxiously or unpleasantly. Individuals are trying to be well mannered or pleasant in accordance to the politeness norms of their own culture. Beyond value and normative differences, the sources of intercultural conflict can include disputes over territorial claims, religious rights, language policies, uneven majority-minority power bases, scarce resources, different approaches to conflict, and biased intergroup membership perceptions and prejudice.

Assumption 2: Intercultural conflict involves varying degrees of biased intergroup perceptions and attributions in assessing what transpires in an ongoing conflict episode. Intercultural- or intergroup-biased perceptions involve the imposition of ethnocentric evaluations and stereotypic lenses in evaluating a conflict episode. For example, Felipe is using his own ethnocentric lens to evaluate what he believes is the incompetent behavior of Paul. Likewise, Paul is, perhaps, using his own mindless stereotypic lens (e.g., all those Asian tourists are a rowdy bunch) in reading into Felipe's passive-aggressive behavior.

Ethnocentrism refers to our tendency to interpret and evaluate dissimilar others' behaviors using our own cultural standards. Stereotypes refer to the mental pictures we have about a large group of individuals and the exaggerated generalized statements that we use to categorize them. Everyone is ethnocentric to some degree. Rigid ethnocentrism, however, leads to a superior view of defining the ingroup's ways of doing things as civilized and outgroups' ways of doing things as backward.

We also often activate our stereotypes to facilitate interaction predictability with dissimilar others to reduce the unpredictable guesswork and anxiety level (Gudykunst, 1995). Although loose stereotypes of cultural strangers do help us to form an initial broad image of what is going on, rigidly held negative stereotypes can lead to further negative intergroup attributions. Negative stereotypes coupled with biased intergroup attributions often perpetuate further destructive cycles of conflict. They also produce tremendous face threats and pressures in a conflict episode.

Assumption 3: Intercultural conflict involves different face needs. Conflict is an emotionally laden face-threatening phenomenon. Face refers to a claimed sense of desired social self-worth or self-image in a relational situation (Ting-Toomey, 1988, 1994a). Face loss occurs when we are being treated in such a way that our identity claims are challenged or ignored. In Felipe's case, for example, his self-image of being a high-status individual has been bypassed and ignored by Paul, the immigration officer. Felipe is proud of the fact that he has been invited to the United States to attend an important, prestigious international conference. However, his status membership and personal pride, and hence face, are dashed by the routine treatment he receives during his first hour of arrival.

Face loss often causes an individual momentary confusion and embarrassment. It often leads to an impasse in the interaction and sometimes leads to conflict escalations and retaliations. Lim and Bowers (1991) identify three face needs in a conflict-inducing situation: competence face, autonomy face, and fellowship face. *Competence face* refers to the need to be respected for one's positions, abilities, or skills. In Felipe's case, he feels his high-power position and hence role-based credibility has been insulted. *Autonomy face* refers to the need for privacy, boundary, and control. From Paul's perspective, Felipe is interfering with his domain of task control (and simultaneously, disturbing his image of presenting a competent face in front of others). Last, *fellowship face* refers to the need for inclusion and connection. It is likely that if a high-status U.S. official visits the Philippines, Felipe will be there right by the gate to extend his fellowship face to make the U.S. official feel welcome and ease his way through the immigration.

Brown and Levinson (1987), in their politeness theory, contend that the greatest face threat is incurred when (a) there is great social distance between the two conflict parties, (b) there is a great degree of perceived imposition placed by the request from the requestor, and (c) the hearer has more self-perceived power than the requestor. For example, from Felipe's perspective, he is of higher status and the line of questioning by Paul is an imposition. Thus Felipe may experience great face threats and face loss, whereas Paul may experience only mild face intrusions because he views Felipe as only one of the many thousand tourists who flood through the immigration gate that day.

Ting-Toomey (1988) observes that face loss is often recouped by diverse face-saving communication behaviors. For example, individuals can engage in either self-oriented face-saving behaviors or other-oriented face-saving behaviors. Self-oriented face-saving behaviors aim to regain the image a person believes has been damaged or degraded. Other-oriented face-saving behaviors aim to help the other to restore or reestablish his or her desired image (see Chapter 2 for more on face). Oftentimes, conflict resolution and satisfaction cannot be achieved until the face image needs of all concerned conflict parties are dealt with, sensitively and affirmatively.

Assumption 4: Intercultural conflict involves multiple goals, and the goals people have largely depend on how they define the conflict episode. In addition to how we respond to one another in terms of intergroup perceptions and different face needs, we often seek particular outcomes or goals in a conflict episode. Four types of goals are important in an interpersonal conflict: content goals, relational goals, identity goals, and process goals (Wilmot & Hocker, 1998). Content goals refer to external, substantive issues in the dispute. What do we want substantively? Relational goals refer to the preferred relationship states. What sort of relationship do we want (equal-unequal, informal-formal)? Identity goals refer to the desired self-image or face-saving goals. How do we view ourselves and each other in the conflict (respect-disrespect, approval-disapproval issues)? Last, process goals refer to how we prefer to approach and resolve a conflict (see "Conflict Goal Assessments" in Chapter 2 for a more detailed explanation along with examples).

Different goal emphasis is based on our cultural conditioning process and situational factors. Individuals who are conditioned by the values of group harmony may consistently frame conflict from a relational priority perspective. Individuals who are programmed by the values of personal achievement and an action orientation may consistently frame conflict from a content priority viewpoint.

Finally, it is critical to remember that conflict parties stay together in a conflict situation because each person has something that the other person wants or desires; otherwise, the conflict parties would go their separate ways. Even in the most desperate hour of a conflict struggle situation, conflict parties may do well to remember their common-interest goals—such as territorial security, identity respect, or combined power resources—and discover the various options available to them in negotiating and pooling their differences together.

Assumption 5: Intercultural conflict involves divergent procedures and styles in approaching the various developmental phases of the conflict. During intercultural conflict, parties use conflict styles that are consistent with their cultural values. For some cultures, conflict with another party should be confronted directly and steps should be taken to resolve the conflict in a mutually acceptable manner. In other cultures, conflict should be avoided to preserve relational harmony. The cultural preferences for certain conflict styles are, of course, mediated by many situational and relationship factors (see Chapter 2).

To engage in a culture-sensitive inclusive conflict approach, the international community needs to adopt a paradigm shift in its usual conflict management practice. As Lederach (1997) notes, conflict mediators need to focus their attention on "discovering and empowering the resources, modalities, and mechanisms for building peace that exist *within* the cultural context" (p. 95). Many examples of divergent conflict modalities can be identified. From Somalia, an extraordinary example exists whereby

> women functioning as forerunners . . . prepared the way for clan conferences—guided by elders and massaged by poets—that led to local and regional peace agreements. [Furthermore, f]rom Mozambique is the example of the UNICEF-funded "Circus of Peace," built on traditional arts, music, and drama, which targeted and incorporated children at the village level in conflict resolutions and peacebuilding activities. (Lederach, 1997, p. 95)

Although the roads to peace are diverse and the conflict modalities are rich and vast across cultural lines, the ultimate goal of universal peace without violence remains a common vision.

Assumption 6: Intercultural conflict is a situationally dependent phenomenon. Intercultural conflict does not happen in a vacuum. Intercultural conflict interaction is always situationally dependent. A situation frames the roles, expectations, norms, rules, and scripts of conflict. A situation includes both the concrete features (such as furniture arrangements or strategic seating arrangements in mediating a conflict) and psychological features (such as perceived formal-informal dimensions) of a setting. Every conflict episode occurs in an interactive situation. An interactive situation typically includes several gestalt features: (a) physical setting and artifacts (e.g., an office mediation setting is very different from a courtroom hearing setting); (b) roles in which different people must play different parts (e.g., the hard bargainer role versus the soft bargainer role in a business conflict); (c) rules of procedure and behavior (e.g., rules for conflict brainstorming or ground rules for opening a conflict dialogue); (d) goals of the participants (e.g., what are the expected goals or desired end states to be achieved in a particular team conflict); and (e) relevant social competence skills (e.g., what are the appropriate and effective skills needed to resolve this particular conflict) (Burgoon, Buller, & Woodall, 1996).

The interpretations that we attach to the various features of an interactive situation are strongly influenced by the meanings we attach to these components. We acquire the meanings and priorities to these situational components via the primary socialization process within our own ethnic group and culture. To understand an intercultural conflict holistically, we need to practice both situational and systems thinking.

Assumption 7: Competent intercultural conflict management demands systems thinking. A system is an interdependent set of components that constitute a whole and simultaneously influence each other. The structure of a system is the pattern of interrelationships among key components in the system. The structure in a conflict system is developed out of the choices people make consciously or unconsciously over time. Systems thinking includes looking at perceptions, thinking patterns, emotions, behaviors, meanings, and embedded contexts. In practicing systems thinking in effective conflict management, we should remember the following (Bateson, 1972; Watzlawick, Beavin, & Jackson, 1967; Wheatley, 1999; Wilmot & Hocker, 1998):

1. *Wholeness:* Think of the entire relationship system, family system, or team system. For example, what is the impact of this conflict on the entire relationship system? On the team system? How should we deal with the conflict? What are the short-term and long-term implications of this conflict to the entire system?

2. *Interdependence:* How are we interdependent on one another in this conflict? How are the subsystems dependent on one another?

3. *Links and loops:* The cause and effect of a conflict may not be closely related in time and space. For example, in an intimate conflict, the most effective solution may be the most subtle, and the search for the cause may be further away than is immediately apparent.

4. *Boundaries:* Do we allow new ideas or feedback to flow into the system? Do we prefer to handle conflict in-house? Or do we go out-of-house to look for possible solutions or expert advice?

5. *Stability/change:* Do we value stability or change in our relationship system or organizational system? How can we instill change in an overly stable environment? Alternatively, how can we introduce stability in an overly chaotic conflict system?

6. *Conflict patterns:* How do our underlying conflict attitudes and interaction patterns constrain our conflict options? How do they promote added values and creativity?

7. *Equifinality:* How can the divergent conflict approaches lead us to a common solution? How can we use a similar approach but arrive at different end goals or innovations?

In the case above, Felipe and Paul would benefit by practicing systems thinking. Felipe would do well to recognize that Paul is constrained by the boundaries of his job. Examining the situation, Felipe could see that the patterns of interactions among customs officers and entrants are similar. Although that would not support his status, it would help him to realize that a change in thinking pattern and behavior may be necessary. On the other hand, Paul would do well to recognize that Felipe is in a new country and may not be aware of the rules. Certainly, as the interaction *loops*, he should be aware that Felipe is experiencing high anxiety and frustration due to multiple cultural and situational factors. Paul might modify his attitude (or tone of voice) to afford some respect to Felipe while still maintaining the requirements of his job. Alternatively, it is incumbent upon the host who had invited Felipe in the first place to brief him on the entry protocol of the U.S. immigration office before Felipe's arrival in the United States for the first time.

Conflict systems thinking requires us to pay attention to the interconnectedness of the cultural level, individual level, situational and relationship level, and the process and outcome level of intercultural conflict management. It also emphasizes the interconnected use of conflict management tools such as effective facework negotiation, mindful reframing, and collaborative dialogue (see Chapter 6). In commenting on the importance of a systems approach to deal with organizational change, Wheatley (1999) observes:

> A system is composed of parts, but we cannot understand a system by looking only at its parts. We need to work *with the whole of a system*, even as we work with individual parts or isolated problems. From a systems consciousness, we understand that no problem or behavior can be understood in isolation. We must account for dynamics operating in the whole system that are displaying themselves in these individual moments. (pp. 139-140)

Systems consciousness requires us to be mindful of the interdependent components of the overall system, to be alert to the recurring patterns within and beyond the conflict system, and to be able to understand the simultaneous interface between the individual parts and the systems-level attributes. Systems thinking in conjunction with flexible conflict practice will help an individual to manage the conflict more satisfactorily and productively across cultural lines. As Rosen et al. (2000) conclude,

> The globally literate mind is a flexible mind. It remains agile and nimble as we learn to travel across boundaries and borders. Comfortable with chaos and change, it is able to contain conflicting and often opposing forces while creating cohesion and harmony from disparate parts. . . . By combining linear, logical reasoning with circular, systematic thinking, the global mind prepares us for the twenty-first century world. (p. 374)

In summary, this chapter has outlined the basis for understanding intercultural conflict from a culture-based competence perspective. We discussed reasons why we should study intercultural conflict, the elements of culture, and assumptions of intercultural conflict. In this book, we expand on this information and attempt to provide the knowledge and skills for interpreting and managing intercultural conflict. In the next chapter, we outline a culture-based situational model that explains the interconnection of cultural and situational features that affect the conflict communication process. In Chapters 3 to 5, we summarize how the elements of our model work in various contexts including interpersonal-intimate relationships (Chapter 3), work groups (Chapter 4), and between managers and employees (Chapter 5). In Chapter 6, we conclude the book by identifying specific dimensions of conflict competence that can be used to improve the management of intercultural conflict.

2

INTERCULTURAL CONFLICT

A Culture-Based Situational Model

Competent conflict management requires us to communicate adaptively and flexibly in diverse conflict situations. It requires us to be sensitive to the differences and similarities across a wide range of cultural and situational factors that affect the intercultural conflict episode. Effective conflict negotiation demands that we be mindful of our own ethnocentric biases when making hasty judgments of other people's conflict styles. It also demands that we be attuned to the multiple layers of the antecedent, process, and outcome of an intercultural encounter episode.

Although the study of intercultural conflict is a complex phenomenon, understanding conflict along a cultural variability perspective serves as the beginning step in understanding conflict variations among different clusters of cultures. A *cultural variability perspective* emphasizes the value variation dimensions of individualism-collectivism and power distance and how these dimensions influence conflict management processes. These value dimensions, in conjunction with individual personality attributes and situational factors, influence the expectations and attitudes we hold in approaching or side-stepping various conflicts in our everyday lives. Cultural value dimensions, as mediated through situational features, affect the way we experience the conflict, define the conflict, and attribute meanings to the micro-events that take place in the conflict.

Many factors affect our competent management of an intercultural conflict episode. To explain these factors, we need a model to organize, relate, and explain concepts in a coherent fashion. This chapter introduces a culture-based situational model and examines some of the cultural, personal, and situational factors that shape face-to-face intercultural conflict. We identify four clusters of factors in this model: (a) primary orientation factors: cultural value patterns, personal attributes, conflict norms, and face concerns; (b) situational and relationship boundary features: intergroup boundaries, relationship parameters, conflict goal assessments, and conflict intensity; (c) conflict communication process factors: conflict styles, facework strategies, emotional expressions, and conflict rhythms; and (d) conflict competence features (see Figure 2.1).

The primary orientation factors refer to factors that create primary differences between cultural members in an intercultural conflict episode. In addition, because of these primary orientation factors, our interpretations of different situational and relationship features may differ across cultures and individuals. Situational and relationship features, in turn, serve as moderating variables that influence our conflict communication process. As a result of these processes, individuals evaluate the conflict in terms of satisfaction, productivity, effectiveness, and appropriateness. To develop our competencies in managing differences in an intercultural conflict episode, we should learn to attune to the primary orientation factors that create the initial conflict condition.

A CULTURE-BASED SITUATIONAL CONFLICT MODEL: PRIMARY ORIENTATION FACTORS

In conflict episodes that include two polarized intercultural parties, the participants often carry with them different cultural lenses and values, face concerns, and distinctive conflict styles in dealing with

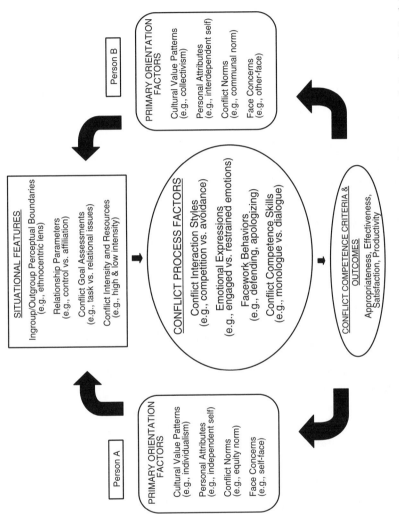

Person B

PRIMARY ORIENTATION
FACTORS

Cultural Value Patterns
(e.g., collectivism)

Personal Attributes
(e.g., interdependent self)

Conflict Norms
(e.g., communal norm)

Face Concerns
(e.g., other-face)

SITUATIONAL FEATURES

Ingroup/Outgroup Perceptual Boundaries
(e.g., ethnocentric lens)

Relationship Parameters
(e.g., control vs. affiliation)

Conflict Goal Assessments
(e.g., task vs. relational issues)

Conflict Intensity and Resources
(e.g., high & low intensity)

CONFLICT PROCESS FACTORS

Conflict Interaction Styles
(e.g., competition vs. avoidance)

Emotional Expressions
(e.g., engaged vs. restrained emotions)

Facework Behaviors
(e.g., defending, apologizing)

Conflict Competence Skills
(e.g., monologue vs. dialogue)

CONFLICT COMPETENCE CRITERIA &
OUTCOMES

Appropriateness, Effectiveness,
Satisfaction, Productivity

Person A

PRIMARY ORIENTATION
FACTORS

Cultural Value Patterns
(e.g., individualism)

Personal Attributes
(e.g., independent self)

Conflict Norms
(e.g., equity norm)

Face Concerns
(e.g., self-face)

Figure 2.1. An Intercultural Conflict Episode: A Culture-Based Situational Conflict Model

the escalatory conflict spirals. These different conflict lenses and patterns often affect the core expectations and attitudes indicating how an intercultural conflict should be approached, managed, and resolved. In an intercultural conflict situation, different conflict lenses often sustain the conflict and serve as major obstacles to genuine intercultural and interpersonal understanding. By understanding the larger cultural grounding and situational features that influence the use of various conflict styles and facework behaviors, we can understand the logic that motivates actions by intercultural others. We begin with a discussion of primary cultural value patterns.

Cultural Value Patterns

The hidden dimensions of intercultural conflict often stem, in part, from differences in cultural values that give rise to different ideals that determine how conflicts should be managed. Although national cultures differ in many value orientations, two value frameworks that have received consistent attention from intercultural researchers are individualism-collectivism and power distance (Gudykunst & Ting-Toomey, 1988; Hofstede, 1991; Ting-Toomey, 1999; Triandis, 1995a).

Individualism refers to the broad value tendencies of people in a culture to emphasize individual identity over group identity and individual rights over group obligations. Hofstede's (1991) and Triandis's (1995a) research indicates that individualism is a cultural pattern found in most northern and western regions of Europe and in North America. By comparison, *collectivism* refers to the broad value tendencies of people in a culture to emphasize the group identity over the individual identity and ingroup-oriented concerns over individual wants and desires. The cultural pattern of collectivism is common in Asia, Africa, the Middle East, Central and South America, and the Pacific Islands. One third of the world population is represented by cultures with high individualistic value tendencies, whereas the remaining two thirds of the people lie in cultures with high group-oriented value tendencies (Triandis, 1995a).

Individualism is expressed in interpersonal conflict through the strong assertion of personal opinions, the effective display of personal emotions, and the importance of personal accountability for any problem or mistake. Collectivism, on the other hand, is manifested in interpersonal conflict through the representation of collective opinions or ideas, the restraint (as opposed to effusiveness) of personal emotional expressions, and the protection of ingroup members, if possible, from being held accountable for the conflict.

For cultures that emphasize values of self-initiative and doing (e.g., the larger U.S. culture), the ideal ways of constructive conflict management are to talk it out and perhaps to brainstorm creative solutions to the problem. In comparison, for cultures that emphasize values of relational harmony and uncertainty avoidance (e.g., the larger Japanese culture), the ideal ways of competent conflict management are to talk around the point for the sake of preserving relational harmony and perhaps even avoid the conflict altogether.

Another value framework that national cultures differ on is power distance (Hofstede, 1991). *Small power distance* refers to broad value tendencies of people in a culture to emphasize individual credibility and expertise, democratic decision-making processes, equal rights and relations, and equitable rewards and punishments based on performance. Small power distance index values are found, for example, in Denmark, Norway, Sweden, Israel, and New Zealand. *Large power distance* refers to broad value tendencies of people in a culture to emphasize status-based credibility and experience, benevolent autocratic decision-making processes, asymmetrical role-based relations, and rewards and punishments based on age, rank, status, title, and seniority. Large power distance index values are found, for example, in Japan, Malaysia, Mexico, Venezuela, and many Arab countries (Hofstede, 1991).

In small power distance cultural situations, children can contradict their parents and speak their own minds. They are expected to learn to be verbally articulate in order to defend their own viewpoints and positions. Parents and children attempt to work toward achieving an open or democratic family decision-making system. In contrast, in large power distance cultural situations, children are expected to obey their parents. Good, well-behaved children are the ones who respect and obey the words of their parents, grandparents, and older siblings. Parents and grandparents often assume the authority roles in the family decision-making process.

In small power distance work situations, power is often distributed more widely and evenly across different management levels. Subordinates expect to be consulted, and the ideal boss is a resourceful democrat. By comparison, in large power distance work situations, the power of an organization is centralized at the upper-management level. Subordinates expect to be told what to do, and the ideal boss plays the benevolent autocratic role. In a study of pilots and flight attendants in eight nations, findings show that five Asian nations collectively endorse "top-down communication and coordination, a preference for autocratic leadership" in the cockpit (Merritt & Helmreich, 1996, p. 17). Although the United States scores on the low side of power distance, it is not extremely low. Hofstede (1991) explains that "U.S. leadership theories tend to be based on subordinates with medium-level dependence needs: not too high, not too low" (p. 42).

Intercultural conflicts often arise between members who ascribe different meanings to the twin concepts of respect and power. Small power distance members respect self-empowered individuals who actively seek solutions to the conflict problem and encourage individual resourcefulness to solve the problem. On the other hand, large power distance members respect individuals who are well connected in their networks and are able to find the proper people in the proper channels to resolve the conflict.

Hofstede (1991) has also determined that individualism and power distance are two separate but correlated conceptual dimensions. Countries high in individualism also tend to be small in power distance. Countries high in collectivism also tend to be large in power distance. Individualistic, small power distance cultural patterns can be found primarily in Northern European and Northern American regions. Collectivistic, large power distance cultural patterns can be found primarily in Latin American, African, and Asian regions.

Personal Attributes

An alternative way to understand individualism and collectivism and power distance focuses on how individuals within a culture conceptualize the sense of self. We must remember that within-culture variations exist in each culture. In individualistic cultures, there are those who act just like collectivists. Likewise, in collectivistic cultures, there are people who behave just like individualists. We must also keep in mind that behavior is only a partial indicator of a person's identity. To understand a "full-fledged" independent or interdependent person, we must also examine the thinking and affective pattern of this individual. Markus and Kitayama (1991) argue that our self-conception within our culture profoundly influences our communication with others: Individuals with a strong independent sense of self tend to see themselves as autonomous, self-reliant, unencumbered, and as rational choice makers; individuals with a strong interdependent sense of self tend to see themselves as ingroup-bound, obligatory agents, and as relational peacemakers. Both types of self-construal exist within a culture. Overall, however, independent concepts of self are more common in individualistic cultures, and interdependent concepts of self are more common in collectivistic cultures.

Independent-self individuals tend to make sense of their environment through autonomous-self lenses. In comparison, interdependent-self individuals tend to make sense of their surrounding through ingroup-self lenses. Independent-self types tend to worry about whether they present their unique self credibly and competently in front of others. Interdependent-self types tend to be more attuned to what others think of their face image in the context of ingroup-outgroup relations. When communicating with others, high independents believe in voicing their personal opinions, striving for personal goals, and assertively expressing their conflict needs. On the other hand, high interdependents tend to be more circumspect in an interpersonal conflict situation. They prefer self-restraint and self-monitoring strategies to approach a conflict in order not to bring relational chaos or disharmony. They practice other-centered communication in anticipating the thoughts and feelings of the other person in the conflict situation (Gudykunst et al., 1996).

Juxtaposed to the above self-construal idea, we can examine power distance from a personal level. Individuals and their behaviors can be conceptualized as either moving toward the "horizontal-self" spectrum or the "vertical-self" spectrum. Individuals who endorse horizontal self-construals prefer informal-symmetrical interactions (i.e., equal treatment) regardless of one's position, status, rank, or age. In comparison, individuals who emphasize vertical self-construals prefer formal-asymmetrical interactions (i.e., deferential treatment) with due respect to one's position, title, and age. As Triandis (1995a) observes,

> This [conceptualization] means that people will seek different kinds of relationships and when possible "convert" a relationship to the kind that they are most comfortable with. Thus, a professor from a horizontal-based self may convert a professor-student relationship to a friend-friend relationship, which may well confuse a student from a vertical-based self. (p. 164)

Although horizontal selves tend to predominate in small power distance cultures, vertical selves tend to predominate in large power distance cultures.

Conflict Norms

Cultural values and personal attributes influence the norms that we use in a conflict interaction episode. Norms are the prescriptive standards that we apply to assess culturally "reasonable" or "unreasonable" behaviors in a conflict situation. Norms are implicit or explicit guidelines for evaluating competent or incompetent conflict behavior, such as listening to a high-status person's perspective during a conflict. They are reflected through our expectations of what constitutes appropriate or effective actions in a given setting. Norms are driven by the underlying beliefs and value patterns in a cultural system.

According to past research (Leung & Bond, 1984; Leung & Iwawaki, 1988), individualists tend to prefer the use of the *equity norm* in dealing with reward allocation. In comparison, collectivists prefer the use of the *communal norm* in ingroup conflict, thereby preserving ingroup harmony. For example, individuals with an equity norm would distribute points in a group project based on individual merit, whereas individuals with a communal norm would distribute the points for a group project evenly. The equity norm emphasizes the importance of individual reward and cost calculations and the importance of obtaining equitable rewards in resolving the problem. The communal norm, in contrast, stresses the importance of taking ingroup expectations into calculation and of determining how to satisfy the face needs of the ingroup members involved in the conflict.

Cultural norms guide the expected scripts that we ought to use in a conflict scene. Violations of our expectations often produce further interpersonal tensions and intrapersonal dissonance. However, without culture-sensitive knowledge, we may not even be aware that we have violated another cultural group's conflict expectations. Under the pressure of an emotionally vulnerable conflict situation, we may cling ever more closely to our own conflict scripts and routines for protection and solace. Learning how to deal with conflict constructively means we have to attend to the concept of face.

Face Concerns

Hu (1944) provided one of the earliest definitions of face when he argued that there are two types of face in Chinese culture: *lien* and *mianzi*. *Lien* refers to the moral character of an individual, whereas *mianzi* refers to the social status achieved through success in life. The two concepts can be viewed as interdependent constructs; they can also be understood separately. To understand the concept of face on the deep level, we have to understand the moral conditioning or moral drives (e.g., shame, guilt) of the self. However, in the context of explaining intercultural conflict, the concept of face is cast at a midrange level—that is, the concept of a negotiated social self-image.

Face is an important social self-concept in China (Gao & Ting-Toomey, 1998), Japan (Morisaki & Gudykunst, 1994), Korea (Lim & Choi, 1996), Colombia (Fitch, 1998), Mexico (Garcia, 1996), and many Arab countries (Katriel, 1986). Morisaki and Gudykunst (1994), for example, pointed out that there are two types of social face in Japanese culture; one is *mentsu* and the other is *taimen*. *Mentsu* is similar to the social status concept of *mianzi* in Chinese culture, whereas *taimen* refers to the appearance or impression one presents to others.

Although the concept of face originated in Eastern cultures, people in all cultures share aspects of face. Face can be lost, saved, and protected. All members of a society want to present and protect their own public images (Brown & Levinson, 1978; Goffman, 1959). Previous studies indicate that the concept of face is used across cultures; however, the meanings and usages are different depending on the culture (Condon, 1984; Ting-Toomey, 1988).

We define *face* as the claimed sense of favorable social self-worth and the simultaneous assessment of other-worth in an interpersonal situation (Ting-Toomey & Kurogi, 1998). It is a vulnerable resource in social interaction because this resource can be threatened, enhanced, bargained over, and maintained. Face is a cluster of identity- and relational-based issues that simmer and surface before, during, and after the conflict process. Face is associated with respect, honor, status, reputation, credibility, competence, network connection, and relational obligation issues. Face has simultaneous affective (e.g., feelings of shame and pride), cognitive (e.g., calculating how much to give and to receive), and behavioral levels.

Face consists of three dimensions: (a) locus of face—concern for self, other, or both; (b) face valence—whether face is being defended, maintained, or honored; and (c) temporality—whether face is being restored or proactively protected (Rogan & Hammer, 1994; Ting-Toomey & Cole, 1990). We focus our discussion on the locus of face because it is the primary dimension of face and determines the direction of the subsequent conflict messages. *Self-face* is the protective concern for one's own image when one's own face is threatened in the conflict situation. *Other-face*, on the other hand, is the concern for accommodating the other conflict party's image in the conflict crisis situation. *Mutual-face* is the concern for both parties' images, the image of the relationship, or all three (Ting-Toomey, 1988; Ting-Toomey & Kurogi, 1998).

Whereas individualists or independents tend to be more concerned with protecting or preserving self-face images during an ongoing conflict episode, collectivists or interdependents tend to be more concerned with either accommodating the other-face images or saving mutual-face images during a conflict. This line of reasoning is drawn from the cultural variability dimension of individualism-collectivism. In applying the value dimension of power distance, overall, small power distance and horizontal-self individuals tend to engage in asserting and saving self-face images in a conflict scene, whereas large power distance or vertical-self individuals tend to observe the facework respect-deference interaction. However, many situational features mediate between the locus of face on the one hand, and facework strategies and behaviors on the other. We turn now to examine this critical set of mediating factors in conflict: situational and relationship boundary features.

SITUATIONAL AND RELATIONSHIP BOUNDARY FEATURES

Situational and relationship boundary features refer to two aspects: (a) the physical setting and work activity in a particular interaction and (b) the nature of the relationship that you have with the other party. To manage intercultural conflict mindfully, we have to understand the features that mediate between the primary orientation factors on the one hand, and the conflict communication process factors on the other. How individuals draw ingroup-outgroup boundaries, how they perceive the nature of their relationship, and how they evaluate the different goal types will have a profound influence on the conflict styles and facework behaviors exhibited in an intercultural conflict episode. We discuss each of these features in this section.

Ingroup-Outgroup Perceptual Boundaries

The drawing of an ingroup-outgroup boundary involves intergroup perceptions and attributions. Intergroup perception is the process of selecting cues from the social environment, organizing the cues into some coherent pattern, and interpreting and dissecting the pattern into a dichotomy of "Us versus Them." According to Triandis (1995a), *ingroups* are groups of individuals "about whose welfare a person is concerned, with whom that person is willing to cooperate without demanding equitable returns, and separation from whom leads to anxiety" (p. 9). Ingroups are usually characterized by members who perceive a common fate or shared attributes among them. *Outgroups* are groups of individuals that are perceived as disconnected, unequal, or threatening in some way. Outgroups are groups that carry very different characteristics or attributes, and often, these attributes are in conflict with one's ingroup standards.

It is important to note that members of collectivistic cultures make a greater distinction between ingroups and outgroups than do members of individualistic cultures (Triandis, 1995a). It usually takes time, patience, and a long-term commitment to move from the outgroup to the ingroup boundary in a collectivistic-based culture. Collectivists tend to practice greater other-face concerns with ingroup members and greater self-face concerns with outgroup members. In contrast, individualists have greater self-face concerns in dealing with *both* ingroup and outgroup members. For highly important conflicts, both collectivists and individualists prefer the use of the equity norm when competing with outgroup members for needed resources. For example, both individualistic and collectivistic managers from different companies would compete with each other for a contract by showing that they deserve it more than other bidders. For less important conflicts, however, collectivists prefer the use of the communal norm with either ingroup or outgroup members, opting for maintaining surface relational harmony over getting too "worked up" dealing with irritants (Leung & Iwawaki, 1988).

The ingroup-outgroup bias is influenced by group-based and individual-based ethnocentrism and prejudiced tendencies. The stronger we view the outgroup members as our "enemies," the more tightly we hold on to our negative stereotypes and prejudiced images, the more likely we will be to use competitive and sabotaging conflict strategies in dealing with outgroup members. Our sociohistorical scripts have programmed us to attend to cues that match our preconceived expectations about outgroup members' conflict actions.

Relationship Parameters

Another feature of situational and relationship boundary features is relationship parameters. *Relationship parameters* can be understood in terms of three dimensions: competition-cooperation, affiliation-control, and trust-distrust (Lewicki & Bunker, 1995; Rubin & Levinger, 1995). In an intercultural conflict episode, conflict combatants may emphasize different features of the perceived relationship parameters. Relationship parameters affect how we frame a conflict. Framing is critical to how two conflict parties view one another and how they view their relationship and the conflict task. Framing directs our attention and steers our focus to what is at stake in a conflict.

The first set of relationship parameters concerns the competitive-cooperative dimension. If members frame the relationship as purely competitive, they are likely to use conflict and facework strategies that enhance individual (or ingroup) gains and minimize individual (or ingroup) loss. If members frame the relationship as somewhat cooperative in nature, they are more likely to maximize mutual gains and less likely to push away the other conflict party in their negotiation behavior.

At some point, conflict disputants may realize that the conflict is a mixed-motive arrangement that requires both cooperative and competitive moves—especially if the relationship is highly inter-dependent. If two disputants each have something that the other wants or needs, then some degree of cooperation will be essential, whether it is dividing the resources equally, trading off different re-sources, or expanding the resource pie collaboratively.

The second set of relationship parameters concerns the affiliation-control dimension. *Affiliation* involves social ties and intimacy is-sues, as well as relational rapport and support. On the other hand, *control* involves social dominance and submission issues, as well as respect and deference orientations.

For example, an intercultural couple may argue over time spent together—the collectivistic wife wants to spend more time with her family, whereas the individualistic husband wants the couple to have more private time together. The wife perceives the conflict relationship as a high controlling one, whereas the husband views the conflict relationship as a low affiliative problem. Depending on the culture, relationship affiliation can be expressed through a vari-ety of behaviors. For instance, some individuals may perceive direct eye gaze or close personal space as affiliative, whereas in another culture these may be considered as aggressive and intrusive. Likewise, what is considered a decisive action move by one party, such as a loud and take-charge tone of voice, can be viewed as overbearing and insulting by another party in an intercultural conflict episode.

A third set of relationship parameters is the trust-distrust dimen-sion. Trust is often viewed as the single most important element of a good working relationship (Fisher & Brown, 1988). Whereas *trust* is about reliability and sustained faith issues, *distrust* is about reli-ability violations and sustained skepticism issues. When trust is nonexistent, disputants will often second-guess each other's inten-tions and actions. In a tension-filled intercultural conflict scenario, adversaries will often view the relationship with distrust because interpersonal faith is broken and the other party is perceived from an outgroup—one of the distant "them."

Interpersonal trust begins with one side's perception that the other's verbal or nonverbal gesture is reliable or trustworthy. This perception is often followed by direct experience that the other's action is highly dependable. Repeated reliability and dependability across time further cultivate attachment accompanied by faith in the other person's responsiveness to one's needs (Rubin & Levinger, 1995). Thus, trust building depends heavily on reliable words and dependable actions. Being trusted by someone means promises that are kept and commitments that are honored. It also means we have the sustained faith that the other conflict party will perform as promised. For individualists, trust may be tested in a short to medium time frame, a monochronic basis. For collectivists, however, trust may entail a long-term, polychronic focus that entails mutual patience and longitudinal network reciprocity (see the "Conflict Rhythms" section in this chapter for definitions and description of monochronic and polychronic).

If conflict parties do not trust each other, they tend to move away (cognitively, affectively, and physically) from each other rather than work together with each other to resolve the conflict (Ting-Toomey, 1997). When we do not trust someone's words or actions, we also tend to tune out. We may hear the words, but we are not taking them in. Thus, lack of trust can lead to lack of faith and hope in resolving the conflict situation constructively. Trust building is both a mind-set and a communication skill. Well-developed and well-founded trust is critical in any effective and appropriate management of intercultural conflict.

Conflict Goal Assessments

A third situational feature is conflict goal assessments. People experience conflict in intimate and nonintimate relationships across a diverse range of cultures. How we perceive the conflict, whether we choose to engage in or disengage from it, and how we attribute different weights to the different goals in a conflict episode can vary greatly across cultural lines. The perceived or actual conflict differences often rotate around the following goal issues: content, relational, and identity (Wilmot & Hocker, 1998).

By *content conflict goals* we mean the substantive issues external to the individual involved. For example, an intercultural couple might argue about whether they should entertain their visiting in-laws at home or in a restaurant. They might disagree whether they should raise their children as monolinguals or bilinguals. Intercultural business partners might argue about whether they should hold their business meetings in Mexico City or Los Angeles. Recurrent content conflict issues often go hand-in-hand with relational conflict goals.

By *relational conflict goals* we refer to how individuals define, or would like to define, the particular relationship (e.g., nonintimate vs. intimate, formal vs. informal) in that conflict episode. Nonintimate-intimate and formal-informal are two ways individuals might relate to one another. In the business setting, for example, one business partner from the United States might opt to scribble a note and fax it to another international partner from Japan. The latter might well view this hastily prepared communication as a cavalier and unfriendly gesture. The Japanese partner may have perceived and experienced face threat and relationship threat. However, the U.S. American business partner may not even realize that he or she has committed a faux pas by sending this offhand message. The U.S. American perceived the informal note as signaling affiliation or friendliness to minimize the formal relationship distance.

Identity-based goals revolve around issues of validation-rejection, approval-disapproval, respect-disrespect, and valuing-disconfirming of the individuals in the conflict episode. In a given interaction, identity goals are directly linked to face-saving and face-honoring issues. Over the course of many interactions, identity goals are broadly linked to the underlying beliefs and value patterns of the culture and the individuals. Thus, to reject someone's proposal or idea in a conflict can mean rejecting that person's deeply held beliefs and convictions. For example, when an interfaith couple is arguing about which religious faith they should instill in their children, they are, at the same time, assessing which religious faith is more or less "worthwhile" in the family system.

From the partner's conflict response, each would assess whether his or her underlying beliefs are being valued or devalued. Beliefs and values are strongly tied to one's conception of identity or self-image.

To the extent that the couple can engage in a constructive dialogue about this important issue, the conflict can act as a catalyst for their relationship growth. To the extent that the dyadic interaction spirals into negative loops (e.g., the more the wife wants to talk about it, the more the husband seeks to avoid the topic), the conflict can be detrimental to both individuals' sense of self-worth. Likewise, in the case of deciding where an international business meeting should take place, the conflicting parties may be arguing over a concrete topic such as a location site; however, they are also testing their self-images or face in front of the other. The decision to hold the business meeting in country X may be interpreted as enhanced power or increased status for the business representatives of that country. In this way, identity goals are tied closely to culture-based face-orientation factors.

Identity-based conflict goals often underlie content-based and relational-based conflict issues. On the overt level, people may be arguing or disagreeing over content or relational issues; however, beneath the surface rest identity conflict problems. From the collectivistic cultural perspective, relational conflict goals usually supersede content goals. The reasoning from the collectivistic point of view is that if the relationship is in jeopardy and mutual-face images have been threatened, there is no advantage to spending time talking about content issues. In contrast, from the individualistic perspective, content issues usually supersede relational issues. The reasoning from the individualistic perspective is that we can use actions and concrete steps to resolve the content goal problem decisively and have closure to the problem. An action orientation and a content problem-solving mode reflect the individualistic conflict worldview. By tackling the content problem first, individualists then can relax and deal with an interpersonal relationship problem. At the heart of all recurring conflict problems often rest unresolved identity conflict issues.

Conflict Intensity and Resources

The final situational feature is conflict intensity and resources. *High intensity conflict* means that high stakes are involved in the conflict and gains and losses can severely affect the individual, the organization, or both. The calculation of gains and losses can be content based, relationship based, or both. In contrast, *low intensity conflict* means that low stakes are involved and low incentives and costs are tied to the process and outcome. Conflict intensity holds both cultural-overlap and cultural-distinctive meanings.

The cultural-overlap meanings can be that both group membership teams realize that if they do not find a way to work collaboratively together they will lose their jobs. The cultural-distinctive meanings can involve collectivists wanting to emphasize the relationship trust issue and individualists wanting to consider substantive solution. As a result, individualists and collectivists may develop different "punctuation points" of what constitute the salient aspects of the conflict, as well as the scarce resources that are involved in the conflict episode.

Conflict resources refer to tangible or intangible rewards that people strive for in the dispute. The rewards or commodities may be scarce, or perceived as scarce, by individuals in the conflict. Perceived scarce resources may spark the initial impetus for conflict. Tangible resources may include a salary increase, a promotion, a new office, or a bonus vacation trip. Some tangible commodities are indeed scarce or limited (e.g., only one promotion for three finalists). Other tangible resources are only perceived to be limited (e.g., not enough computers for everyone when abundant supplies are hidden in a storage room) rather than involving actual scarcity.

Intangible resources, on the other hand, may include deeply felt desires or needs such as psychological/emotional security, inclusion, connection, respect, control, and meaning issues. Many recurring conflicts between disputants involve unmet (or frustrated) intangible needs rather than conflicting tangible wants. Scarce intangible resources can be real or perceived as real (e.g., two children fighting for the perceived scarcity of attention of their parent) by individuals in the conflict episode. Both tangible and intangible resources can be managed constructively or destructively, depending on whether the disputants are willing to spend the time and energy probing the underlying concerns, expectations, and needs of the other conflict party as well as focusing on their own needs and interests. Taking the time to clarify one's own needs and expectations, taking the time to probe the needs and interests of the other conflict party, the willingness to suspend "quick fix" solutions, and the willingness to explore creative alternatives and options may lead to resource expansion and collaboration. Furthermore, conflict parties may want to learn to reframe or refocus their perceptions and realize that the resources are not as limited as they imagine. Through competent conflict communication skills, the conflict parties may invent creative avenues to generate additional resources for mutual gains or mutual trade-offs.

We have discussed the situational and relationship factors that moderate the effect of primary orientation components of cultural values and face concerns on one hand, and the conflict communication process component on the other. We now turn to a discussion of the salient conflict process factors.

INTERCULTURAL CONFLICT COMMUNICATION: PROCESS FACTORS

Drawing from the conceptual explanations of Ting-Toomey's (1988; see also Ting-Toomey & Kurogi, 1998) face negotiation theory, we examine the process-based factors of conflict interaction styles and conflict facework behaviors. We conclude the section by examining two additional factors—conflict emotional expressions and conflict rhythms—in the intercultural conflict process. The four factors are the communication behaviors that individuals employ during intercultural conflict.

Conflict Interaction Styles

Conflict interaction style refers to patterned responses to conflict in a variety of dissenting conflict situations (Ting-Toomey, 1994b,

1994c). Findings in many past studies indicate that people display consistent styles across a variety of conflict situations in different cultures. Conflict style is learned within the primary socialization process of one's cultural or ethnic group.

Many researchers conceptualize conflict styles along two dimensions (Blake & Mouton, 1964; Putnam & Wilson, 1982; Thomas & Kilmann, 1974). Rahim (1983, 1992) bases his classification of conflict styles on the two conceptual dimensions of concern for self and concern for others. The first dimension illustrates the degree (high or low) to which a person seeks to satisfy his or her own interest or own face need. The second dimension represents the degree (high or low) to which a person desires to incorporate the other's conflict interest. The two dimensions are combined, resulting in five styles of handling interpersonal conflict: dominating, avoiding, obliging, compromising, and integrating (see Figure 2.2).

Briefly, the *dominating* (or *competitive/controlling*) style emphasizes conflict tactics that push for one's own position or goal above and beyond the other person's conflict interest. The *avoiding* style involves eluding the conflict topic, the conflict party, or the conflict situation altogether. The *obliging* (or *accommodating*) style is characterized by a high concern for the other person's conflict interest above and beyond one's own conflict interest. The *compromising* style involves a give-and-take concession approach to reach a midpoint agreement concerning the conflict issue. Finally, the *integrating* (or *collaborative*) style reflects a need for solution closure in conflict and involves high concern for self and high concern for other in conflict substantive negotiation. It should be noted that, in the U.S. conflict management literature, obliging and avoiding conflict styles often take on a Western slant of being negatively disengaged (i.e., placating or flight from the conflict scene). However, collectivists do not perceive obliging and avoiding conflict styles as negative. Typically, these two styles are employed to maintain mutual-face interests and relational network interests (Ting-Toomey, 1988).

Furthermore, the five-style model misses subtle nuances of conflict behavior. Therefore, we have added three other conflict styles to account for the potentially rich areas of cultural and ethnic

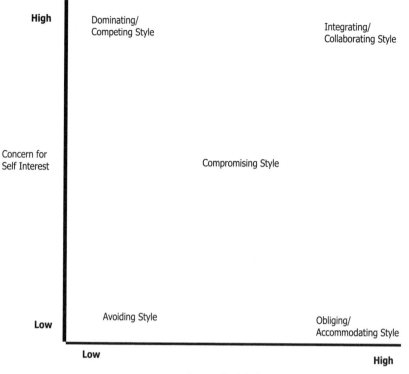

Figure 2.2. A Five-Style Conflict Grid: A Western Approach

differences in conflict: emotional expression, third-party help, and neglect (Ting-Toomey et al., 2000). *Emotional expression* refers to using one's emotions to guide communication behaviors during conflict. *Third-party help* involves using an outsider to mediate the conflict. *Neglect* is characterized by using passive-aggressive responses to sidestep the conflict but at the same time getting an indirect reaction from the other conflict party. Further conceptual discussions and measurements of these eight conflict styles can be found in Ting-Toomey et al.'s article (2000). Based on our research in recent years, we have refined and updated the model to an eight-style conflict model (see Figure 2.3).

Face-negotiation theory helps to explain how individualism-collectivism, power distance, and self-construals influence conflict style (Ting-Toomey, 1988, 1997; Ting-Toomey & Kurogi, 1998).

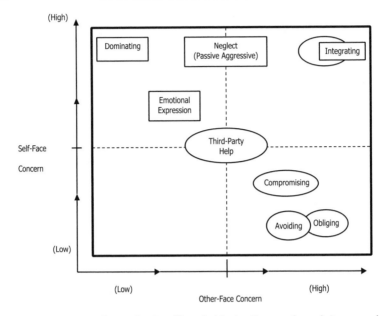

Figure 2.3. An Eight-Style Conflict Grid: An Intercultural Approach

The premise of the theory is that members who subscribe to individualistic values tend to be more self-face oriented and members who subscribe to group-oriented values tend to be more other- or mutual-face oriented in conflict negotiation. In addition, cultural members who subscribe to small power distance values tend to be more sensitive to horizontal face treatment, and cultural members who subscribe to large power distance values tend to be more attuned to vertical face treatment (Ting-Toomey & Kurogi, 1998). Parallel to the cultural-level predictions, personal attributes such as independent/interdependent self and horizontal/vertical self also assert a strong influence on conflict styles. Finally, different situational contexts and goals call for different rituals of conflict styles and facework appropriateness and effectiveness.

The face orientations, influenced by the various cultural and individual factors, affect conflict styles. Research across cultures (e.g., in China, Hong Kong, Japan, Korea, Taiwan, Mexico, and the United States) clearly indicates that individualists tend to use more self-defensive, controlling, dominating, and competitive styles in

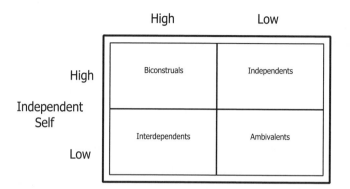

Figure 2.4. A Self-Construal Typological Model

managing conflict than do collectivists. By comparison, collectivists tend to use more integrative and compromising styles in dealing with conflict than do individualists. Furthermore, collectivists tend to use more obliging and avoiding styles in task-related conflicts than do individualists (Chua & Gudykunst, 1987; Ting-Toomey et al., 1991; Ting-Toomey et al., 2000; Trubisky, Ting-Toomey, & Lin, 1991).

On the personal attributes level, independent-self individuals tend to use more dominating conflict styles than interdependent-self individuals, whereas interdependent-self individuals tend to use more avoiding, obliging, integrating, and compromising styles than independent-self individuals (Oetzel, 1998b). Further research helps to illustrate how self-construals affect conflict styles by considering four types that result from a combination of the two components of self: biconstrual, independent, interdependent, and ambivalent (Ting-Toomey, Oetzel, & Yee-Jung, in press) (see Figure 2.4). Overall, it seems that the biconstruals have a wide range of conflict repertoires to deal with different conflict situations. They appear to be more flexible and adaptable in handling different conflict issues than the other three self-construal types. In addition, biconstruals, independents, and interdependents prefer to use integrating and compromising conflict styles more than do ambivalents. Finally, ambivalents prefer to use neglecting conflict style more than do biconstruals, independents, and interdependents.

Conflict Facework Behaviors

A closely related concept to conflict style is facework behavior. *Facework* is the combination of communication strategies used to uphold, support, and challenge self-face and the other's face. Facework can be specific behaviors of a broad conflict style. For example, the integrating conflict style reflects a need for finding a solution during conflict and involves both parties working together to substantively resolve the issue (Rahim, 1983). Facework behaviors consistent with the integrating style include (but are not limited to) listening to the other person, respecting the feelings of the other, and sharing personal viewpoints. During conflict, facework has a variety of functions. Facework is employed to resolve a conflict, exacerbate a conflict, avoid a conflict, threaten or challenge another person, protect a person's image, and so on. These functions are part of the process of maintaining and upholding face. Facework is linked closely with identity and relationship conflict goal issues.

In examining facework strategies in saving self-face or giving consideration to the other's face, research indicates that whereas individualists tend to use self-oriented face-saving strategies in conflicts, collectivists tend to use other- or mutual-oriented face-saving strategies in such situations. In addition, individualists (e.g., U.S. European American respondents) tend to use more direct face-threatening conflict behaviors than collectivists, whereas collectivists (e.g., Taiwanese and Chinese respondents) tend to use more indirect other-oriented face-saving conflict behaviors than individualists (Cocroft & Ting-Toomey, 1994; Ting-Toomey et al., 1991). Self-face is reflected through behaviors such as defending a position and confrontation of the other party's position. Other-face is reflected through behaviors such as avoiding the conflict, seeking a third party to help resolve the conflict, and giving in to the other party. Mutual-face is reflected through behaviors such as attempting to solve the problem with the other person, compromising, signaling relational solidarity, having private discussions with the other party, and apologizing for behavior (Oetzel, Ting-Toomey, Masumoto, Yokochi, & Takai, in press).

In terms of ethnic facework behaviors in the United States, African Americans are influenced simultaneously by individualistic and collectivistic values. At the same time that traditional African values are collectivistic (e.g., community, interdependence, being one with nature, and church/religious participation) and large power distance oriented (e.g., respecting grandparents and pastors) (Asante & Asante, 1990), African Americans are in constant struggle against the power dominance of whites in the white-privileged American society. The white-privileged social position refers to a general favored state of whites holding ower over other minority groups in all key decision-making avenues (McIntosh, 1995). There is also a tendency for whites to view racism episodes as individual acts rather than as part of a problematic, power imbalance institutional package. Thus, assertive facework styles may be one method for African Americans to uphold self and ingroup membership pride and to handle daily racism with self-face protection dignity.

Overall, African American facework patterns are influenced strongly by cultural/ethnic values, social class, and reactions to racial oppression factors. As a complex, diverse group, African Americans have an integrative system of individualistic and collectivistic values. They also subscribe to hierarchical power distance values in some domains (e.g., proper respect for hierarchical family structure) and strive for horizontal power distance values in other domains (e.g., in the workplace). Thus, their facework practice can range from self-face protection mode (especially with outgroup members) in expressing individual self-dignity, and mutual-face protection mode (especially with ingroup members) in displaying ingroup solidarity during racist conflict episodes (Collier, 1991).

In terms of Asian American facework orientations, it has been found that the philosophy of Confucianism strongly influences proper facework enactment (Ting-Toomey et al., 2000). Confucius was a Chinese philosopher of practical ethics who lived from 551-

479 B.C. His practical code of conduct emphasizes hierarchical societal structure and appropriate family role performance. Confucianism remains the fundamental philosophy that underlies many Asian cultures (e.g., in China, Taiwan, Singapore, Korea, and Japan). Some core Confucian values include a dynamic long-term orientation, perseverance, ordering relationships by status, being thrift centered, having a sense of shame, and emphasizing collective face saving (Chen, 1997; Gao & Ting-Toomey, 1998; Hofstede, 1991).

A collective or interdependent sense of shame includes the constant awareness of other people's expectations of one's own performance, concerns for face-losing behaviors, and being mindful to fulfill the basic obligations of one's own role in the hierarchical scheme of family or workplace setting. Asian Americans who adhere to traditional Asian values tend to use a self-critical or self-effacing mode to handle a disagreement. Their intention by using the self-effacing mode is to preserve relational or group harmony. Given the diversity of the Asian American population, we should also pay close attention to the country of origin, immigration experience, acculturation, generation, language, family socialization, and ethnic and cultural identity salience factors that create tremendous distinctions between and within these multiple groups.

In the context of traditional Latino/Latina Americans' conflict practices, tactfulness and consideration of others' feelings are considered to be important facework norms. Tactfulness is conveyed through the use of other-oriented facework rituals such as the use of accommodative (i.e., smoothing over), status-related, or compromising facework behaviors (Garcia, 1996). For example, in Mexican American culture, the term *respeto* connotes honor, respect, and face that we accord to the listeners in accordance with their roles and hierarchical statuses. The family is at the center of all events and planning. Facework is closely related to family loyalty, honor, name, respect, and extended family inclusion (from blood relatives to nonblood relatives such as the best man [*padrino*], maid of honor [*madrina*], and godparents [*compadre* and *comadre*]) and relational pride issues. Similarly, in Colombia, *respeto* or face is conferred through the following means: (a) by acknowledging hearer status (e.g., through the use of a title); (b) by maintaining interpersonal distance, showing that the speaker does not presume intimacy; and (c) by adhering to a code of conduct named *culto* (well-mannered behavior), staying formal in address (e.g., through the use of a title plus the first name, say, Don Pedro; even the first name alone might be an option) (Fitch, 1998), or both. Thus, well-mannered and diplomatic facework behaviors in the context of managing midrange types of conflict are preferred in the Latin cultures. Collectivism and large power distance values are the underlying drives that frame the Latino/Latina facework expectations. With the tremendous diversities under the Latin American label, we will do well to increase the complexity of our understanding of the values and distinctive facework patterns of each group (e.g., Puerto Rican group, Cuban group, Mexican group).

Divergent conflict styles and facework behaviors create different attributional biases in the conflict actors. In attributing meanings to collectivistic, indirect facework behaviors, individualists tend to view collectivists in the conflict as trying to sidestep genuine issue discussions. Conversely, collectivists would tend to perceive individualists as too pushy, rude, and overbearing because of their confrontational, face-threatening postures. Intercultural conflict parties should learn to cultivate appropriate and effective facework management skills in dealing with intergroup conflicts. Facework management skills (see Chapter 6) basically address the fundamental core issue of identity respect before, during, and after a conflict episode. All human beings like to be respected and be approved of in their daily interactions. However, what constitutes respectful and disrespectful behaviors, or approval and disapproval facework actions, very likely differ from one culture to the next.

Conflict Emotional Expressions

Regarding norms of emotional expression, conflict is an emotionally distressing experience. In two extensive, detailed reviews of culture and emotions (Mesquita & Frijida, 1992; Russell, 1991), clear cross-cultural emotional expression and interpretation differences are uncovered. Based on these reviews, we can conclude that cultural norms, or *cultural display rules*, exist in conflict, which regulate displays of aggressive or negative emotional reactions such as anger, fear, shame, frustration, resentment, and hostility. For example, in many Western, individualistic cultures, open expressions of emotions in conflict are viewed as honest, engaging signals. However, in many Asian, collectivistic cultures, maintaining restrained emotional composure is viewed as the self-disciplined, mature way to handle conflict. This norm does not mean, however, that collectivists deal with each other harmoniously all the time. As Triandis (1994) observes,

> In collectivist cultures . . . norms are very powerful regulators of behavior. . . . [Japanese returnees] after spending some time abroad are frequently criticized, teased, and bullied by their peers . . . for non-Japanese behaviors such as having a sun tan or a permanent-wave hairstyle. . . . The threat of ostracism is an especially powerful source of fear in collectivist cultures. (p. 302)

In the United States, it has been found that African Americans tend to be more emotionally expressive and engaging in their conflict approach, whereas European Americans tend to be more emotionally restrained and detached in their conflict discussion (Ting-Toomey, 1986). According to Kochman (1981), the "'Black mode' of conflict is high-keyed: animated, interpersonal, and confrontational; whereas the 'White mode' of conflict is relatively low-keyed: dispassionate, impersonal and non-challenging" (p. 18). Overall, African Americans prefer affectively engaging, self-face assertion modes in conflicts, whereas European Americans often prefer analytically distancing, self-face management modes.

The animation and vitality of African American expressive behavior stems, in part, from the "emotional force or spiritual energy that Blacks habitually invest in their public presentations and the functional role that emotions play in realizing the goals of Black interactions, activities, and events" (Kochman, 1990, p. 195). In addition, the ethnic socialization experiences of African Americans within the larger American culture well may contribute to their emotionally expressive conflict style. African American parents report more frequent discussion of prejudice issues and counter-prejudice strategies with their children than Japanese American and Mexican American parents (Phinney & Chavira, 1995).

In comparison, Native Americans prefer the use of restraint and self-discipline in emotional expressions. Some of the value patterns of Native Americans that have been identified by researchers are (a) sharing—honor and respect is gained by sharing and giving; (b) cooperation—the family and tribe take precedence over the individual; (c) noninterference—they are taught to observe and to not react impulsively, especially in meddling with other people's affairs; (d) time orientation—they tend to be present oriented rather than future oriented, and life is to be lived fully in the present; (e) extended family orientations—a strong respect for elders and their wisdom and generational knowledge; and (f) harmony with nature—they tend to flow with nature and not want to control or master their outer environment (Herring, 1997; Sue & Sue, 1999).

Given these value patterns, we can infer that in terms of emotional expressions, Native Americans tend to be more other- and mutual-face sensitive in dealing with disputes in their everyday lives. Out of consideration for the other person's face, they use more emotionally understated expressions in trying to resolve their conflict peacefully. They are also likely go to a third-party elder to solicit wisdom to resolve the conflict issue and, thus, help each other to maintain face. Collectivism and large power distance values frame many Native Americans' emotional expression styles. However, given the fact that there are more than 500 Native American groups, any generalizations should serve only as preliminary cultural knowledge (rather than rigid stereotyping) that helps us to be more mindful and flexible in generating alternative viewpoints in interpreting an entangled conflict situation. We should realize that, for example, Native Americans who live on or near reservations are more likely to subscribe to traditional values, whereas other Native Americans may adhere to predominant, mainstream values or a set of bicultural values.

Conflict Rhythms

Individuals vary in terms of their tempos, pacing, and rhythms in managing various conflict schedules and issues. In *monochronic-time* (M-time) cultures, time is experienced and used in a linear way. "Comparable to a road. . . . M-time is divided quite naturally into segments; it is scheduled and compartmentalized, making it possible for a person to concentrate on one thing at a time" (Hall & Hall, 1987, p. 16). Intercultural researchers have identified Germany, the Scandinavian countries, Switzerland, and the United States as prime M-time examples. In comparison, *polychronic-time* (P-time) cultures are characterized by the "simultaneous occurrence of many things and by a great involvement with people. There is also more emphasis on completing human transactions than on holding schedules. . . . P-time is experienced as much less tangible than M-time, and can better be compared to a single point than to a road" (Hall & Hall, 1987, pp. 17-18). Many African, Asian, Latin American, Eastern European, Caribbean, and Mediterranean cultures are prime examples of P-time cultures. It also appears that cultural members who subscribe to individualistic value patterns also favor a monochronic-time approach to conflict. Conversely, cultural members who subscribe to collectivistic value patterns also tend to favor a polychronic-time approach to conflict.

Monochronic-time people prefer to deal with conflict from a linear-sequential approach (either through inductive or deductive means); polychronic-time people prefer to handle conflict from a spiral-holistic viewpoint. For M-time individuals, conflict management time should be filled with problem-solving or decision-making activities. For P-time individuals, time is an idea governed by the smooth implicit rhythms in the interaction between people. When conflict occurs between two P-time individuals, they will be more concerned with restoring the disjunctive rhythms in the interaction than in dealing directly with issues of substance.

M-time people tend to emphasize agenda setting, objective criteria, and precise time schedules to accomplish certain conflict goals. P-time people, in contrast, tend to work on the relational

atmosphere and the contextual setting that frame the conflict episode. For M-time individuals, effective conflict negotiation means
reaching and implementing tangible conflict outcomes within a
clearly established timetable. For P-time individuals, the arbitrary
division of clock time or calendar time holds little meaning for them
if the relational rhythms between people are out of sync.

In sum, we have reviewed four processes relevant to intercultural
conflict: conflict styles, facework behaviors, conflict emotional
expressions, and conflict rhythms. The primary orientation factors
and situational features influence these processes. Subsequently,
these processes are used to evaluate the competence of the intercultural conflict. That is, individuals determine the appropriateness, effectiveness, satisfaction, and productivity of the conflict
through the communication processes employed by them and the
other parties. We discuss intercultural conflict competence in the
next section.

INTERCULTURAL CONFLICT
COMPETENCE: FOUR CRITERIA

Conflict processes, such as conflict styles, face behaviors, and conflict rhythms, affect the rating of intercultural conflict competence.
What is intercultural conflict competence? Intercultural conflict
competence refers to applying the intercultural knowledge we have
learned in a skillful manner. It refers to a transformative learning
process in connecting intercultural knowledge with competent conflict practice. To be a competent conflict communicator, we need to
internalize and adapt our knowledge of intercultural theories into
appropriate and effective application. This section is organized in
two parts: (a) appropriateness and effectiveness and (b) satisfaction
and productivity.

The criteria of perceived appropriateness, effectiveness, satisfaction, and productivity are inferred through the exchange of messages between people of different cultures and the outcome that is
generated as a result of such exchange. Competent exchange of

messages means that both intercultural communicators perceive that they and their messages are being understood in the proper context and with the desirable effects. When interested conflict parties experience communication appropriateness and effectiveness, the experience can cue relationship satisfaction and team productivity.

Appropriateness and Effectiveness

Appropriateness refers to the degree to which the exchanged conflict behaviors are regarded as proper and match the expectations generated by the insiders of the culture. Individuals typically use their own cultural expectations and scripts to approach an intercultural interaction scene. They also formulate their impressions of a competent conflict communicator based on their perceptions of the other's verbal and nonverbal behaviors in the particular conflict setting. Whereas insiders have worked out a smooth script of how to approach a conflict episode, outsiders may be completely baffled by what seems like a dishonest or hypocritical way of conflict expression.

The first lesson in conflict competence is to "tune in" to our own ethnocentric evaluations concerning improper dissimilar behaviors. Our evaluations of proper and improper behavior stem, in part, from our ingrained cultural socialization experiences. To understand whether appropriate communication has been perceived, it is vital to obtain competence evaluations from the standpoint of both the conflict parties and interested observers. It is also critical to obtain both self-perception and other-perception data. We may think that we are acting appropriately, but others may not concur with our self-assessments.

Appropriate conflict behaviors can be assessed through understanding the underlying values, norms, social roles, expectations, and scripts that govern the conflict episode. The criterion of communication appropriateness works concurrently with the criterion of communication effectiveness. When we act appropriately in a conflict scene, our culturally proper behaviors can facilitate communication effectiveness. By signaling to the other party that we are willing to adapt our behaviors in a culture-sensitive manner, we convey our respect for the other's cultural frame of reference.

Effectiveness refers to the degree to which conflict adversaries achieve mutually shared meaning and integrative goal-related outcomes. Effective encoding and decoding processes lead to mutually shared meanings. Mutually shared meanings lead to perceived intercultural understanding. During a conflict episode, perceptual filters and "noises" often distort our ability to comprehend what transpires in a conflict scene. Ineffective encoding and decoding by one of the two communicators can lead to further intercultural or intergroup polarization.

Interaction effectiveness has been achieved when multiple conflict meanings are attended to with accuracy, and mutually desired interaction goals have been reached. Interaction ineffectiveness occurs when content or relational meanings are mismatched, and intercultural noises and clashes jam the communication channels.

Satisfaction and Productivity

Individuals tend to be more satisfied in interaction scenes in which their desired identity images are elicited or validated. They tend to experience dissatisfaction when their desired identity images are denied or disconfirmed. Thus, to the extent that the important identities (e.g., cultural or gender) of the conflict communicators have been positively addressed, they will experience interaction *satisfaction*. To the extent that important identities of the communicators have been bypassed or patronized, they will experience interaction dissatisfaction.

To achieve conflict interaction satisfaction, we have to understand the cultural premises that surround the use of exchanged messages in the conflict negotiation process itself. We have to realize that cultural values, such as individualism-collectivism and power distance, frame the culture-specific functions of conflict styles and behaviors in a particular intercultural conflict episode.

For example, for individualists, conflict interaction satisfaction is related to individual-based conflict expressions and personal self-worth and credibility issues. For collectivists, on the other hand, conflict interaction satisfaction is closely tied with relationship validation and acknowledgment, ingroup loyalty and support. Furthermore, for small power distance conflict situations, individual respect and personal openness can move the two conflict parties closer together. On the other hand, for large power distance conflict situations, hierarchical respect together with verbal and nonverbal discretion can often facilitate interaction smoothness and satisfaction.

After a protracted conflict discussion, conflict parties would like to feel they have accomplished something. *Productivity* is closely related to outcome factors, such as the generation of new ideas, new plans, new momentum, and new directions in resolving the conflict problem. In an unproductive conflict, both sides feel that they have wasted their time and energy by being involved in the conflict in the first place, and that both sides have lost sight of the original goals in the conflict episode. In a productive conflict, both sides feel that they have mutual influence over the conflict process, and they both think that they have gained something as a result of the conflict. Whereas an unproductive conflict discussion reflects a win-lose (to lose-lose) orientation to conflict, a productive conflict discussion reflects a win-win orientation to conflict (see Table 2.1).

Conflict parties who practice a win-lose orientation in approaching an intercultural conflict often ignore or suppress cultural differences, bypass or invalidate salient identities of the other conflict parties, focus exclusively on self-interest conflict goals, and react mindlessly and defensively in a conflict situation. In contrast, conflict parties who practice a win-win orientation to conflict tend to accept and respect cultural differences, validate salient identities of their conflict opponents, hold a collaborative mind-set, attempt to uncover deep-seated needs and interests in the other conflict parties, and try to practice mindful conflict management skills. In unproductive conflict discussions, conflict parties often strive for a win-lose outcome and may even end up with a lose-lose outcome. During these unproductive discussions, they often feel that their conflict goals have been ignored, critical relationship issues are

Table 2.1 Win-Lose Versus Win-Win Conflict Orientation:
Core Characteristics

Win-Lose Conflict Orientation	*Win-Win Conflict Orientation*
Ignore Cultural Differences	Respect Cultural Differences
Identity Devaluation	Identity Validation
Win-Lose to Lose-Lose Attitude	Win-Win Collaborative Attitude
Insensitivity to Conflict Context	Sensitivity to Conflict Context
Impose Self-Interest Conflict Goals	Uncover Mutual-Interest Conflict Goals
Argue and Defend Self-Interest Conflict Position	Uncover Deeper Conflict Needs and Assumptions
Competitive or Passive Aggressive Conflict Mode	Collaborative or Give-and-Take Compromising Mode
Engage in Mindless Behaviors	Practice Mindful Conflict Skills
Rigidity of Conflict Posture	Willingness to Change

side-stepped, and conflict stalemate is the only outcome. In productive conflict discussions, by comparison, conflict members often feel that their conflict goals have been fully addressed, important relationship issues are acknowledged, salient content issues in the conflict have been dealt with affirmatively, and a synergistic, win-win outcome can be accomplished.

The criteria of communication appropriateness, effectiveness, relationship satisfaction, and productivity can serve as evaluative yardsticks of an intercultural interaction episode. A competent conflict communicator is one who manages conflict meanings appropriately and effectively, and at the same time, transforms the conflict relationship to a higher level of satisfaction and productivity. All four criteria are contingent on our development of the dimensions of knowledge, mindfulness, and competent conflict management skills in a wide variety of intercultural encounter situations (see the following chapters; in particular, see Chapter 6 for competent conflict management skills).

CONCLUSIONS

In this chapter, we presented a culture-based situational model of intercultural conflict. This model explicates that the values of individualism-collectivism and small-large power distance, and how these are linked to individual self-construals, affect our underlying worldviews about an intercultural conflict episode. In addition, situational and relationship parameters moderate the effect of cultural- and individual-level factors on the one hand, and conflict process-level factors on the other. The conflict processes then influence the degree to which we feel whether or not the conflict was managed competently by us and others.

Before any actual conflict negotiation begins, conflict disputants often frame the conflict in ways that are consistent with their underlying beliefs, values, biases, and expectations. This frame or lens provides a focus on what is at stake in a conflict. This polarized framing process, however, is often automatically activated yet unexamined. Thus, in any conflict situation, we need to intentionally or mindfully "catch" ourselves as we slip easily into our habitual conflict scripts and reactions. It is important to point out here that not even an insider of a culture can fully explain or interpret every detail of conflict management practice in her or his own culture. The best chance an outsider has is to always underestimate her or his knowledge and always be willing to learn more about the new culture and its rich and divergent approaches to conflict resolution process.

In this book, we argue for the importance of understanding cultural values as a starting point to understand self, conflict, and culture and the complex role that situational and relational factors add to an intercultural disputation process. We believe that to manage an intercultural conflict effectively, we need a "big picture" framework to guide our systematic analysis of the emerging features that unfold in a conflict scene. We hope that the culture-based situational conflict model will help you to be more alert and sensitive to the combined culture-based and situationally based factors that shape your own conflict response and the response of the culturally dissimilar others.

3

INTERCULTURAL-INTIMATE CONFLICT IN PERSONAL RELATIONSHIPS

Intercultural dating or marriage is fertile ground for culture clashes and shocks. At the same time, it is a hopeful arena for honoring and reconciling cultural differences. According to a recent census report, there are more than 1.3 million racially mixed marriages in the United States. The tally did not include interethnic marriages (e.g., Chinese with Japanese) within the same race. The highest rate of intermarriage occurs between European American males and Asian American females, and the lowest rate is that between European American males and African American females (Wehrly, Kenney, & Kenney, 1999).

A little less than 25 years ago the Supreme Court (*Loving v. Commonwealth of Virginia*, 1967) struck down laws against interracial marriage. Intergroup history, racism, and fears were some of the factors why antimiscegenation laws were passed in the United States as early as 1664 (Wehrly et al., 1999). Many reasons explain why we should understand how intercultural and interracial pairs handle the various pressures and conflicts in their relationship lives.

First, according to a recent Gallup Poll, more than twice as many teenagers of all races in the United States reported a willingness to date interracially (in comparison to a similar poll in 1980). They are also more open to developing multicultural friendships than their parents' generation. Second, partners who are in an intercultural personal relationship face many external and internal stressors. Some of these stressors are a result of the relationship itself, whereas other stressors develop because of cultural/ethnic value differences. Third, the culture-based situational model (as discussed in Chapter 2) can explain some of the underlying reasons for these intercultural-intimate frictions. Understanding some of these cultural and situational factors helps individuals to be more sensitive to their cultural conflict lenses. Intergroup research indicates that close relationship development between races facilitates interpersonal empathy and dispels rigid stereotypes. The more intercultural friends get to know each other on an intimate level, the more they appreciate both the commonalities and differences between them.

Personal relationships of any kind, however, often involve disagreements and emotional frustrations because we have such high hopes pinned on these exclusive relationships. Having conflicts with our intimate partners is not an index of a poor relationship. Rather, how we manage the frictions and how we signal our cultural and interpersonal sensitivity may very well affect the quality of our relationship. We focus our discussion here on intimate conflicts between romantic relationship pairs because this is the one domain that creates entangled misunderstandings more than any other relationship type. Personal relationship is defined in this chapter as any close relationship that exhibits a certain degree of relational interdependence, commitment, and positive sentiments. Intercultural-intimate conflict is defined as any antagonistic friction or disagreement between two romantic partners due, in part, to cultural or ethnic group membership differences.

This chapter is divided into five sections. First, primary orientation factors revolving around cultural values and normative differences in intimate conflict are explored. Second, situational features of ethnocentrism, prejudice, and racism surrounding intercultural-intimate conflict are illustrated. Third, process factors such as intimate conflict responses and relational face-preservation strategies are summarized. Fourth, outcome factors of relationship commitment and stability/satisfaction are discussed. The chapter ends with a set of guidelines for dealing with intercultural-intimate conflict effectively.

INTERCULTURAL-INTIMATE CONFLICT: PRIMARY FACTORS

Many sources contribute to an intercultural-intimate conflict. Some of the salient sources include cultural/ethnic value clashes, prejudice and racism issues, and distinctive intimate conflict styles. In terms of marital conflict, researchers have discovered that work stress, money, sex, housework, and a new baby are the most typical areas of discord (Gottman & Silver, 1999). These are the frequent "emotional tasks" that couples have to deal with in their everyday lives and often signal that they may have very different cultural and personal perspectives in approaching these issues. We discuss the impact of cultural value differences and conflict norm differences in shaping an intimate conflict in this section.

Different Cultural Value Orientations

Let us look first at the following critical incident:

Michael and Mabel have been married for 6 years. For most of those 6 years, they have been a happily married, loving couple. Michael is a 33-year-old German American and works at a high-tech firm in Silicon Valley. Mabel is a 30-year-old Chinese immigrant who is a pharmacist and works in a nearby hospital. The couple has a 3-year-old son, Micky. For the past 3 years, Mabel has spent countless hours at the immigration office, applying for her parents and younger brother to emigrate from China to the United States. Michael has been very supportive of Mabel throughout this process. At long last, her parents and younger brother finally gained entrance to the United States. They have been here for 8 months, living across the street from the couple. The grandparents are delighted to be reunited with their daughter, and they dote on their only grandson. When Michael and Mabel are at work, the grandparents baby-sit Micky. Because the grandparents do not speak English, they speak only Chinese to Micky. To their delight, Micky has been picking up Chinese quickly.

Recently, Michael and Mabel have had many tense moments and communication difficulties relating to the in-law issue. To begin with, Michael feels he is never alone with Mabel in the house anymore. His in-laws are always there. Mabel and her parents chatter constantly in Chinese. They also laugh in that strange Chinese tone. To make matters worse, Micky has now started to speak to him in Chinese rather than English! Michael feels very left out in his own house. He hears the Chinese laughter from the kitchen and he feels like an outsider. He loves his family and he wants things back to normal—the way it was. He decides to have an upfront, honest talk with Mabel about his frustrations.

He asks Mabel to please tell her parents to reduce their visits from every day to only on the weekends. Moreover, they should really call them ahead of time rather than just popping in to visit. He asks Mabel to register Micky in a nearby English-speaking preschool so that he can play with other English-speaking children. Although Mabel nods "uh-huh" to all his comments, nothing seems to change. Her parents continue to visit unannounced every day and often cook up strange-smelling Chinese food in the kitchen. Michael feels increased frustration in his own house.

Meanwhile, from Mabel's viewpoint, she cannot understand how Michael can be so selfish. Her parents are new immigrants to this country. They have no friends and they do not drive. She is glad that Micky has a chance to learn Chinese from her parents. Before their arrival, she spoke to Micky only in English so that Michael could be included in the conversation. Now that her parents are here, she feels that her Chinese roots are taking hold again. She hopes that by ignoring Michael's "ridiculous" requests, he'll eventually forget about them and come to his senses. Although at one point she yells back at Michael for raising his voice and making another of his "off-the-wall" comments, often she ends up only staring at Michael in silence. She does not want to upset her parents who are playing with Micky in the next room. Inwardly, Mabel grows increasingly resentful. She loves Michael, but at the same time she feels that her marriage is spiraling out of control. She feels misunderstood all the time. She desperately needs some help and advice to handle her marital crisis.

How would you explain Michael's frustration and Mabel's stress? Can you draw upon some of the ideas in Chapter 2 to help Michael and Mabel to understand each other's cultural and interpersonal conflict viewpoint? What would you recommend Michael and Mabel to do in order to deal with their conflict constructively? Let us use this case to discuss more fully the culture-based situational conflict model.

Individualism-Collectivism Values Analysis. Cultural value orientations such as individualism and collectivism may help to serve as a beginning step to explain the in-laws critical incident. To begin with our analysis, Michael (a German American) probably subscribes to a set of individualistic, "I-identity" values. His personality may also have strong independent-self value tendencies. In comparison, Mabel (as a traditional Chinese immigrant) subscribes to a set of group-oriented "we-identity" values. Her personality has strong interdependent-self value tendencies. In this incident, culture and personality factors intersect and form different motivational bases for the different conflict responses between Michael and Mabel.

Michael longs for the relational privacy and intimacy he has experienced prior to his in-laws' (and also baby's) arrival. Because of the frequent unannounced visits by his in-laws, Michael feels that the privacy in his own "castle" has been violated. As an independent-self individualist, Michael places a high emphasis on the separation between his own immediate family and that of his in-laws. Michael knows that even his own parents (who happen to live only half an hour away) will never just pop in without first calling. However, Mabel, who is an interdependent-self collectivist, tends to define family in both immediate and extended family terms.

Mabel grew up in a traditional Chinese family setting where close family relatives would often visit each other's houses without prior announcement. They also often helped out with needed household chores and child care activities. For many of the traditional Asian families, doing things or chores for each other on a daily basis is a natural part of practicing interdependent collectivism. Mabel could not grasp the concept of privacy from an individualistic angle. Her sense of self is closely intertwined with her own immediate and extended family.

Small-Large Power Distance Values Analysis. Although Michael comes from a moderate power distance family background, Mabel comes from a large power distance family context. Michael was taught early in his childhood life to be respectful of his parents and, at the same time, to "speak up" if he disagreed with his parents' or a teacher's viewpoint. In any conflict, he was taught to persuade his opponent with logical arguments and concrete evidence. Furthermore, he was taught at school and in competitive sports to win at all costs, rather than give in to his opponents. Meanwhile, Mabel was taught that a good child is an obedient child, and that she should always act respectfully, and be observant in anticipation of the needs and wishes of her parents and grandparents.

Mabel learned early in her childhood life that she should never question or contradict her parents' (or teachers') words and actions. She was naturally quite alarmed when Michael asked that she should inform her parents to call before visiting their house. From her viewpoint, her house and her parents' house are the same. Her mind-set does not have a dividing line between her parents' family and her own family. Moreover, coming from a vertical-self value perspective, she knows that her parents will be very upset and hurt if she even dares to raise the issue of calling before visiting.

Intimate Conflict Norms and Face Concerns

Whereas Michael used an equity norm in dealing with the conflict situation, Mabel used the communal norm to smooth over the conflict episode (e.g., by using the "uh-huh" response to signal "I hear you" but not necessarily "I agree with you"). With Michael's increasing frustration, he decided to use the low-context "upfront" mode to talk to Mabel. Michael loves Mabel; from his perspective, all he wants is for his in-laws to respect his family privacy and home territory. He believes that after a hard day's work, he deserves some quiet, romantic time with his wife and peace within his house.

Michael is, overall, more concerned with pursuing his "self-face" need above and beyond Mabel's (and her family's) face needs. His increased frustrations led him to decide to confront Mabel openly with his concerns. Mabel, meanwhile, used either an "uh-huh" response or high-context nonverbal gestures to deal with Michael's mounting discontent. She hopes that by not making a big deal out of all these issues, she can preserve family and relational harmony. Overall, Mabel used an other-face mode (i.e., not further provoking Michael and also not upsetting her own parents or Micky) in dealing with the simmering conflict situation with avoidance spiral tactics.

Drawing from the literature of personal relationship conflict (Rusbult, 1987), Michael, as an independent-self individualist, used a relational equity model to approach the intimate conflict situation. On the other hand, Mabel, as an interdependent-self collectivist, used a communal-based model to interpret the intimate conflict problem. The term *relational equity model* emphasizes the importance of using norms and rules that focus on fairness (i.e., calculating what one deserves in a relationship) in resolving personal conflict issues. A relational equity model is also more outcome based (e.g., own individual happiness and satisfaction) rather than process based (e.g., tending to feelings and relationships). On the other hand, a *communal-based model* refers to the importance of using norms that focus on ingroup and relational harmony in handling conflicts. It is also more a process-based and an other-focused orientation (e.g., being sensitive to the ingroup face needs during a conflict) than an outcome-based and a self-focused orientation.

We have drawn on the primary orientation factors (see the culture-based situational conflict model in Chapter 2) to pave our way to understanding the simmering conflict patterns that exist between Michael and Mabel. Cultural and personal values such as independent/interdependent self values, power distance values, and self-face and other-face concerns have been applied to understand the in-laws incident. We now turn to the features that mediate between the primary orientation conflict factors on one hand, and the conflict process factors on the other.

INTERCULTURAL-INTIMATE CONFLICT: SITUATIONAL FEATURES

Cultural and individual primary orientation factors go hand-in-hand with situational features such as ethnocentrism and biased attributions, prejudice and racism, and goal types in shaping our interpretations of an intimate conflict situation. We first discuss ethnocentric lenses and biased attributions that commonly occur in viewing an intercultural-intimate conflict.

Ethnocentric Lenses and Biased Attributions

Biased attribution often stems from rigidly held ethnocentric boundaries. Ethnocentrism means that we hold views and standards and make negative judgments about other groups based on our own group's values and practices. Even in the most intimate relationship, our ethnocentric tendencies can surface, especially during unpleasant relationship periods (e.g., Michael was disturbed by all the strange-smelling Chinese food in his kitchen and, moreover, by his son Micky speaking to him in Chinese). When our intimate relationship is under stress, we tend to retreat into our ethnocentric shells for security. Thus, cultural and interpersonal issues are often simultaneously at work when we are involved in an intercultural-intimate conflict struggle.

According to attribution research (Sillars, 1980; Vangelisti, 1994), when we are in prolonged conflicts with our intimate partners, we often view the cause of the other's conflict behavior as global (overall), stable (over time), internal (dispositional or personality locus), and intentionally motivated (a purposeful offensive act). Assigning negative dispositional attributions to our partner's conflict behavior, while crediting our own conflict behavior as situationally based, can create a polarized win-lose conflict climate in our intimate relationship (see Figure 3.1).

For example, Michael could attribute Mabel's noncompliance behavior (i.e., not requesting her parents to call before visiting) as her not caring about the relationship overall. Furthermore, he might see her as a thoughtless/vengeful person and that she intentionally wants to spite him for all past hurts. Such global, negative dispositional attributions can also provoke further defensive and aggressive (and also passive aggressive) behaviors toward the partner during an intimate conflict episode. In interpersonal-intimate conflict research, research studies have consistently shown that, during stressful conflict periods, we often attribute the cause of conflict to our partner's negative traits (e.g., He is selfish) and the cause of our own behavior to situational pressure (e.g., I'm undergoing lots of work stress) (Cupach & Canary, 1997; Kashima & Triandis, 1986).

Conversely, individuals who explain the offensive behavior of a partner in unstable (i.e., a rare occurrence), external (i.e., situational pressure), and unintentional terms (i.e., not intentionally motivated to hurt) tend to manage their conflicts much more

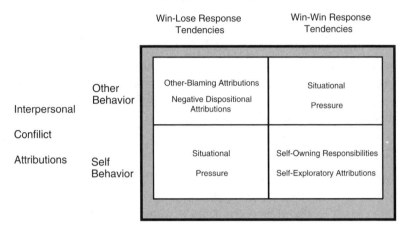

Figure 3.1. Interpersonal Conflict Attributions: Win-Lose Versus Win-Win Response Tendencies

constructively than individuals who generalize the cause of the conflict as global and stable. It seems that intimate partners who learn to accept some responsibility for a conflict and are willing to explore their own role in the conflict situation can move the conflict to a win-win mode more readily than individuals who are too ready to lash out and blame their partners. From a win-win orientation, these individuals who accept some responsibility are also more willing to use a situational attribution perspective to explain their partners' conflict behavior and also suspend snapshot attacks on their partners' personality traits.

Thus, if both Michael and Mabel can learn to reframe their attributions from a negative dispositional approach to a situational attribution viewpoint, both may come closer to understanding each other's conflict viewpoint. A situational attribution approach also allows both parties to save face and to honor each other's situational space. For example, Michael and Mabel can both attribute their stress, in part, to the arrival of the in-laws and their initial adjustment period to a new baby. They can learn to be more empathetic to each other's conflict lens. They have to learn to create a shared meaning frame of what it means, for example, to be a family—from both perspectives. Michael and Mabel can learn to make sense of the conflict situation by expanding their perspectives to

include both cultural and situational factors that surround the simmering conflict issues.

Encountering Prejudice and Racism

Of all the contrasts that interracial couples bring to their relationship, the most visible and inescapable is that of their race.
Whereas interethnic (or interfaith) couples of the same race can
choose how and when they will reveal their differences to outsiders,
interracial couples display obvious visible differences. An African
American and white interracial couple are a visually different couple because of their different skin colors and facial features. Interracial couples must find different ways to deal with the family and
social reactions as well as with each other's reactions toward the
role of race in their relationship.

Although the outsiders' emotional reactions can range from
complete acceptance to utter ostracism, the couples' reactions in
considering race as a factor in their relationship can also range from
deep understanding to total dismissal. Conflicts can often arise
when intercultural and interracial couples have to deal with the
dilemma of whether or not to talk about matters of race or racism in
their surrounding environment and within their own relationship
context.

Although prejudice is about biased, inflexible prejudgments and
antagonistic feelings about outgroup members, racism is about the
personal/institutional belief in the cultural superiority of one race
and the inferiority of other races (Jones, 1997). It also refers to the
practice of power dominance of a "superior" racial group over
other "inferior" races. Couples often encounter their initial conflicts when they speak to their respective parents about their plans
for marriage. Their respective family's reactions can range from responses of support, acceptance, rejection, or fear, to outright hostility. For example, let us look at Gina's family response from the following interview excerpt (Gina is a white female planning to marry
an African American male) (McNamara, Tempenis, & Walton,
1999):

Well, when I told my parents, they both looked kind of shocked and then my father sort of blew up. He was yelling and screaming and told me that I had just thrown my life away and was I happy about that. But the whole time, I didn't hear my mother say anything against us. Later, after my father went to bed, she came up to me and told me that while she couldn't go against my father's wishes, she just wanted to make sure that I was happy. (p. 76)

Consider James's family response (James is an African American male planning to marry a white female) (McNamara et al., 1999):

My father was absolutely against my marrying a White woman. He said I was a traitor to my race and that I was not giving Black women a chance at a wonderful life. He would not talk to Donna, would not see her under any circumstances, and we did not talk to each other for over five years. (p. 84)

It appears that for many of the white families, the core emotion of fear underlies the many reasons for their opposition to interracial marriage. Their reasons can include societal or community disapproval, fear for the general physical and emotional well-being of the couple, fear of ostracism, and self-esteem issues for their biracial grandchildren (Frankenberg, 1993). As one white female comments (Crohn, 1995),

I am sitting in a small restaurant with my daughter, my husband, my grandson, and my son-in-law. I look at my two-year-old grandson. I have a warm feeling and think to myself, "This is my first grandchild." Then my pleasure dissolves into anxiety as I realize that everyone in the restaurant is looking at us. My grandson is brown. My son-in-law is black. And my daughter is no longer mine. (p. 190)

In terms of societal reactions, one of the most common problems experienced by interracial couples are stares by strangers. In addition to the stares, prejudicial treatment by some restaurant servers, real estate agents, and racism within their own workplace deeply disturb the couple's relationship. For example, listen to Russell's (an African American husband) comments (McNamara et al., 1999):

> We go into a restaurant, together, with our children. We will order the meal and when we are done, the waitress hands us separate checks. Like she is saying "There is no way you two could be together." And here we are sitting with our children, who are obviously fair-skinned: whom does she think they belong to? (p. 96)

Let us look at another interview excerpt, this one about Sean (an African American husband) dealing with a real estate agent (McNamara et al., 1999):

> Oh it happens all the time. You call them up and they'll be nice and everything and take all the information down for you. Then you meet them down at the house and you can just see it in their eyes. They want no part of this situation. And I don't think all of them are racists. I think the nature of their job keeps them from lending money or selling property to Black folks. But it is still steering, however you want to define it. (p. 97)

Steering refers to the real estate practice wherein an agent steers prospective tenants or buyers away from an all-white neighborhood into one composed primarily of minorities. Research also indicates that banks and other lenders are much more likely to reject a mortgage to a minority-looking family than to a comparable white family (McNamara et al., 1999).

Most interracial couples have developed various coping strategies to deal with prejudiced and racist situations. These coping strategies include ignoring/dismissing (especially minor offenses such as staring or nasty comments), normalizing (to think of themselves and appeal to others to treat them as "normal" couples with marital ups and downs), and withdrawing (avoiding places and groups of people who are hostile to interracial couples). In addition, they also use education (outreach efforts to help others to accept interracial couples), confrontation (addressing directly the people who insult or embarrass them), prayers (relying on faith to solve problems), and humor (to add levity in a distressing situation) to ease or ward off the pains of racism (McNamara et al., 1999). These coping strategies can be viewed as face-recuperating moves by the interracial couples when their self-respect and relational identity as a couple are being downgraded or insulted. Partners usually use ignoring/dismissal coping strategies to deal with minor face-threats, and use more direct—such as education and confrontation—coping strategies in countering major face-threats.

Finally, simply because the partners are in an intimate relationship, there is no guarantee that they are free of racism or matters of race in their own evolving relationship. In times of anger and conflict, couples may have expressed racial epithets or racial attitudes to vent their frustrated feelings that can seriously hurt each other. Although some of the words may have been exchanged in a joking/teasing or sarcastic way during an intimate conflict, those words or phrases can be taken as hurtful, racist comments. The following interview excerpt, for example, from Gregory (an African American male married to a white female), is revealing:

> Joyce will ask me sometimes about "Why aren't you on time?" and I'll say, "Well, you've been married to me for so many years, don't you understand the concept of CPT? When you gonna learn CPT? [he explained that CPT stands for "colored people's time."] . . . Or if Joyce makes a meal that I find rather "flat" in taste, I might get sarcastic and say things like, "This is White people's cooking; why don't you learn how to cook colored?" It comes out that way, sort of sarcastically.
>
> Joyce's response: I think now it's a joke. I think initially when we were first together, it was more hurtful. (Rosenblatt, Karis, & Powell, 1995, pp. 230-231)

Sometimes a white partner's indifference to or ignorance of a racism issue may perpetuate a racist worldview. Gloria (an African

American female married to a white male) says in an interview excerpt (Rosenblatt et al., 1995),

> I told him someone yelled, "nigger." I was on the corner down there; I was with the baby, just driving by. And his first reaction is, "Well, what did you do to provoke that?" . . . And I thought, "That's the difference between being Black and White. Why would I have to do anything to provoke it? (p. 240)

The white partner's insulated stance toward racism issues reflects his lifelong privilege of being a white male in a dominant, white society (McIntosh, 1995). The concept of white privilege refers to the invisible systems that confer dominance or power resources on whites. Thus, white males can walk down the street at night or drive their cars routinely without the need for awareness of potentially racist remarks directed at them without cause, or be particularly concerned with racial profiling issues by the police on the highways.

Fortunately, not all European American males have such a chilling, indifferent reaction to racism issues faced by their intimate partners. As Adam (a white male married to an African American female) commented (Rosenblatt et al., 1995),

> It takes being open to your own racism. It's all well and good to be sensitive to others in how they react to you, but you ought to be a little bit sensitive when you can and recognize your own mistakes, try to learn why what you've just said or done offended your partner. . . . [F]or example, there's an experience where Wanda would say, "Yeah, I understand that," and I say, "I don't understand it. What was happening? Help me out here." (p. 243)

When two intimate partners bring to their relationship strong identities as members of two different minority groups, they are hypersensitive to identity conflict issues. The following heated debate between Alan (with a strong sense of African American identity) and Sara (with a strong sense of Jewish identity) illustrates this point (Crohn, 1995):

Alan: How can you know what it means to be discriminated against? You grew up in a comfortable, safe neighborhood. You got to choose whether or not you revealed to others that you were Jewish. My ancestors were brought here as slaves.

Sara: I can't believe you're saying this stuff. You know that I lost great-aunts and great-uncles in the Holocaust. You don't have any monopoly on suffering. What right does the past give you to say how we lead our lives? (p. 171)

Alan and Sara's identity conflict issues—cultural, racial, and religious—obviously tapped into very intense, core emotions in their own identity construction. They will need time to really get to know the identity meaning of each other and to find meaningful ways to connect to each other's cultures as well as their own.

Because the discussion of any racial or religious identity issue is so complex and emotionally charged, most couples opt to avoid the topic altogether. However, refraining from dealing with salient identity issues (especially salient from the beholder's viewpoint) is like "buying peace for your relationship on a credit card. You may enjoy the temporary freedom from anxiety you 'purchased' by avoiding the difficult topics, but when the bill finally comes due, the 'interest' that's accumulated in the form of resentment and regret may be devastating" (Crohn, 1995, pp. 183-184).

In dealing with prejudice and racism outside their relationship, some couples may talk about dealing with racism issues as a lifetime project whereas others dismiss them as inconsequential. Some reinforce the idea that in order to deal with prejudice issues they have to learn to be honest with the prejudices that they carry within themselves. Other couples try to keep matters of race as a small part of their relationship, with their attention focused more on "love, grocery shopping, raising children . . . doing the laundry, planning vacations, washing the dishes, and all the details of a shared life" (Rosenblatt et al., 1995, p. 249).

Partners in an intercultural-intimate relationship can often wonder whether their conflict during the ebb and flow of their relationship is a result of genuine differences of opinion, personality clashes, cultural/ethnic value differences, or the prejudiced attitude of one of the partners. To achieve a genuine understanding of these intertwined issues, couples have to learn to listen, to probe, and to listen some more. They have to learn to develop unconditional acceptance and trust—to trust the first-hand experience of their partners—whether it is about racism or prejudice issues. The intimate partners need to be mindfully present during those moments—to comfort, to bolster and uplift the spirit of their partners, and to be unconditionally supportive and empathetic.

Punctuating Different Conflict Goals

Intimate conflict, especially if the same conflict theme recurs, often involves multiple conflict goals. Revisiting the arrival of the in-laws incident with Michael and Mabel, we see that whereas the conflict content issue is about the in-laws' visitation protocol, the conflict situation is really about incompatible relational and identity conflict goal issues. The implicit relational conflict goal is complex—from Michael's relationship with Mabel to his relationship with his in-laws, plus his relationship with his 3-year-old son, Micky. As indicated in Chapter 1, if we want to engage in a coherent analysis of a conflict situation, we have to think in terms of interdependent systems analysis among all the individuals and patterns involved in the conflict situation.

Relationship conflict goals are intertwined with identity conflict goals. Although both Michael and Mabel in the critical incident are stressed about their marital relationship, they are also experiencing increased identity frustrations. For example, Mabel feels that Michael should be more appreciative and supportive of her Chinese cultural identity, including allowing their son to learn how to speak Chinese. She thinks Michael should be grateful to her parents because they are teaching Micky to speak Chinese, helping to babysit, and even doing cooking chores so that the couple can enjoy a nice dinner when they return home from work. Michael, on the other hand, feels that his identity needs for personal privacy time and family privacy time are not being respected. Even though the couple may be quarreling about content conflict issues such as the need to call before visiting or that Micky should speak English to his father, the deeper core issues in this intimate conflict situation are about relational and identity conflict goal issues.

According to sex differences in intimate conflict research in the United States (Wood, 1997), whereas males tend to punctuate or emphasize content or substantive issues in an interpersonal conflict fight, females tend to punctuate relational or socioemotional issues in a conflict. These different punctuation points of conflict are learned early on in the games that boys and girls play in the family and within the school (Maltz & Borker, 1982; Tannen, 1990, 1994). In the United States, for example, boys' games (e.g., baseball, football) typically involve fairly large groups, and the games usually have clear substantive objectives, distinct roles and rules with decisive win-lose end goals. When boys fight with each other, they argue over "objective" facts, "impartial" procedures, and win-lose content goals.

By comparison, girls' games (e.g., playing house, jumping rope) tend to involve dyadic pairs or small groups. They often involve fluid discussion about who is going to play what roles in the playing house game. Through active give-and-take relational negotiation, the girls' games often promote relational compromises and collaborations. Thus, girls (and females in general) tend to be more in tune with relational conflict goal issues. The *process* of playing and the art of negotiating different roles tend to be more important than clear win-lose substantive outcomes. Games that boys and girls play during childhood, their family socialization processes, their school experiences, mass media influence, and the larger cultural environment are some of the factors that account for their different goal emphases.

Although males and females are sometimes aware of their clashes over different content and relational goal orientations, they tend to operate unconsciously or mindlessly about their identity goal needs and wants. To express clearly one's own identity conflict goals and needs, one has to know what one wants in an intimate relationship.

Learning to be honest with oneself can be an emotionally unsettling experience because we may not like what we have uncovered or we may be disappointed at the unmet needs. In a quality intimate relationship, individuals have to learn to be emotionally vulnerable and accessible to the self and to their intimate partners. They have to take time to understand their self-identity issues and also take the time and commitment to deeply understand the multiple identity issues that confront their partners.

INTERCULTURAL-INTIMATE CONFLICT: PROCESS FACTORS

Primary cultural factors and the situational conflict features shape the styles and responses in dealing with an intercultural-intimate conflict. We discuss emotional expressions, conflict responses, and intimate facework strategies in this section.

Intimate Emotional Expressions

Intimate conflict is, essentially, an emotionally distressing experience. Whereas independent-self individualists are inclined to engage in ego-based emotional expressions during a conflict, interdependent-self collectivists are inclined to emphasize other-focused emotional expressions (Markus & Kitayama, 1991). For example, in the case of Michael and Mabel, Michael is more concerned with protecting his self-pride and asserting his discontent emotions. Mabel, for her part, is more concerned with protecting relational face and family network face (e.g., by sparing her parents the embarrassing arguments and, hence, hurting their feelings). Ego-based emotions can include the protection of self-pride, vulnerabilities, and hurts. Other-focused emotions can include the concerns with the intimate partner's feelings, other-focused shame issues, and network emotional reactions during a conflict.

In addition, even if Mabel's parents have heard their arguments, they would most likely pretend not to have heard anything. Because

Mabel's parents are interdependent collectivists, they would also help their daughter to save face by not mentioning anything to Mabel or Michael. However, they may use nonverbal facial expressions or silence (or even overly polite smiling expressions) to indicate their emotional displeasure with Michael. Coming from a large power distance value culture, they would expect that Michael could read their nonverbal signals accurately and actually would act nicer to their daughter or to them. Unfortunately, in this particular story, Michael, coming from a moderate power distance value environment, has not yet learned to decode the subtle, nonverbal messages from his in-laws (or for that matter, decode the silence of Mabel) with cultural accuracy. As mentioned in Chapter 1, intercultural conflict often involves unintentional clashes and miscued attributions.

Overall, although both individualists and collectivists may experience a wide spectrum of emotions in an intimate conflict, they may internalize more strongly different types of emotions under different conflict conditions. Although Michael's inner emotions are that of outward-directed frustrations and a sense of unfairness, Mabel's inner emotions are that of inward-directed resentments and a sense of shame or embarrassment. Whereas Michael's emotional reaction is that Mabel should stand up to her parents more, Mabel's emotional reaction is that Michael should learn self-discipline and self-restraint to reign in his negative emotional outbursts.

Individualists and collectivists may also choose to deintensify or dramatize different types of facial expressions to achieve specific conflict interaction outcomes. A smile or silence, for example, can carry different connotations in different cultures. In the Chinese or Japanese culture, a smile can be used to signal friendliness, but it can also be used to mask embarrassment, hide displeasure, or suppress anger. Likewise, the meaning of silence can carry different connotations. In many Asian group-based cultures, the use of silence or *ma*—in conjunction with very subtle nonverbal facial cues—can connote disapproval to approval, refusal to acceptance, and shame to appreciation. The strategic use of smile or silence in

these Asian cultures reflects mutual-concern face-saving emotions. Although insiders learn to master the cultural decoding rules of these nonverbal emotional cues at a very young age, it may take outsiders many years of experience before they can accurately decode some of these complex emotional displays during a conflict.

Overall, culture plays a powerful role in terms of the types of emotions that should be displayed or suppressed in different conflict situations. Individualistic cultures tend to encourage the display of a wide range of extreme positive to extreme negative emotions in everyday lives. Individualistic value tendencies encourage the spontaneous display of emotions to reflect one's inner state or mood. In comparison, collectivistic cultures tend to encourage the display of moderately positive emotions such as friendliness and agreeableness in everyday interaction routines. Group-based cultures tend to suppress the overt display of extreme negative emotions such as anger and disgust, even in an intimate conflict situation. If one is a good nonverbal cultural detective, however, one can detect the displeased emotions through very subtle, microfacial expression or tone of voice. To be competent conflict communicators, both parties need to be observant of the emotional nonverbal cues that the facial, body, and vocal language that their intimate partners display.

Relational Conflict Responses

In any relationship, information openness and closedness acts as a critical gatekeeper in moving a relationship to greater or lesser intimacy. Openness refers to the disclosure or revelation of feelings concerning the different facets of the self. Closedness refers to the regulation or concealment of feelings concerning different aspects of the emotional self.

According to Barnlund's (1989), Gudykunst's (1998), and Ting-Toomey's (1991) research, although intimate partners in individualistic cultures tend to subscribe to the ideology of openness, intimates in collectivistic cultures tend to subscribe to the ideology of verbal information closedness. These trends may continue during

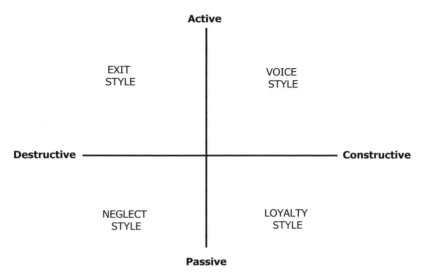

Figure 3.2. Intimate Conflict Modes: Four Styles

an intercultural-intimate conflict. An individualist (e.g., Michael) often prefers to confront the conflict with a low-context conflict style, and a collectivist (e.g., Mabel) often prefers to avoid the conflict with a high-context conflict mode.

In addition, in intimate conflict style research, there are four intimate conflict modes: exit, voice, loyalty, and neglect (Healey & Bell, 1990; Rusbult, 1987). These four modes or styles are categorized under the active-versus-passive dimension and the destructive-versus-constructive dimension (see Figure 3.2).

Based on research studies in the larger U.S. culture, *exit style* refers to an active, yet destructive, conflict response when one party directly hurts the other conflict party with intimidation or threatening strategies such as shouting or exiting the scene (or the relationship) abruptly. *Voice style* refers to an active and constructive conflict response when one party tries to improve the conflict situation by talking out the problem with his or her conflict partner. *Loyalty style* means a passive, yet constructive, conflict response when one party uses a wait-and-see attitude and attempts to accommodate the wishes of the other conflict partner. Finally, *neglect style* means

a passive and destructive conflict response when one party uses avoidance or passive-aggressive strategies in ignoring the partner's wishes or requests.

In relating the exit/voice/loyalty/neglect conflict responses to Michael and Mabel's intimate conflict styles, we can say that Michael uses the voice style in the hope of resolving the conflict problem, whereas Mabel uses a mixture of neglect/loyalty style in the hope that the conflict issue will disappear. The interpretations and the meanings that are attached to these four intimate styles definitely reflect an individualistic, Western orientation—in terms of what constitutes constructive versus destructive conflict responses, and active versus passive conflict reactions. For example, from Mabel's perspective, Michael's voice style definitely is being viewed as an aggressive, destructive conflict response in dealing with the in-laws issue. In contrast, from Michael's perspective, Mabel's neglect/loyalty style surely is being interpreted as a passive, destructive conflict approach. However, from both viewpoints, they likely would see their own intimate conflict styles as constructive. Thus, our cultural and personal baseline (habitual) level of how we deal with a variety of conflict situations asserts a strong influence in terms of how we frame the meanings of different intimate conflict styles.

In relating face-negotiation theory (Ting-Toomey & Kurogi, 1998) to interpret these four intimate conflict styles, we can view voice as an assertive-aggressive, self-face maintenance mode, whereas neglect is a passive-aggressive, self-face maintenance mode. There are two layers to the voice conflict style: whether one acts assertively (i.e., voicing one's own needs and disclosing one's own conflict emotions in an open manner) or aggressively (i.e., expressing one's own need and emotions at the expense of overlooking the need or shutting down the emotions of the other conflict party). These will influence whether a constructive or destructive conflict solution can be achieved. More importantly, whether one actually invites the other conflict party to voice her or his concerns and share her or his conflict emotions will profoundly affect the intimate conflict process and outcome. In addition, the neglect conflict style also has two possible layers. One can passively neglect without working constructively toward a mutually shared solution or one can strategically neglect to make time to think of a creative outcome.

Finally, loyalty (i.e., as an obliging strategy) and exit (i.e., as an avoidance strategy) can also straddle between other-face accommodation and mutual-face maintenance conflict responses. For example, the exit style can be viewed or reframed as a constructive conflict response when one is emotionally flooded (or emotionally muted) and a cooling down or time-out period is desperately needed to defuse the escalating verbal abuses or relational hurts. How we frame or reframe some of the perceived behaviors in the intimate conflict episode plays a decisive role for how we want to approach or avoid a particular intimate conflict situation. If we are willing to give the relationship a chance to continue or if we can catch ourselves mindfully responding to an explosive conflict scene, we may be able to change the direction and the emotional intensity of the conflict negotiation process.

Intimate Conflict Facework Strategies

The kindling, development, and integration (or the erosion) of an intimate interpersonal relationship involve continuous, active management of relational facework issues (Cupach & Metts, 1994). In managing intercultural-intimate conflicts in the course of a long-term relationship, the ability to manage one's own and the other party's identity image in a satisfactory manner will have a profound impact on the relational conflict outcome. When an intimate partner's sense of identity esteem or self-worth is being threatened in a conflict situation, he or she may resort to defensive or passive-aggressive acts. Recurring win-lose to lose-lose conflict spirals are relationally threatening. Prolonged aggressive to passive-aggressive conflict patterns can produce an identity invalidation climate in an intimate relationship.

In an intimate conflict situation that revolves around in-laws, work stress, or children issues, when our intimate partner consistently disagrees with our viewpoints, we often view his or her disagreement as an identity rejection gesture. The more personal the relationship, the more vulnerable and defensive we are in interpreting the face-threat moves. Thus, competent interpersonal facework should strive to foster mutual identity respect and buttress against contempt. Facework is integral to "managing challenges and dilemmas of relationships. At its best, effective face support permits us to achieve (however fleeting) relationship nirvana. At its worst, persistent face loss can create bitter enmity and personal agony" (Cupach & Metts, 1994, pp. 15-16).

Intercultural-intimate conflict entails face-threat behaviors, face-loss behaviors, and face-saving behaviors. In an intimate conflict situation, we can threaten our own face by losing an argument, losing our temper, getting caught in a lie, or breaking a promise. We can also threaten the other conflict party's face through making direct personal criticisms, making him or her look stupid, insulting or ridiculing him or her, or blaming the other for causing a problem (Cupach & Canary, 1997). When face-threats escalate in intensity and severity, intimate partners become defensive and close-minded and are more likely to engage in hurtful put-downs or exiting the conflict scene all together.

Ting-Toomey and Kurogi (1998) reason that for independent-self individualists, when their face is threatened or damaged, they tend to engage in self-face recuperating moves such as defending and aggressive facework tactics. For interdependent-self collectivists, when their face is attacked, they tend to use avoidance facework moves such as making concessions, obliging, pretending/neglecting, or even involve a third-party intermediary to resolve the intimate conflict. Both individualists and collectivists may resort to integrative facework behaviors such as compromising, apologizing, and private discussion, if they are able to place a higher priority over mutual-face issues (Ting-Toomey, 1994b, 1994c).

Finally, whereas individualists would draw a clear privacy line between themselves and the external world regarding their marital conflict process, collectivists may blur that distinction between the private world and the family kinship world. When faced with a recurring conflict situation, individualists often prefer to go to a neutral third party or counselor for relational therapy and advice.

They often feel safe disclosing emotions to a professional expert whom they believe is well trained to guide them in resolving their marital crises. For collectivists, however, going to therapists or counselors for marital advice means "airing the dirty laundry" in the public arena and can cause the couple or the family to lose tremendous face. Thus, even in the third-party, help-seeking arena, special attention needs to be paid to the different attitudes and expectations that intercultural-intimate partners hold toward the role of a third-party mediator.

To conclude, to the extent that mutual face is supported in an intimate conflict, a satisfying conflict outcome is attainable. As relationships grow in intimacy, partners presumably work harder to enhance their partners' face and demonstrate attunement and attentiveness for their partners at a more profound level. When relationships break down or dissolve, however, one or both partners "exhibit a competitive orientation in which one's own face [often] takes precedence over the partner's. However, even in the face of a disintegrating relationship, partners can assist each other in saving face" (Cupach & Metts, 1994, pp. 97-98). Effective mutual face saving can be accomplished through culture-sensitive collaborative dialogue, mindful listening, and affirming the other's sense of self-worth in the relationship (see Chapter 6). Constructive conflict responses can directly affect the outcome dimensions of an intimate relationship.

INTERCULTURAL-INTIMATE CONFLICT: OUTCOME DIMENSIONS

We discuss two outcome dimensions that are related to an intercultural-intimate conflict process: relational commitment and relational stability/satisfaction.

Relational Commitment

Johnson (1991) proposes that there are two types of marital commitment: personal and structural. *Personal commitment* means the individual's desire or intent to continue the marital relationship based on their subjective feelings, sentiments, and personal experiences. *Structural commitment,* on the other hand, means the individual takes into consideration various external social reactions, nuclear family, and extended family reactions in keeping the marital relationship stable or enduring.

In completing our analysis of the in-laws critical incident, we can predict that Michael (as an independent-self individualist) places a higher emphasis on the personal commitment aspect of his marital relationship than does Mabel. Meanwhile, Mabel (as an interdependent-self collectivist) would place a higher priority on the structural commitment aspect (e.g., the reactions of her parents to her marital quarrel) of the marital relationship than does Michael. This does not mean that personal commitment is not important to Mabel; it simply means that although both aspects are important, one aspect outweighs the other in terms of ranking.

Because interdependent types tend to be more ingroup-bound and obligation-based, the ingroup reactions and advice on whether the couple should stay together or dissolve the relationship would also have a strong impact on the recipient. Intercultural frictions arise when one partner subscribes strongly to the ideology of personal commitment and the other partner subscribes strongly to the ideology of structural commitment. The former will crave more privacy away from the partner's network and its incessant intrusions, whereas the latter will experience split loyalty and conflict in dealing with two intertwined relationships. Supportive mutual face-saving behaviors and responsive identity confirmation messages can enhance both personal and structural commitment in the intimate relationship. Frequent negativity patterns (e.g., complain-complain, complain-defend, attack-attack, and defend-attack patterns) in intimate conflicts destroy a relationship (Ting-Toomey, 1983).

Relational Stability and Satisfaction

According to interracial couple marital research, education level appears to be the best predictor of a stable interracial marriage. The higher the educational level of both partners, the more stable or long-lasting the interracial marriage (Billingsley, 1992). Moreover, most interracial couples tend to share similar social, educational, and occupational characteristics. In counseling hundreds of inter-ethnic and interfaith couples to strengthen marital satisfaction, Crohn (1995) has the following five suggestions: (a) Clarify your different cultural codes—learn the hidden cultural rules that shape self's and the cultural partner's behaviors; (b) deal with the tough cultural and racial issues in time—face your fear and learn to talk with each other in a culture-sensitive manner; (c) sort out the confusion about your cultural, racial, and religious identities—acknowledge and come to terms with your multiple identities; (d) be aware of the social context of your relationship—understand societal prejudice and racism issues; and (e) find your own path and help your children find theirs—help them to develop a secure sense of self-esteem and encourage them to experiment with their multi-ple identities.

Although Gottman's (1999) marital conflict research has focused primarily on mainstream white couples in the U.S. culture, his rich conflict research findings nevertheless may shed light on issues for intercultural or interracial couples. After studying 650 marital cou-ples and tracking their marriages for 14 years, he has uncovered six major signs that indicate a divorce will ensue:

1. Harsh conflict startup—the first 3 minutes of any marital dispute (the harsher the startup, the more doomed the out-come) will determine the tone of the rest of the conversa-tion.
2. The Four Horsemen of the Apocalypse—criticism (e.g., with global character attack), contempt (e.g., mockery and sneering), defensiveness (e.g., self-defense and blaming other), and stonewalling (e.g., tuning-out or indifferent response).
3. Emotional flooding—meaning that your partner's nega-tivity is so overwhelming that it leaves you shell-shocked and prompts you to disengage emotionally.

4. Stressful body/physiological language—increased heart rate and sweating make it impossible to have a productive, problem-solving discussion.

5. Failed repair attempts—failure to put on the brakes to deescalate the tension during a touchy discussion.

6. Bad memories—couples tend to recall negative events and have pervasive negative thoughts about their marriage.

Gottman was able to predict in 91% of the cases whether a couple's marriage would succeed or fail based on the emergent signs of unproductive conflict communication.

Gottman and Silver (1999) suggest that the key to handling all marital conflicts competently is communicating unconditional acceptance of your partner's core personality. They comment, "You must make your partner feel that you are understanding. If either (or both) of you feels judged, misunderstood, or rejected by the other, you will not be able to manage the problems in your marriage" (p. 149). Furthermore, in satisfying marriages, couples appear to have developed a deep friendship in their relationship. They have a profound, mutual respect for each other and they enjoy each other's company. These couples tend to know each other intimately—they are "well-versed in each other's likes, dislikes, personality quirks, hopes, and dreams. They have an abiding regard for each other and express this fondness not just in the big ways but in little ways day in and day out" (pp. 19-20). As a final example, let us listen to the following comments by an African American male who is married to a white female (McNamara et al., 1999):

If I had to pick the perfect wife that I could have, she is very close to it. . . . She knows me better than anyone else and I think she helps me a lot too. I like to talk to her and trust her and the fact that we both trust each other was there from the start. I know that she is really sensitive to issues of race and that is because we have experienced so much together. But I also know how difficult that has been for her. So I always try to keep her feelings in the front of my mind. I can't do anything about my race, but I can do something about how it affects her, at least sometimes I can. She does the same for me, which means that we are always thinking of each other. That's one of the reasons why I think we have lasted for so long—we are a lot stronger because we are really sensitive to the problem. . . . [S]he has taught me how to chase away the demons that get to me about racism. I used to get so angry and be so volatile and now I realize that if I want this relationship to last, I have to let some of that go. And she has been able to help me do that. (p. 150)

For intercultural-intimate couples, a fundamental acceptance of the cultural/racial and religious aspects of their partner's identity, a mutual willingness to explore cultural codes, and a mutual openness in discussing racism issues can facilitate greater relational satisfaction. Whether we are in an intimate intracultural or intercultural relationship, we will do well to regard each interpersonal relationship as if it is an intercultural one. We can then learn to be more attuned to the different cultural values, religious beliefs, or family backgrounds that shape the mindset and the habits of the heart that intimate partners bring into their unique relational culture.

In concluding their interviews with interracial marital couples, Rosenblatt et al. (1995) summarize three relationship blessings that their interviewees mentioned in their interviews: (a) enrichment— the enrichment of self, partner, and children that comes from the joining of different races, cultures, and perspectives; (b) weathering racist opposition—as individual and couple, being able to get past racism and getting to better places with family members who had initially opposed the relationship; and (c) healing—healing individual hurts and wounds from racism, and practicing forgiveness in a society that has been strained by racism.

Intercultural-intimate relationships reveal the kinds of possibilities that are created when individuals bring different facets of the cultural self together and are committed to making the process work. Intercultural matches present us with a microcosm of the larger world in which intergroup conflict and cooperation is played out—constructively or destructively—in the most intimate forum.

INTERCULTURAL-INTIMATE CONFLICT: PRACTICAL GUIDELINES

We have walked through the culture-based situational model (see Chapter 2) with specific analyses and examples in the intercultural-intimate conflict arena. We summarize the main ideas in this section and propose four competencies in managing intercultural-intimate conflict.

Intercultural-Intimate Conflict: A Summary

In analyzing an intercultural-intimate conflict situation in depth, six observations can be gleaned. First, cultural values of individualism-collectivism and power distance often create relational frictions within the intimate dyad and between their respective families. Second, an intercultural-intimate conflict often involves different face contents (e.g., autonomy face, relationship face, or family/network face) and different face interaction styles (low- vs. high-context; overt verbal vs. subtle nonverbal). Third, biased attributional tendencies (especially in using negative dispositional attributions such as blaming and direct criticism) can often propel the conflict episode to either escalatory or avoidance conflict spirals. Fourth, prejudice and racism issues can create further divides and collusions in an already fragile personal relationship. Fifth, from cultural value difference to racism issues, many of such differences are face-related problems, an underlying call for identity respect, consideration, recognition, pride, and relational worthiness. Sixth, the communication competencies or skills that we use to handle the cultural, personal, and situational aspects of the conflict transactions will dramatically shape the outcome dimensions of an intimate relationship.

Translating our culturally grounded knowledge into mindful practice, sustained faith that the relational crises or storms will blow over, and a pervasive positive assessment of the relationship itself may help us to tackle our intimate conflicts on a step-by-step basis. Developing a systems consciousness in looking at the "big picture" of the relationship, emphasizing the rewards or positive qualities of the relationship more so than the costs, and cultivating individual interests and hobbies so that the relationship has room to "breathe" or rejuvenate, may also help the developmental growth of the relationship on a holistic level.

Intimate Conflict Management: Four Competencies

The following four competencies can serve as concrete reminders intimate partners can practice in their everyday conflict situations.

Decoding Cultural Aspects of an Intimate Conflict. To manage an intimate conflict constructively, intimate partners need to understand the underlying beliefs and values that drive their own conflict decisions. They need to spend time reflecting and probing their own culturally and individually derived values, needs, wants, and expectations in the relationship. They also need to take time to understand, on a profound level, their partners' beliefs, values, needs, and wants that frame their conflict behaviors and frustrated emotions. It takes tremendous time, patience, and emotional vulnerability to really know one's own deep-seated emotions and pulses. It also takes enormous time, energy, commitment, and integrity to really know and simultaneously understand or grasp the core beliefs and values that anchor our intimate partners' hearts and conflict rhythms.

The most we can do in any intimate conflict relationship is to underestimate our understanding and be willing to learn more and be surprised by our partners. With the information in this chapter, we believe that an initial cultural value analysis can be gained through understanding value patterns such as individualism-collectivism, small and large power distance, and culture-based sex role socialization processes. We want to further emphasize that although each culture or ethnic group has certain system-level characteristics, individuals within a culture or ethnic group, of course, exhibit rich and diverse personality tendencies (e.g., introvert vs. extrovert) and individual attributes. Furthermore, situational features add further layers of complexity to the people to whom we are attracted. Thus, understanding our cultural partner holistically requires multiple layers of cultural-level, personal-level, and situational-level knowledge.

Developing a deep friendship with our partner—knowing her or his deepest dreams, fears, triumphs, failures, hopes, and strivings—would help to develop a strong foundation to weather the relational conflicts and storms. In addition, nurturing a strong fondness and appreciation for our partner, that is, keeping positive thoughts about our partner on a daily, habitual basis, would serve as a shield to counteract major relationship crises and stressors (Gottman & Silver, 1999). Developing a core set of shared relationship beliefs and visions (e.g., willingness to sacrifice materialistic needs to serve the underprivileged) may serve as support during difficult times in the maturing relationship.

Listening to the Voices of Identity. Our conceptions of our own cultural/racial identity evolve across time. At times, our sense of cultural or racial identity can be clear and unmistaken. At other times, it may create great confusion or ambivalence for our partners or for us. There is also a danger that what is a matter of social class or gender, for example, could be taken as a matter of race. All these identity issues are intertwined (Ting-Toomey, 1993).

In times of confusion, however, we should take time to listen truthfully to ourselves, to listen to our own voices in terms of where and why the confusion arises. In addition, we need to clarify for our partners why their interpretation may have an alternative source (e.g., My interpretation is that this is not a race issue, the way I see it is that this is a gender difference issue because . . .). The timing, the pacing, the situation (e.g., following a racist episode, when your partner is convinced that it is a racist act, you should accept his or her experience without reservation), and the tone we use to promote our alternative interpretation can easily turn the conversation into a constructive or destructive one.

In negotiating our cultural/racial or religious identity with our partners, we have to learn to know ourselves first. We have to acknowledge the evolving nature of our own identity development and the different (i.e., conscious or unconscious) choices we have made over the years. The more we learn to be honest with ourselves, the more likely we can learn to be vulnerable with our intimate partners. We can learn to self-disclose incrementally about our own doubts, ambivalence, pride, and identity change. We should also invite our partners to tell their stories, images, struggles, and identity triumphs. Mindful listening and sharing our identity stories during the developmental course of our relationships can foster deep trust and intimacy. By listening to our own and our partner's identity voices, we can prioritize what we consider precious and valuable in our personal and relational lives.

Helping Children to Develop a Secure Identity. One of the major conflict stressors in any intercultural-intimate relationship is the topic of raising children. In any intercultural or interfaith marriage, both parents and children have multiple options to choose from and to follow. Some of the factors that influence the choice are these: Does one parent have a greater intensity of identification with her or his cultural or racial group (or religious faith) than the other? What degree of involvement do members of the immediate and extended families play in the child's life? What is the cultural and religious composition of neighborhoods and schools? Do parents reach a mutually satisfactory consensus about an identity path for the family and in raising the child?

The children of intercultural or interracial marriages face different cultural/racial identity issues at different stages of their life cycle development. There are basically four forms of identity these children or adolescents can choose to identify themselves with, or they can also create their own unique combinations. The four identity forms in which many bicultural or biracial children find themselves are (a) majority-group identifiers—majority identifiers identify primarily with the parent who is from the dominant culture or religion, and they may or may not publicly acknowledge the identity of their other parent (in this case, a minority-group background); (b) minority-group identifiers—minority identifiers identify primarily with the parent who is a minority-group member, and they may either acknowledge that their other parent is from a different background or they may deny (or minimize) their dual heritage background; (c) synthesizers—synthesizers acknowledge that they are influenced by the different aspects of their parents' cultural backgrounds, and they are able to synchronize and synthesize the diverse aspects of their parents' values into a coherent identity; and (d) disaffiliates (i.e., "none of the above" identifiers)—disaffiliates try to distance themselves or claim not to be influenced by their parents' cultural backgrounds, and they often create their own identity labels and rebel against any existing label that is imposed on them as part of a particular racial or cultural group (Crohn, 1995). Children or teenagers at different developmental stages may experience different identity emotions and opt for different identity forms, shaped by their parents' attitudes, peer group reactions, self-identity explorations, and the larger society's support or rejection of their identity search process.

Some practical guidelines to deal with childrens' and adolescents' confusions about cultural and racial identity issues are as follows. First, try to take time and make a commitment to work out a family identity plan as early in your relationship as possible; understand the salient aspects of your own and your partner's cultural/racial and religious identity (Crohn, 1995). Second, learn to listen to your children's identity stories and experiences; their ambivalence is oftentimes part of a normal, developmental process. Learn not to judge or be hurt by their truthful revelations. Third, try to provide your children with plenty of cultural enrichment opportunities that celebrate the diversity of both of your cultures; offer them positive experiences to appreciate and synthesize the differences. Fourth, be truthful in dealing with prejudice and racism issues; nurture a secure sense of personal self-esteem and self-worth in your children regardless of how they wish to identify themselves. Parents should model constructive, assertive behaviors in confronting prejudice and racism issues. Fifth, recognize that your children will grow up and choose their own path; keep the dialogue open and let your children or teenagers know that you will always be there for them. A secure home environment, multiple sources of pride and self-esteem, listening to their stories with patience and interest, giving them room or space to grow, and finding meaningful ways to relate to who they are and are becoming are some very basic means that parents can use to signal their heartfelt caring and mindful presence in their children's lives.

Turning Toward Each Other Instead of Away. Finally, in managing any intercultural-intimate conflict effectively, couples have to learn to give *and* save face for each other, and also to take time to see each on an eye-to-eye, face-to-face, and breath-to-breath mutuality level. In emphasizing the marital principle of "turning towards each other instead of away," Gottman and Silver (1999) observe that couples should display genuine interest in what their intimate partners are telling them during a conflict episode. Although it is all right that intimate partners voice their conflict complaint or dissatisfaction, it is not acceptable to blame or criticize their partners' personalities and intrinsic attributes, therefore arousing defensiveness and hurts. Couples should learn to complain about the *behaviors* of their partners yet continue to affirm the self-worth and intrinsic values of their loved ones.

Intimate partners should also learn to signal their understanding and empathy through affectionate words, soothing phrases, and nonverbal gestures during an escalatory conflict spiral. Sometimes a tender nonverbal gesture (e.g., a gentle touch or hug) can dramatically lower the physiological alarms in the body of their partners. When intimate partners are coaxed into a relaxed state of readiness, they are more open and less defensive in discussing the conflict problem constructively. Thus, gentle humor or tactful face moves may help to warm up the relationship climate and diminish direct face-threats.

Finally, in any intercultural-intimate conflict, it is difficult to pursue all "my needs" or all "your needs" and come up with a neat conflict resolution. In most intimate conflicts, constructive conflict couples tend to cultivate multiple paths in arriving at a mutually satisfying destination. They also tend to use trial-and-error techniques and arrive at a give-and-take, mutual-face honoring process and outcome. For many effective conflict bridgebuilders in dealing with their own conflicts, they also accept the "messiness" of the conflict situation and sometime even opt to "let it go" without any close-ended resolutions. These conflict peacemakers learn to listen to their partners' viewpoints with patience and they are open to reconsidering their own position. They share conflict emotions in a constructive, culture-sensitive manner. They use gentle inquiries to understand their partners' cultural conflict lenses. They also actively invite their partners to tell their conflict images and stories.

These competent conflict partners are more attuned to the complexity of self-identity and other-identity issues. They are also more in sync and secure with themselves, and hence, they are more comfortable and resourceful in dealing with bicultural and multicultural identity issues without being emotionally overwhelmed. Finally, these intimate partners are also more committed and energized to seek creative and renewed ways of connecting—in a true partnership journey of intercultural surprises and discoveries.

INTERCULTURAL
CONFLICT IN DIVERSE
WORK GROUPS

Group interaction is prevalent in many organizations. Recently, we have seen teams and groups becoming formal aspects of many organizations. Indeed, many courses at universities require group projects, and many businesses have implemented team structures. This increased use of teams has occurred for several reasons. First, many managers and teachers believe that "two heads are better than one" and that groups can help increase productivity and creativity (Larson & LaFasto, 1989). Second, the movement of many organizations to self-managed teams to reduce the number of layers in the hierarchy has increased the number of work groups (Barker, 1993). As a result, participants in many organizations, including employees in businesses, governmental agencies, and students in schools and universities, are working in team situations on a daily basis. Because of this shift, organizations are now requiring individuals to have teamwork skills.

As we noted in Chapter 1, many nations around the world have seen a change in demographics. Coupled with the trend toward teams, members from different ethnic and cultural groups are interacting in groups on a daily basis. Furthermore, organizations have seen an increase in the creation of international joint ventures. A joint venture occurs when two companies combine forces in a cooperative effort to create, manufacture, and market a product. In an international joint venture, one company enters a foreign country and works with a company in that country; this allows the advantages of sharing costs and risks, as well as having the local partner's knowledge of consumer tastes and business practices (Barkema & Vermeulen, 1997). The international joint venture results in a global business team composed of members from multiple countries and companies. Such global business teams are another example of culturally diverse people working together in a group.

Conflict is inevitable in any group. Any time a group of people is brought together to make a decision or to solve a problem, differences of opinions and disagreements are common. Groups composed of ethnically and culturally diverse members, however, likely experience more conflict than groups composed of culturally homogeneous members (Cox, 1994). Increased conflict can be expected because of value differences, procedural differences, and differences in communication styles (Cox, 1994; Nadler, Keeshan-Nadler, & Broome, 1985). If conflict is more prevalent in diverse groups, why don't managers create homogeneous groups? Culturally diverse groups have advantages over homogeneous groups when conflict is managed effectively. The benefits of diversity include increased creativity and improved problem solving; overall, the benefits of diversity outweigh the disadvantages (Cox & Blake, 1991).

This chapter explores how cultural diversity in a group influences conflict. Specifically, we start by defining a group and providing a model of a group. Then, we examine what causes conflicts in diverse groups. We discuss how culture and cultural diversity influence conflict behavior and outcomes in groups. Finally, we offer

some recommendations for effectively managing conflicts in culturally diverse groups.

WHAT IS A GROUP?

Small Group: Features and Types

Several features define a group and distinguish it simply from a
collection of individuals. First, size is an important element. There
need to be at least three people, but the group needs to be small
enough so that each person can be aware of and have some reaction
to the other members (approximately 15-20 people maximum)
(Brilhart, 1978). Second, individual members must define themselves as a group (Socha, 1997). Third, for a collection of individuals to be a group, they must interact with one another (Socha,
1997). Finally, the members of the group must be interdependent.
Interdependence refers to the fact that group members affect and
are affected by other group members. Having a common goal and
influencing other members are factors of interdependence. In essence, a group is "a collection of three or more individuals who
interact about a common problem or goal so that they exert mutual
influence over one another" (Wilson & Hanna, 1993, p. 6).

There are numerous types of groups: (a) commercial (e.g., consumer groups), (b) educational (e.g., study groups), (c) familial (e.g.,
immediate and extended family), (d) health and welfare (e.g., support groups), (e) occupational (e.g., quality circles and commit-
tees), (f) political/civic (e.g., city council), (g) recreational (e.g.,
sports team), (h) social (e.g., gangs and sororities/fraternities), and
(i) spiritual (e.g., Bible study) (Socha, 1997). A student group completing a project for a class is an example of an educational group.
A search committee whose purpose is to hire a new department
manager represents an occupational group. This chapter focuses on
conflict within a group that is engaged in some type of work and
thus cuts across many of these types.

Small Group Interaction: A Systems Model

A group can be thought of as a social system consisting of inputs, processes, and outcomes, with the inputs influencing the processes that, in turn, influence outcomes (Ellis & Fisher, 1994). The inputs of the group are the features present at the outset of a group's discussion and include the cultural and individual characteristics of the members, as well as characteristics of the group such as its composition or the task it is completing. The processes are the communicative behaviors or the interactions that occur among group members, including behaviors such as turn taking, decision making, and conflict. The outputs of the group are what the group achieves or produces and include both task and relational outcomes. Task outcomes are the work of the group and tend to be measured in terms of productivity or quality, whereas relational outcomes are gauged by the quality of relationships among the members and tend to be measured in terms of satisfaction or cohesion (Bales, 1950; Oetzel & Bolton-Oetzel, 1997).

Inputs, processes, and outputs affect one another and are shaped by the group's environment. First, the inputs of the group influence the process. For example, the cultural background of individuals affects whether conflict is expressed directly or indirectly (Ting-Toomey, 1985, 1988, 1991). Second, the processes affect the outcomes. Research has shown groups that manage conflicts with cooperative conflict styles are likely to make better decisions than groups that manage conflicts with competitive conflict styles (Dace, 1990; Deutsch, 1969; Pood, 1980). Third, the output of the group influences the inputs through feedback. If an individual is satisfied with the group's processes, that person will likely have a positive attitude toward group work and be more apt to cooperate with the other members on future tasks. Finally, the environment influences the group (Putnam & Stohl, 1990). A group does not operate in a vacuum. Rather, it works within the confines of a larger organization or community. A group at a workplace, for instance, is constrained by the available resources and work norms of the organization. Thus, if the organization has limited resources, the group

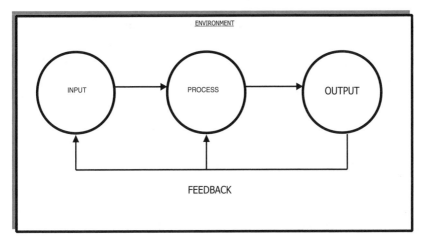

Figure 4.1. Small Group Interaction: A Systems Model

may feel the need to compete with other groups for those resources. Figure 4.1 provides a model of a group as a system.

The systems model of a small group is consistent with the culture-based situational model we presented in Chapter 2. The input in the culture-based situational model equals the primary orientation and the situational feature factors. The process in the culture-based situational model matches the conflict interaction styles, emotional expressions, facework behaviors, and conflict competence skills. The output parallels the conflict competence criteria and outcomes. Finally, the environment corresponds to the situational features, in which feedback is represented by the arrows that connect the various features. The model provides the framework for which we can understand conflict in culturally diverse groups. In the next section, we examine why conflicts occur.

SOURCES OF CONFLICT IN A CULTURALLY DIVERSE GROUP

At the heart of any conflict are opposing issues. There are myriad topics, attitudes, values, and behaviors for which opposing issues may develop. Cox (1994) identifies five critical sources, or causes of conflict, in intergroup relationships that are applicable for culturally diverse groups: (a) cultural differences, (b) assimilation versus ethnic identity maintenance, (c) power imbalance, (d) competing conflict goals, and (e) competition for scarce resources. We briefly describe each of these.

Cultural Differences

As we noted in Chapter 1, cultural differences are a prevalent source of contention in intercultural conflict. We communicate and process information based on the set of values that a cultural group holds (Earley, 1997; Triandis, 1995a). Intercultural conflict often results because of misunderstandings related to different world-views and communication styles that result from cultural differences. It is not uncommon for members of individualistic and collectivistic cultures to misunderstand one another during conversations (Ting-Toomey, 1997). One source of misunderstanding is the tendency for individualists to use direct communication styles and collectivists to use indirect styles. A collectivist may use indirect messages to hint at what they want or think (e.g., saying, "This proposal has some merit" to indicate that the idea may not be the best one), whereas individualists likely interpret the messages as direct statements (e.g., thinking, "She likes that proposal").

Different perceptions from cultural groups also may lead to conflict. African American and European American managers tend to have different cognitive orientations (Cox, 1994). In a study of a large corporation, 62% of African American men and 53% of African American women agreed that qualified European Americans were promoted in the company more rapidly than equally qualified African Americans, compared with 4% of European American men and 7% of European American women. In contrast, 12% of African American men and 13% of African American women agreed that qualified African Americans were promoted in the company more rapidly than equally qualified European Americans, whereas 75% of European American men and 85% of European American women believed this to be the case (Alderfer &

Smith, 1982). These findings illustrate startling differences in perceptions about promotion decisions that could potentially lead to
conflicts when discussing hiring and promotion problems in an
organization.

Assimilation Versus
Ethnic Identity Maintenance

A second source for conflict in culturally diverse groups is the
competing needs of assimilation and preservation of cultural/ethnic
identity (especially minority group identity). Assimilation refers to
the process of accepting the cultural values of the larger society and
de-emphasizing ethnic traditions and norms, whereas preservation
of cultural/ethnic identity refers to the process of maintaining
ethnic traditions and values (Berry, Kim, & Boski, 1987). Minority
group members are usually more aware of, and concerned with,
preserving cultural/ethnic identity than are majority group members (Cox, 1994; Ting-Toomey et al., 2000).

For minority members, the perceived imbalance in power and
inaccessibility to power within a society lead them to draw clear
boundaries between the dominant power-holder group and the
nondominant fringe group (Orbe, 1998). In response to these discrepancies in power, minority group members often emphasize a
strong cultural/ethnic identity to preserve customs, rituals, and a
positive self-identity. Majority group members often do not understand the need for positive ethnic identity affirmation that minority
group members feel and may be concerned, even annoyed, by such
efforts to differentiate themselves from the work group. This friction may lead to conflict between members who feel everyone
should sacrifice themselves for the good of the group (i.e., assimilation) and those who feel group members can be themselves and
remain a member of the group (i.e., preserve cultural identity).

For example, a work team is composed of two European Americans and three Mexican Americans and supervised by a European
American manager. The Mexican American members speak Span-
ish to each other during work (not during meetings for which all
members are present). The European American manager may see

108 MANAGING INTERCULTURAL CONFLICT EFFECTIVELY

this practice as not conforming to the company norms and therefore institutes an English-only policy during work hours. The Mexican American members likely see this policy as threatening their identity given the importance of language for ethnic identity maintenance. This example also demonstrates the importance of power in intercultural conflict.

Power Imbalance

A third source of conflict in culturally diverse groups is power discrepancy. Power, and the distribution of power, is a critical resource in an organization. One measure of power is the proportion of representation in a group or organization. Minority group density "refers to the percentage representation of a minority group in the total population of a social system" (Cox, 1994, p. 145). If a minority is not equally represented in a group, power is unequal, and there is a great potential for conflict and misunderstanding (Kanter, 1977; Larkey, 1996). In a situation where one cultural group has a majority, the potential exists for members of the majority group to form a coalition, and in turn, to force others in the group to go along with the coalition.

For instance, three European Americans and one African American are on a task force to discuss the usefulness of creating an African American support group to increase the number of African American managers at a company. If the three European Americans do not agree that this is a good policy, they can easily impose a decision on the African American member by a majority vote. It is important to note that coalitions are not the only possible outcomes in this situation; rather, the likelihood of a coalition forming increases if there is an inequality in the representation of the cultural groups.

Competing Conflict Goals

A fourth source of conflict is competing goals. During interactions among groups with members from different cultures, it is likely that there are different goals. For example, members of collectivistic cultures tend to have goals of establishing and maintaining strong interpersonal relationships, whereas members of individualistic cultures tend to have goals of being efficient and getting the work done (Hofstede, 1991; Oetzel & Bolton-Oetzel, 1997).

As a result, individualists have a tendency to want to get to work and finish the task at hand, whereas collectivists will want to spend time getting to know one another and build trust and rapport among one another before beginning the work. These goal differences often lead to a procedural conflict of what is the best way to complete the task.

Competition for Scarce Resources

A final cause of conflict in culturally diverse groups is the competition for allocation of resources. A resource is "any positively perceived physical, economic, or social consequence" (Miller & Steinberg, 1975, p. 65). Resources include factors such as money, land, water, time, and power. Resources historically have been the cause of many intercultural conflicts.

As a case in point, European Americans and Native Americans have had many conflicts over the importance and use of land (Healey, 1997). Furthermore, in the state of New Mexico, the state government and representatives of various Pueblos have been engaged in debates about the revenues, and taxes on the revenues, from Pueblo casinos. And in recent years, leaders of Israel and Palestine have met with various leaders of the world to solve the confrontation about the West Bank. Many of the above interactions surrounding these conflicts take place in groups of representatives from each of the respective groups. These examples of competition over resources also illustrate the importance of context for a group's interaction. Members of work groups bring their cultural backgrounds, history, and political agendas to group meetings.

In summary, there are numerous reasons why members of culturally diverse groups have conflict. Cultural values and historical relationships play a large role in these conflicts. In the next section, we examine the influence of these factors on conflict processes during group interaction.

CULTURE-BASED SITUATIONAL FEATURES: INFLUENCE OF GROUP INPUTS ON CONFLICT PROCESS

This section describes how the input factors of a group affect conflict and conflict behavior in culturally diverse work groups. We examine four features that are elements of the culture-based situational model: (a) group composition (i.e., ingroup-outgroup boundaries), (b) social identity and proportional representation (this factor is consistent with ingroup-outgroup boundaries but provides an explanation different than group composition), (c) other situational characteristics, and (d) cultural value patterns. The first three factors are a part of culture-based situational features, whereas cultural value patterns are a part of the primary orientation factors.

Group Composition: Ingroup-Outgroup Boundaries

Group composition is the makeup of the group membership and varies in degree from homogeneous to heterogeneous. A homogeneous group is one composed of members with similar cultural backgrounds, abilities, and ideas, whereas a heterogeneous group is composed of members with different cultural backgrounds, abilities, and ideas. Imagine that you are a member of a heterogeneous group such as a global business team. There are six members on the team. Two of the members are from the United States but from different ethnic backgrounds. The other four members are from various countries around the world. Your group members have come together for the first time in your company's headquarters in New York. The first meetings occur over the course of a week and are primarily to get the members to know each other, understand the goals of the project, and figure out how to proceed. The project is a joint venture to develop and market new software. What could you expect at the first meeting?

Initially, there is bound to be considerable excitement about the project. After all, it is an important project and your boss chose you and the others. Furthermore, there is a natural curiosity to learn about and work with culturally diverse others. There is also going to be a fair amount of uncertainty about the others. What is going to happen? Are people going to trust you? As you begin to discuss, you realize that there are numerous potential disagreements. First, in what language are you going to conduct the meetings? Is there a common language or will you need interpreters? Second, when are you going to work? You are accustomed to a Monday through Friday schedule, but other members celebrate their religion on Fridays. Speaking of religion, you were hoping to take off the last 2 weeks of the year to celebrate Christmas and New Year's, but other members want to celebrate Ramadan, Passover, and the Chinese New Year. If you celebrate all of your holidays, you have only 9 months to work and the company wants the project completed in a year. Third, how are you going to communicate? Do you use electronic mail, conference calls, or face-to-face meetings? How often do you need to speak? All of these are valid issues, and we have not even focused on the different communication styles. From your perspective, Jing, from China, tends to be indirect and evasive, and Sigried, from Germany, is extremely direct and heavy-handed.

These are some of the factors that face a global business team. A consistent finding about group composition is that culturally heterogeneous groups have less effective interaction processes, or process difficulty, than culturally homogeneous groups (Cox, 1994; Watson, Kumar, & Michaelson, 1993). This *process difficulty* is a communication process that potentially interferes with the productivity of a group and includes high levels of conflict, tension, and power struggles (Watson & Michaelson, 1988). Thus, your global business team is generally going to have more conflicts and misunderstandings than the business team composed of members from the same country and cultural background.

Research studies support the prevalence of conflict and misunderstandings in culturally heterogeneous groups. One study examined 45 student groups working on a task that involved making a decision about hypothetical layoffs for an engineering firm (Kirchmeyer & Cohen, 1992). Most of the groups had four members composed of two men and two women, one of whom was an ethnic minority. Ethnic minorities contributed considerably less to decisions than did nonminorities. This contribution exemplifies process difficulty because the students who are not participating as much as others may have key ideas that could benefit the group. A second study compared the processes of culturally homogeneous and heterogeneous student groups working on four business case studies over the course of a semester (Watson et al., 1993). The homogeneous groups were composed of European Americans, whereas the heterogeneous groups were predominantly composed of an African American, European American, Latin American, and a foreign national from an Asian, African, Middle Eastern, or Latin American country. Homogeneous groups were found to have fewer power struggles, more cooperative interaction, and equal participation compared with the heterogeneous groups. Over a period of 12 weeks, however, the heterogeneous groups made adjustments and had processes at the level of homogeneous groups. This finding demonstrates a key point about cultural diversity: It takes time for culturally diverse members to adjust to one another and to alleviate misunderstandings.

Why do we construct global business teams if they have more conflict than homogeneous teams? As we elaborated on in Chapter 1, there are several reasons. First, quality ideas do not all come from the same country. Global business teams are formed because managers want to include their best personnel regardless of cultural background. Second, global business teams offer advantages of knowing how to market to a diverse clientele. A culturally diverse group will be better equipped to communicate with a diverse consumer base than will a homogeneous group. Finally, cultural/ethnic diversity can benefit group performance because of the infusion of different ideas and approaches to solving problems (McLeod et al., 1996).

Red Earth is a band in Albuquerque, New Mexico, composed of seven members, each with a different cultural/ethnic background (Shively, 1999). Their experiences illustrate these research findings. They have struggled to mesh seven disparate sets of ideas and energies over the course of four years. Christian, one of the members, says, "We're seven different brains. . . . [W]e all think differently, we all have different backgrounds. That's what makes it more exciting—that we are actually making it work." Adrian, another member, explains, "It's a lot of work to write a simple song. There are so many avenues to explore when you are writing and we like to explore them and see what works." Jeff sums up their experience: "Although we fight a lot, in the end there is a unity" (Shively, 1999, p. E14). Essentially, this culturally diverse band produces high-quality music because of their diversity and their ability to manage conflict and focus their diversity into their music.

For diversity to benefit group performance, it is necessary to understand how culture and cultural diversity affect conflict process and to learn how to manage these difficulties. Culturally diverse groups tend to have more conflict than do culturally homogeneous groups. However, the research on group composition does not explain *why* cultural diversity has an impact on conflict. In the following sections, we review several variables that offer explanations for why culture affects conflict behavior in culturally diverse groups.

Social Identity and Proportional Representation

Two critical and closely linked factors relating to ingroup-outgroup boundaries provide important insight into why cultural diversity affects conflict: (a) identity and (b) proportional representation. Identity is one's self-conception and consists of both social and personal identities (Turner, 1987). Personal identity involves views of self that differentiate us from other members of our ingroups, whereas social identity involves views of self we share with other members of our ingroups (Turner, 1987). Social identity includes groups such as gender, national culture, and ethnic culture. Proportional representation focuses on the makeup of the group and whether or not there is equal or unequal representation of relevant cultural groups (e.g., equal or unequal numbers of men and women or European Americans and Latino Americans).

Social identity theory focuses on how the social categorization of people into arbitrary groups affects interactions among people of different social identities (Tajfel, 1978). Social identity theory states that people practice ingroup favoritism and outgroup differentiation for the purpose of enhancing their social and personal identities. Awareness of membership in a social group is the most important factor for influencing intergroup behavior. This factor derives from an inherent drive to establish a positive social identity achieved through a process of social comparisons that results in a positive bias favoring the ingroup (Tajfel & Turner, 1986; Turner, 1987). When interacting with members of different social groups, individuals tend to engage in social competition to protect a positive social identity (Turner, 1975). A number of factors influence whether people of different social categories will cooperate or compete when working with one another in groups. These conditions include similar status, competing for limited resources, and proportional representation.

How does social identity and proportional representation influence conflict behaviors? We compare two group meetings, both involving European Americans and Latino Americans discussing the implementation of a new proposal. The first group is composed of three European Americans (Trudy, Kate, and Carmen) and one Latina American (Martha). The organization in which they work is predominantly white. The second is composed of three Latino Americans (Frank, Jerry, and Lupe) and one European American (CJ). The organization in which they work is relatively balanced in terms of ethnicity. In both groups, a Latino initiates the proposal.

Group 1

Martha: So, what did you think of my proposal?

Trudy: I think it is really good and could help the company a lot, but there are some problems.

Martha: Problems?

Kate: Yeah, I'm not sure that we can afford to implement it.

Martha: How can we afford not to?

Carmen: I know improving employee morale is important, but if we can't afford the program, we'll have to lay people off and that won't be very good for morale.

Martha: Didn't you look at the figures? We can easily pay for this program. I'm getting the sense that you are trying to sabotage this project. You know how much work I put into this.

Kate: We know and we think we can help you fix it.

Martha: Yeah, so that you can take the credit.

Group 2

Frank: So, what did you think of my proposal?

CJ: I think it is really good and can help out the company, but there are some problems.

Jerry: Problems?

CJ: Yeah, I'm not sure that we can afford to implement it.

Lupe: What do you mean?

CJ: I know improving employee morale is important, but if we can't afford the program, we'll have to lay people off and that won't be very good for morale.

Frank: I'm not sure if we understand the same figures, but from where we stand, we can afford it. Can we take the time to show you?

CJ: Sounds good. Let's meet after lunch.

In both of these situations, the person who has presented the plan faces some minor resistance. In Group 1, Martha becomes defensive and competitive. In contrast, the Group 2 initiators are willing to listen to criticism and talk about resolving the problem. The European Americans in both groups are direct and confrontational to what they see as a potential flaw.

Previous research supports this situation. Two studies were conducted to test the effects of social identity on cooperation and competition in diverse work groups (Espinoza & Garza, 1985; Garza & Santos, 1991). In the first study, European Americans and Latino Americans were randomly assigned to one of two conditions that required them to make a choice in a Prisoner's Dilemma-type game: a 3:1 or 1:3 ratio of ingroup to outgroup composition (same sex). In the second study, European Americans and Latino Americans were randomly assigned to groups in ratios varying from 1:5 up to 6:0. In both studies, they found that Latino Americans competed with the others when they were in the minority condition (1:5, 2:4, or 1:3) and cooperated when they were equal, in a majority, or in an exclusive group. In contrast, European Americans were minimally affected by the changes in ingroup-outgroup balance.

Social identity theory offers an explanation for these differences. Ethnic majority groups (e.g., European Americans) already have a number of socially valued dimensions, such as education and occupation, along which they can positively differentiate themselves. As a result, they do not have to consider the ethnic minority group members in a relevant social comparison and do not feel the need to compete. Conversely, ethnic minority members (e.g., Latino Americans) lack a preexisting positive social identity and therefore perceive the majority group in a relevant social comparison. Some ethnic minority group members consequently feel the need to compete when they are in a numerical minority in order to achieve a positive social identity. To further support this conclusion, most research indicates that Latino Americans cooperate with others because of the importance of collectivism.

From a culture-based situational model perspective, equal representation helps to allow ethnic minority work group members to save face. Recall that, in general, ethnic minority members have a higher concern for preserving ethnic identity (Cox, 1994). In a group that has equal numbers of people from various ethnic groups, it is relatively easy to maintain core ethnic identity because no one ethnic identity will have power within that group. In contrast, in a group with more individuals from one particular ethnic group (usually European Americans in U.S. organizations), there may be a push for the minority members to assimilate with the others. This push would threaten the face of the members who feel strongly about their ethnic identity and may lead to a power struggle or conflict. It should be noted that equal numbers does not guarantee the saving of face and unequal numbers does not guarantee the threatening of face. Face is a dynamic variable that is created and maintained by interacting with others in particular situations.

Additional Situational Features

From the systems perspective, a group is influenced and shaped by its immediate environment or situational features. The nature of work for a group and historical relationships among group members are potential variables that can influence conflict in a culturally diverse group. These variables frame the ingroup-outgroup boundaries and the conflict goals for a group. We discuss the importance of the nature of work and historical relationships among group members on conflict in culturally diverse groups in this section.

The nature of the work a group is performing can affect the conflict behavior of that group. The task structures the activity of the group and thus guides the interaction of group members. One way to categorize group tasks is along the dimension of cooperation and competition (McGrath, 1984). A brainstorming task is an example of a cooperative task. During brainstorming, all of the members contribute to the outcome of the group. The group members share in the benefits and costs equally. A mixed-motive task is an example of a competitive task. A mixed-motive task involves conflicts of interest in which one member of the group gains and another member loses, such as negotiating over the price of an object. The more one sells it for, the less the buyer saves. Competitive group tasks lead to more dominating, avoiding, and third-party help than cooperative tasks (Oetzel, 1999). That is, during competitive tasks, people either "fight" with or "flee" from the others. During cooperative tasks, group members tend to employ integrating, obliging, and compromising conflict styles.

These results appear to be consistent with the culture-based situational model. Competitive and cooperative tasks affect the conflict goal assessments and subsequently influence face concerns and conflict processes. Competitive tasks likely lead to a high self-face concern, and therefore individuals use conflict styles, such as dominating, that will maximize individual gain. Cooperative tasks enable people to enact mutual-face concerns, and therefore, integrating is prevalent.

A history of conflict between cultural groups can also affect conflict behavior (Triandis, 1995b). History of conflict between cultural groups emphasizes the relational parameters (i.e., control-affiliation) of the culture-based situational model. If you have traditionally fought with another culture and then have to come together and work with these people, conflict is likely to be prevalent in your work group. This situation occurs frequently in political negotiations. Let us take an example of a joint venture with a company from a country with which your country has traditionally had difficulties. The venture is appealing because of the economic advantages it may provide your companies. Although you probably would think twice about entering into the joint venture, it may be so beneficial to both companies that it is necessary to launch the venture. Opening meetings are likely to be filled with power struggles and tension. You may fight over where to hold meetings, in what language, what size and shape of table should be used, and so on. This lack of trust leads to an emphasis on self-face protection concerns. In essence, the individuals will be struggling to maintain face in the context of negative historical conflict, which results in unsatisfying group interactions.

Cultural Value Patterns

Although situational features are important elements for understanding how culture affects conflict behavior in culturally diverse groups, they do not provide the complete picture. Cultural value patterns are also important factors. Problems, misunderstandings, and conflicts likely occur in diverse groups because individuals tend to view the interaction from their own cultural perspective (Nadler et al., 1985). For example, during heterogeneous group inter-actions, members use different communication styles and proce-dures that may not correspond to the others' styles and procedures. Differences stemming from contrasting cultural backgrounds of the members of heterogeneous groups lead to different communica-tion processes than in homogeneous groups. These differences cre-ate difficulties and misunderstandings, at least during initial meet-ings. Individualism-collectivism and self-construals are important cultural factors for communication styles and have a significant impact on conflict and conflict behavior in groups.

Three research studies demonstrate how individualism-collectivism and self-construals influence conflict behavior in culturally diverse groups. In the first study, the cooperative and competitive behavior of groups composed of members with individualistic cultural tradi-tions (i.e., European Americans) were compared with groups com-posed of members with collectivistic cultural traditions (i.e., Afri-can Americans, Asian Americans, and Latino Americans) (Cox, Lobel, & McLeod, 1991). Groups composed of members with collectivistic cultural traditions displayed more cooperative behav-ior than groups composed of members with individualistic cultural traditions. Furthermore, when given cooperative feedback, the collectivistic groups were more likely to reciprocate with coopera-tive behavior than the individualistic groups. Cooperative feedback consisted of finding out that other members of the group were working with rather than competing against one another. This situ-ation creates two choices. One could either choose to work to-gether so that both parties benefit equally or there could be compe-tition for individual benefit. What would you do? Would you cooperate as the collectivistic group members tended to do? Or would you compete, as the individualistic group members tended to do? Your answer to these questions provides some indication about your individualistic and collectivistic tendencies.

In the second study, the communication patterns of homoge-neous European American groups (an individualistic culture), homogeneous Japanese groups (a collectivistic culture), and heterogeneous groups composed of two Japanese and two European Americans were compared (Oetzel, 1998a, 1998c). The groups were attempting to make a decision about how to punish a student caught cheating on an exam. There were several interesting findings. First, participants who have an independent self-construal tended to use competitive conflict tactics and initiate conflicts. Second, the individualistic participants used more competitive conflict tactics than did the collectivistic participants. Third, individualistic groups had more competitive tactics and fewer cooperative tactics than did the collectivistic groups.

In the third study, 36 student groups, ranging from culturally homogeneous to culturally diverse, completed three group tasks in an interpersonal communication course (Oetzel, 2001). There were two important findings of this study. First, the level of interdependence in a group (determined by summing the interdependence self-identified by the group members) related positively to the amount of cooperation in a group. Second, the amount of cultural diversity in a group did not affect the level of conflict. Although this finding contradicts our earlier points about group composition, it does demonstrate a key point: Simply because a group is physically diverse does not mean that the group will be diverse in individualism-collectivism and self-construals. There is within-culture variation in addition to between-culture variation.

These studies are consistent with the culture-based situational conflict model that we discussed in Chapter 2—specifically that the notion of cultural variability is clear. Individuals from collectivistic cultures, those who are interdependent, or both typically have high other- or mutual-face concerns. Other- and mutual-face lead these individuals to establish and maintain strong interpersonal relationships within the group. As a result, these individuals attempt to avoid conflict in order not to affect negatively the harmony in the group. If conflict does arise, however, cooperation and obliging are the preferred methods to resolve the conflict because they allow every individual in the group to save face. For example, if I, as a collectivist, offer you concessions that enable you to save face, I will be viewed as strong by other collectivists because I put the group's harmony before personal gain.

In contrast, people from individualistic cultures, those who are independent, or both typically have high self-face concerns. Self-face concern leads these individuals to work for personal initiative and achievement within the group, such as efficient decision making, performing well, and becoming a leader. Achievement within the group allows the individual group members to maintain face because they appear credible. Good performance in a group activity may lead to a good grade in a class or a promotion. Competition and cooperation are the preferred methods for resolving conflict. Cooperation is the ideal that allows every group member to gain something and save face. However, competition is also used because it places self-face concern first and other-face second. The logic behind this is that every individual works for his or her own benefit, so it is necessary to protect one's interests.

At this point, we are going to examine a group dialogue in which individualism and collectivism and self-construals are important. The group consists of two European Americans (William and Ed) and two Japanese (Yoshi and Jiro), all with the same relative status. They are involved in a joint venture to share computer technology. They have come together for the first time.

William: It's good to meet both of you. I should tell you that I'm very excited about this venture. I think it'll be very profitable for everyone.

Ed: I agree. This is going to be a great project.

Jiro: We're very pleased to meet you. Did you have a nice flight?

William: Oh yes, it was fine. I think we should start by discussing the sharing of costs and benefits of the project.

Jiro: We're glad that your flight was good. Is the hotel comfortable?

William: It's fine as well. Thanks for your hospitality. Now, back to the plan. I've taken the liberty to draw up a contract. I'm sure that we can make changes along the way, but I thought that this would save time so we can get down to business. We advocate a 60/40 split—60 for us and 40 for you because it is our technology, but you are providing the facilities. Does this sound good?

Yoshi: We'll need to talk it over with others in our group. Perhaps, we should all get together this week and have a nice traditional Japanese dinner. We'd like to get to know you a little bit more.

Ed: You'll get to know me in time. What's important is to take care of this contract.

Jiro: We understand you must be very tired from your long flight. Perhaps we should take you to your hotel so that you can rest and we can meet over dinner later where we can get to know you better.

William: OK, but please be ready to work on the contract. I want to finish up as soon as possible so that I can enjoy our visit.

In this situation, the U.S. Americans insist on getting down to business, whereas the Japanese want to take some time to get to know the other party. Getting to know each other involves learning about the credibility of the company and establishing a relationship of trust. This difference creates a conflict that both parties attempt to deal with in their own way. The U.S. Americans are very insistent on dealing with the contract; they are competitive in order to accomplish their objectives. The Japanese attempt to resolve the conflict by avoiding direct discussion of the conflict and attempting to establish a relationship. From the Japanese perspective, personal relationships are more important than written contracts. Their attempt to avoid direct confrontation of the problem works temporarily, but it appears that the parties will have another conflict at dinner because of the U.S. Americans' further insistence that the contract be addressed first and the desire of the Japanese to not discuss the contract yet.

Culturally diverse groups do not have to be composed of individualists and collectivists for difficulties to emerge. Individuals from countries classified as individualistic (or collectivistic) can still have difficulties interacting with people from other individualistic nations. Both the United States and Germany, for instance, are classified as individualistic countries; however, they have different approaches to resolving conflict (Clackworthy, 1996). We illustrate this with an example of two U.S. Americans (Lauren and Whitney) and two Germans (Britta and Katarina) discussing a marketing plan for a product they created through a joint venture.

Lauren: I think that we should think about the big picture. I could see our product dominating the market share in 10 to 15 years.

Whitney: I agree.

Britta: Nonsense! That doesn't matter now. Let's focus on what we know now and what we need to do.

Katarina: I agree. We have a budget of $500,000 right now. Our profit per item is $1.00. We need to figure out a way to see 1,000,000 units just to break even.

Britta: I disagree. I think you are overestimating our profit. It will be closer to 95 cents, and thus we will need to sell another 100,000 units.

Katarina: I think you are mistaken. I carefully calculated these figures.

Lauren: I don't think the exact price is important right now, but why don't we split the difference. We should concentrate on our vision.

Whitney: Yeah, I envision a large Internet campaign.

Katarina: Nonsense, if we don't know the details, we cannot set up our goals. Further, the Internet is too uncertain at this point. We'll need to go with more traditional advertising, but we'll come back to that later.

Germans have a tendency to focus more comprehensively on issues and the details during a discussion than do U.S. Americans. Germans take a great deal of time to focus through issues and to hammer out differences. They are very practically focused and direct during conflict. They disagree very honestly and clearly (many U.S. Americans label it as blunt) and some U. S. Americans view this as harsh and heavy-handed (Clackworthy, 1996). In the above conversation, we can see that the Germans are very focused on the details of the cost of the product. Until this issue is resolved, it will be difficult to continue the negotiations.

U.S. Americans, on the other hand, tend to focus on future visions during conflict and are action oriented. Thus, they do not spend considerable time mired in the details. They want to come up with solutions and propose compromises when issues are not resolved. Furthermore, U.S. Americans are generally described as being direct during conflict, but not as direct as the Germans (Clackworthy, 1996). In the above situation, the Americans attempted to focus on the future and to create some pride in their accomplishment. From this point, it is easy to develop a plan of attack.

A final example helps to illustrate differences between two other individualistic groups, but from the same country. African Americans and European Americans have been found to have strong individualistic tendencies (Hecht, Collier, & Ribeau, 1993; Ting-Toomey et al., 2000). Both ethnic groups tend to confront conflict directly and deal with it in an assertive, and sometimes competitive, manner. However, as we noted in Chapter 2, the African American style of conflict tends to be animated, confrontational, emotionally based, and high-keyed, whereas the European American style of conflict tends to be impersonal, dispassionate, factual-based, and low-keyed (Kochman, 1981). In the following example, two African Americans (Damian and Kelvin) and two European Americans (Brian and Todd) are disagreeing about a solution offered by Damian.

Damian: So that's the solution I came up with.

Brian: Sounds pretty good.

Kelvin: (raising his voice) Ah, that isn't going to work. Our boss will tear that apart. We can do better than that.

Todd: (lowering his voice) I don't like it much either.

Damian: (raising his voice) What do you mean? I put a lot of work into this project and I think it'll work.

Kelvin: (raising his voice) I appreciate your effort, but we've got to please the boss, and she clearly said this won't work right now.

Damian: You're crazy. When she sees this, she'll love it.

Kelvin: Man, you are always like this. Remember last year when you came up with that crazy idea? She hated that.

Damian: That's right. Bring up the one time I failed. That's just like you. How about the previous two years, where I got the awards for new innovations?

Kelvin: Yeah, but what have you done for me lately?

Todd: (lowering his voice) Let's get back to the current situation. Why don't we calm down and talk about the facts one by one?

Damian: I am calm.

Kelvin: Yeah, me too.

Brian: (lowering voice) I like the solution, but I think calming down and talking about the facts is a good idea, too.

Brian and Todd do not agree with each other about the solution, but they do agree about the conflict process: talk softly, review facts, and remain dispassionate. They view a calm approach as the least confrontational and the best way to reach a fair, impartial solution. In contrast, Damian and Kelvin speak with loud voices, bring up past issues, and become emotionally involved with their respective positions. They view a high-charged discussion as a way to see who cares about what issue. These two styles conflict because European Americans tend to view the African American style as leading toward aggression, whereas African Americans tend to view the European American style as passive and suspicious (Kochman, 1981).

In summary, there are a number of primary orientation factors and situational features (i.e., input factors) that affect the occurrence of conflict and how that conflict is managed. We have reviewed research about group composition, power and status, situational variables, and individualism-collectivism. Each of these variables affects face concerns, which in turn affect conflict behavior. Understanding these variables helps us to understand how various parties will behave during intercultural conflict. Understanding potential differences may allow us to adjust our behavior to positively affect group outcomes. The communication behaviors individual group members use have a definite impact on the outcomes of groups. We turn to the outcomes in the next section.

COMBINED SITUATIONAL AND PROCESS FACTORS: INFLUENCE OF CONFLICT PROCESS ON GROUP OUTPUTS

As we noted earlier, outputs are the result of a group's interaction. There are many potential outputs such as decisions, satisfaction, group norms, and cohesion. In general, we can say that there are two main categories of group outputs: task and relational outputs (Hackman, 1990; Hirokawa & Salazar, 1991; Oetzel, 1995).

Defining Group Outputs

Task outputs refer to the work of the group, whereas relational outputs refer to the relationships between group members. Task outputs are evaluated in terms of their effectiveness and productivity. Is the decision of high quality? Is the work of the group useful? Did the group solve the problem? Will the work help the individuals to receive a bonus or get a promotion?

Relational outputs are measured in terms of their appropriateness and satisfaction. Were the interactions among the members supportive? Did they adhere to socially appropriate norms? Were the members satisfied with the outcomes? Is the group a cohesive unit? These two measurements combine to give an evaluation of the group's competence (competence = relational appropriateness + task effectiveness; Oetzel, 1995).

Group competence is an inclusive measure of a group's task and relational outputs. However, it is important to note that some individuals emphasize task effectiveness, whereas others emphasize relational effectiveness. Members of individualistic cultures (and people with independent self-construals) place a premium on task effectiveness rather than relational appropriateness. In contrast, members of collectivistic cultures (and people with interdependent self-construals) focus on relational appropriateness over task effectiveness (Hofstede, 1991; Oetzel & Bolton-Oetzel, 1997).

These varying preferences can lead to procedural conflict for the group. Independent individuals want to get to work right away, whereas interdependent individuals want to spend time getting to know one another and establishing personal relationships. Working with the opposite type of individual can be very frustrating because one's expectations for output are not likely to be met easily. Having clarified how we are conceptualizing group competence, the following section describes the relationship between conflict in culturally diverse groups and group competence. We examine the conflict goal assessments and conflict interaction styles in small groups.

Conflict Goal Assessments

Research on conflict goals (content, relational, or procedural) has generally examined which types of conflict help a group to be task effective. Relational conflict is considered disruptive to task effectiveness, whereas content conflict can facilitate group performance (Falk, 1982; Pelled, Eisenhardt, & Xin, 1999). Content conflict is viewed as a way to assist group members to evaluate ideas critically and allow members to be vigilant in their thinking (Hirokawa & Rost, 1992; Janis, 1982). The critical evaluation of ideas ensures that members are making good choices to solve problems or to make a decision. According to Western-based conflict literature, groups that avoid conflict often make poor decisions because of groupthink (Janis, 1982).

Groupthink occurs when a group is insulated, too cohesive, and does not vigilantly examine alternative ideas. These factors increase the likelihood of poor decisions. On the other hand, relational conflict takes away from the effort toward the task at hand, and the members become more concerned with relationships rather than the group decision.

Procedural conflict focuses on the operation of the group—that is, the way meetings are run or the steps that a group is to follow. If Kersti, Lisa, and Maria are discussing what items should go on the agenda, they are engaged in procedural conflict. Procedural conflict can be both beneficial and detrimental depending on whether it leads to the critical evaluation of ideas. Some groups use procedural rules, such as calling for a vote, to avoid discussing a problem.

There is one important note regarding the distinction between content and relational conflicts. The idea that content conflict is beneficial has been supported only in Western (e.g., the United States) contexts. The differences in values and communication behavior between individualistic and collectivistic cultures reveal a limitation in this research. The research assumes that the individuals in a group can separate the content and relational issues. People from individualistic cultures do not have a problem separating the issues. People from collectivistic cultures, however, tend not to separate the person from the conflict because face or relational issues are always involved in conflicts (Ting-Toomey, 1985, 1988).

Furthermore, type of conflict does not determine the level of relational appropriateness. We can imagine a group that deals with an issue in a direct manner. They can be vigilant in discussing ideas but do so in a manner that hurts members' feelings and damages relationships. The group may be task effective, but not relationally appropriate. Thus, to understand the relationship between conflict and group competence in culturally diverse groups, it is important to examine conflict management styles. Conflict can be destructive and constructive depending on how it is managed.

Conflict Interaction Styles

In Chapter 2, we discussed eight conflict management styles; here we focus on the three broad styles (because of their prevalence in group research)—avoiding, cooperating, and competing—and how they relate to task effectiveness and relational appropriateness. Considerable research illustrates that cooperation during conflict benefits a group more than competition and avoidance (Dace, 1990; Deutsch, 1969; Pood, 1980). Other research shows that competition does hold some value, at least for individualists, in that it can stimulate ideas and challenge solutions (Janis, 1982). However, competition can be detrimental for a group because individuals focus on self-centered goals instead of what is good for the group and because it can lead to the deterioration of good working relationships (Deutsch, 1969). Avoidance can be beneficial, especially to collectivists, because avoidance allows individuals to save face and helps to preserve relationships (Ting-Toomey, 1994c). However, avoidance can be detrimental because it can lead to groupthink (Janis, 1982).

Cooperation is viewed as a conflict style that is able to obtain the benefits of both competition and avoidance without accruing any of the costs. Cooperation allows group members to challenge and examine ideas but does so in a manner that respects members' opinions (and thus, face) (Deutsch, 1969). In culturally diverse groups composed of individualists and collectivists, cooperation is necessary. Cooperation is an acceptable approach to both collectivists and individualists, whereas competition is not acceptable to collectivists and avoidance is not acceptable to individualists. This perspective leads group members to learn how to balance the needs of both cultural backgrounds (Oetzel, 1995).

Recent studies illustrate the benefits of cooperation for culturally diverse groups. Cooperation is often labeled constructive conflict. The presence of constructive conflict increases the participation of ethnic minorities in a culturally diverse group (Kirchmeyer & Cohen, 1992). Furthermore, the level of commitment to the group

and the decision for all of the group members is related positively
with the level of constructive conflict. When group members openly
share information, carefully critique ideas, and actively search
for a variety of opinions, these behaviors determine constructive
conflict.

These findings have important implications for culturally diverse
groups. First, the findings illustrate that groups that cooperate can
increase the participation of members, especially minority group
members. Participation is important for group effectiveness because a silent voice is a potential divergent voice that may have
helpful ideas for a group (Nemeth, 1992). Second, cooperation is
also relationally appropriate for a group because it increases commitment. Increased commitment means that group members are
more likely to be motivated and work hard to help the group
achieve and to help create and maintain strong relationships.

A second study examined the impact of cooperation on three
group outcomes—performance, free riding, and satisfaction—in
student work groups ranging from culturally homogeneous to culturally diverse (Oetzel, 2001). Performance is a measure of the
group's task output, whereas satisfaction is a measure of how the
individuals feel about their group. Free riding refers to the degree to
which members of a group shirk their work, forcing others to take
up the slack (Kidwell & Bennett, 1993). Everyone has experienced
being in a group in which one member does not do a fair share of
work and this free riding negatively affects the quality of work for a
group. Furthermore, free riding also negatively affects relational
appropriateness. In fact, some people lose the desire to work in
groups because they do not want to work with people who free ride.
Kidwell and Bennett (1993) showed that cooperation was associated positively with satisfaction and negatively with free riding.
Thus, with more cooperation in the group, members were more
likely to be satisfied and the less likely they were to free ride. No
relationship was found between cooperation and performance.
One implication of these findings is that cooperation can potentially benefit the effectiveness of the group by improving the sharing of work (although this did not directly affect the performance in

the study). In addition, cooperation leads to a positive affect for a group and has great potential for improving intercultural relations in work groups. Although these two studies are important, more research is needed to understand better how conflict in culturally diverse groups is related to group competence.

An example of a free-riding situation can be seen in a group of four students working on a group project for a class. One of the members (Tom) has just missed a group meeting and the other three members (Sara, Rosalinda, and Curtiss) decide to confront him, because they are concerned about potential free riding.

Sara: Hey Tom. We missed you last night. Is everything OK?

Tom: Yeah, it's fine. I just had a lot of schoolwork to finish up.

Rosalinda: Man, I know how that is. This semester has been tough and completing this project sure is taking up some time.

Tom: (surprised) Yeah, did you get a lot done?

Curtiss: We got some ideas completed, but we missed your input. You are really good at organizing the information.

Sara: Yeah, we won't be able to do as well as we want on this project without your help. Is another night better for you?

Tom: Thanks and no. I just needed to catch up. I'll see you later this week, and I'll make sure I'll be there.

Rosalinda: Great! We'll see you later.

In this situation, Tom is greeted by collaborative dialogue as opposed to competition. His fellow group members do not attack him or accuse him; rather, they check to make sure nothing happened and compliment his skills. Tom is more likely to help out with the group than he would be if he were confronted with attacks and threats such as, "I've worked in groups where people don't pull their fair share, and I'm not going to do it again. You had better be there next week or else." The collaborative dialogue allows Tom to save face and thus increases his likelihood of participating fully in the group project.

In this section, we have reviewed three conflict management styles and their effects on group outcomes. We have tried to illustrate the benefits of a cooperative, or constructive, approach to resolving conflict in culturally diverse groups. With this idea in mind, we move to the final section of this chapter.

INTERCULTURAL CONFLICT IN DIVERSE WORK GROUPS: PRACTICAL GUIDELINES

Given the trends toward diversity and teamwork in a variety of organizations, many people will find themselves, at some point, interacting in a culturally diverse group. In this chapter, we explained that culturally diverse groups have a greater potential for conflict than culturally homogeneous groups. Competing goals, competition for resources, cultural differences, power discrepancies, and assimilation versus preserving ethnic identity can cause content, relational, and procedural conflict. We then discussed how group composition, individualism-collectivism and self-construals, social identity-proportional representation, and situational features affect conflict communication behavior in groups. Finally, we explained, in general, how cooperation is beneficial and competition or avoidance can be detrimental for culturally diverse groups. We conclude by offering the following suggestions for group members of culturally diverse groups to improve their management of conflict. These suggestions also may apply, of course, to culturally homogeneous groups.

Be Aware of Group Composition

The group's composition plays a key role for conflict in terms of its size and proportional representation. If you are creating a group for a project, try to provide equal numbers of all the cultural/ethnic groups involved. For example, if you are a teacher and have a limited number of students from ethnic minority groups, it may be better to pair them up and place them in a group with a pair of students from the ethnic majority group. This grouping will help to maintain a positive social identity for the group members and thus increase the likelihood of cooperation. In addition, the group needs to be relatively small (approximately three to six members). The more people there are in a group, the more difficult it is to coordinate among all of the members. Difficulty in coordination is another avenue for conflict. Thus, a small number provides maximum opportunities for all of the members to communicate with each other, develop relationships, and learn to deal with and respect differences.

Allow Culturally Diverse Groups
Sufficient Time to Develop

As previous research has shown, culturally diverse groups need time to overcome difficulties and work efficiently (Watson et al., 1993). The band Red Earth, discussed earlier, has taken 4 years to overcome obstacles and release its first CD. Although every group may not need 4 years to become efficient, efficiency will not happen overnight. Teachers and managers need to be aware that culturally diverse groups need some time to learn to work together and should try not to impose deadlines shortly after the creation of the group. Time pressure increases tensions and tends to lead to competition among group members.

Use Culture as a Bridge,
Not as a Weapon or Fortress

Cultural differences become the greatest obstacles to a negotiated agreement when one member fears that the other side will seek to impose its culture or use it to dominate (Salacuse, 1993). The metaphors of culture as a weapon and as a fortress help to illustrate these situations. Culture becomes a weapon when "one party perceives the other side's culture as presenting the risk of forcibly changing the 'shared and enduring meanings, values, and beliefs that characterize' the first party's ethnic group" (Salacuse, 1993, p. 203). An example of culture as a weapon is for a dominant, powerful culture to assume that a weaker culture admires or envies the dominant culture. In response, the other party may become defensive and use its own culture as a fortress to protect itself from a cultural onslaught. One method of using one's culture as a fortress is to demonize the other side. Overall, the more one treats its culture as a weapon, the more the other will retreat within its cultural fortress (Salacuse, 1993).

Alternatively, culture can be a bridge between two sides during intercultural group meetings. To build the bridge, members must avoid the weapon or fortress options. Instead, members should try to understand how their culture is perceived and avoid statements that the other side might interpret as arrogant or dominant. To build bridges, members should (a) seek common historical elements or personal elements, if they exist, between group members; (b) demonstrate interest in and respect for the other's culture by asking questions; and (c) demonstrate acceptance and respect of cultural differences. Essentially, these behaviors allow a group member to give face to the other parties and demonstrate mutual concerns.

Seek Out Superordinate Goals

Superordinate goals are those that are common to both parties and transcend the immediate goals of the situation. For example, if two university departments are arguing over limited dollars used to teach two separate classes (the immediate goal of getting the money), the departments can try to see if they can share the money and teach both sets of students with one class through an innovative, collaborative learning format. The effectiveness of superordinate goals is contingent on finding an overarching common goal. Superordinate goals are often very common but often not found because parties tend to try to protect their own interests.

In sum, these four suggestions offer concrete ways for members and managers of culturally diverse groups to improve the management of conflict. These concepts emphasize communication that bridges parties and gives or maintains face, as opposed to defeating conflict opponents. The four guidelines detail the importance of practicing collaborative dialogue and proactive problem-solving techniques (see Chapter 6) rather than a monologue approach in managing interdependent small group conflicts.

5

INTERCULTURAL CONFLICT BETWEEN MANAGERS AND EMPLOYEES IN ORGANIZATIONS

Much of our lives is inextricably bound to organizations. We work in organizations, belong to numerous social organizations, attend universities, and are governed by organizations. What do we mean by an organization? An organization is "a collection, or system, of individuals who commonly, through hierarchy of ranks and division of labor, seek to achieve a predetermined goal" (Tubbs & Moss, 1994, p. 352).

We often think of an organization as a separate, tangible entity that exists apart from the individuals. For example, we say, "I work for the University of New Mexico" or "Intel is a great place to work." However, organizations do not exist separately from their individual members. It is not just a container in which humans interact. An organization is defined by the interaction between its members. Humans organize to complete activities. Communication organizes and coordinates these activities to allow us to achieve common goals. "When we organize, we define and arrange positions or roles in complex relationships. We engage in concerted action with one another by coordinating these roles in order to accomplish some purpose" (Daniels, Spiker, & Papa, 1997, p. 2).

Conflict is a pervasive and inevitable element in the process of organizing. The very idea of coordinating our actions with others leads to conflict. A manager and employee, for example, may disagree over the role that each will play in the organization. With the demographic changes occurring around the world, it is possible that conflict will be even more prevalent. Scholars of organizational diversity have argued that increased diversity because of culture, gender, age, and other differences will lead to a net benefit for organizations if managers are able to manage diversity effectively (Cox, 1994; Cox & Blake, 1991; Daly, 1998; Loden, 1996; Thomas, 1990).

In this chapter, we explore interpersonal conflict between managers and employees. We describe a model that includes four approaches to conflict management. We then examine the face-negotiation of manager-employee conflicts in multinational organizations and culturally diverse organizations in the United States.

CONFLICTS BETWEEN
MANAGERS AND EMPLOYEES

Many reasons explain why managers and employees have conflicts. Some examples of conflict between managers and employees include (a) an employee's disagreeing with the result of a manager's performance review, (b) an employee's unwillingness to work overtime, and (c) a manager's objecting to the way an employee is speaking (i.e., not liking the communication style of the employee).

We limit our discussion to manager-employee conflicts for two reasons. First, research on interpersonal conflict in organizations has focused primarily on conflict styles in manager-employee relationships. Second, the previous two chapters focused on conflicts in group settings and interpersonal relationships. These settings involve conflicts among coworkers and intimates whereby the individuals are of the same status. Conflict between a manager and an employee is unique because it represents a situation in which the disputants occupy different positions and therefore have different power and status. Power is the ability to influence the behavior of others, often because of the control of resources (Dahl, 1957), and status denotes a position, or relative rank, within a hierarchy (Daniels et al., 1997). Power imbalance and status challenge often contribute to conflicts between managers and employees in an organization.

The manager has more power and higher status than the subordinate. The manager has an assigned status and, typically, is able to influence the behavior of employees through the control of resources such as pay raises, performance evaluations, and promotions. As a result, managers often rely on forcing (i.e., dominating style) as the preferred method of handling conflict with employees (Morley & Shockley-Zalabak, 1986; Putnam & Poole, 1987; Putnam & Wilson, 1982). Forcing is particularly characteristic of managers who perceive themselves as lacking skill or expertise. Unskilled managers often quickly resort to dominating or forcing-controlling conflict styles to deal with noncompliant subordinates (Conrad, 1983, 1991; Fairhurst, Green, & Snavely, 1984). On the other hand, employees tend to use avoiding and accommodating styles during conflict with managers (Putnam & Wilson, 1982).

These findings are consistent with the culture-based situational conflict model. Managers are likely to have high self-face concerns corresponding with their status and power, whereas employees are likely to have high other-face and self-face concerns that are necessary for maintaining their job and position. The high self-face of managers results in a preference for forcing with an occasional collaborating style. In contrast, the high self- and other-face concerns of employees result in avoiding and accommodating in order to maintain a good relationship with the boss and to preserve their jobs. Avoiding and accommodating allow the employee to support the face of the manager. It is important to note that this line of research has been conducted only in large, or relatively large, power distance cultures. Small power distance cultures (or small power distance organizations) may not have strong distinctions or hierarchical distance between managers and employees. We discuss these issues in a later section of this chapter.

At the heart of any conflict are opposing issues. In the previous chapter, we discussed five sources of conflict in intercultural relationships: (a) cultural differences, (b) assimilation versus ethnic identity maintenance, (c) power imbalance, (d) competing conflict goals, and (e) competition for scarce resources. These issues also apply to conflicts between manager and employees. For example, a boss who asks an employee to work overtime (when that employee does not want to) has a different goal than the employee. The boss wants more work time from the employee, whereas the employee wants to go home. The resource of time is in competition between the parties. In addition, the minority employee may start wondering whether the boss asks for the overtime because he or she is from a particular ethnic group and, therefore, of course, he or she would comply with the request. Thus, situational features (e.g., stereotypes and prejudice) interact with primary orientation factors (e.g., cultural/ethnic values) and shape workplace conflict processes. In the next section, we introduce a model to explain conflict styles for managers and employees from different cultural backgrounds.

PRIMARY ORIENTATION FACTORS: A MODEL OF CONFLICT APPROACHES

Managers and employees around the world employ a number of interaction styles and facework behaviors to resolve their conflicts. To explain these various communication behaviors, we offer a model that includes two of the basic cultural value patterns of the culture-based situational model we introduced in Chapter 2: individualism-collectivism and power distance. The overlay of these two dimensions results in four predominant approaches to conflict: impartial, status-achievement, benevolent, and communal. The *impartial approach* consists of an individualistic and small power

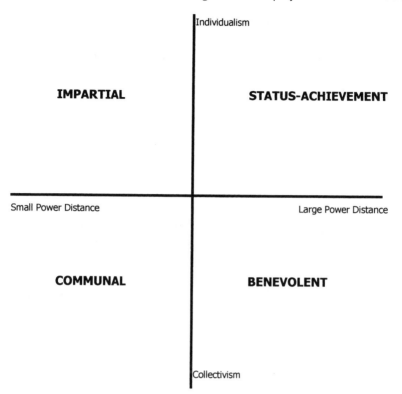

Figure 5.1. Organizational Conflict Management: Four Approaches

distance orientation; the *status-achievement approach* consists of an individualistic and large power distance orientation; the *benevolent approach* consists of a collectivistic and large power distance orientation; and the *communal approach* consists of a collectivistic and small power distance orientation. Figure 5.1 displays the model.

In this section, we describe each of these approaches as it relates to conflict between managers and employees. We explain the values, roles, and communicative behaviors associated with each approach and describe which national cultures, predominantly, fit each approach. We want to offer a few caveats before continuing. First, any model that attempts to categorize a variety of cultures is going to gloss over unique features of each culture. The model organizes a variety of behaviors, but it will not explain every behavior. Second, the model does not reflect the gradients that occur between countries. Third, it is important to understand that although we discuss predominant approaches in each culture, individuals of that culture may have a unique approach to addressing an organizational conflict issue because of many complex, situational features.

Impartial Approach

The impartial and benevolent approaches are the two most common approaches observed around the world (Hofstede, 1991). Managers with the impartial approach tend to see themselves as independent and at the same status level as others (Triandis, 1995a). That is, these managers think of themselves as unique, separate from all others, and yet similar to other individuals in terms of status. Two values that pervade this approach are freedom (to be a unique individual) and equality. Countries that predominantly reflect the impartial managerial approach include Australia, Canada, Northern European nations (e.g., Scandinavia and Germany), Israel, the United States, and Great Britain. The United States and Great Britain also have tendencies that reflect the status-achievement approach, especially in business settings, which we discuss in the next section.

Managers from individualistic, small power distance cultures are expected to have a personally developed style based on their work experiences but also to treat everyone the same regardless of status, title, or rank (Brislin, 1993; Smith, Dugan, Peterson, & Leung, 1998). During conflict, managers often use impartial rules and guidelines to resolve the issues. If interpersonal conflicts arise between a manager and an employee, the manager has a tendency to deal with the conflict in a direct, up front manner. Employees are expected to directly articulate their conflict concerns as well. If an employee has a problem, he or she is expected to bring the problem to the manager's attention. These patterns are consistent with a self-face-oriented perspective because of its emphasis on direct conflict expressions and a straightforward approach to substantive conflict issues. Both the manager and the employee also tend to rely on the principle of impartiality to resolve the conflict problem objectively.

The following example will help illustrate this perspective and the subsequent three other approaches in turn. Two employees are having a conflict about their responsibilities on a project. They are unable to resolve the disagreement. From the impartial approach, after trying to resolve the dispute themselves unsuccessfully, the employees then need to bring the conflict to the attention of the boss. The manager likely confronts the issue directly and brings the disputants together. The manager encourages the disputants to open up and share individual perceptions of the issues. Generally, the manager plays the role of mediator and tries to be objective and encourage the employees to find their own solution. In the impartial approach to mediation, managers often prefer to remain professional and detached (Donohue & Bresnahan, 1994). If, however, the dispute is affecting work performance, the manager may play the role of arbitrator. A decision is based on an objective weighing of the facts and not the interpersonal relationships that the manager has with the workers (Kolb, 1989). This mediation or arbitration process reflects the impartial approach values of fairness, directness, and neutrality. Thus, the concept of impartial approach, which connotes an individualistic value stance, is really an impersonal, objective approach to managing workplace conflicts.

The effectiveness of the impartial approach relies on the ability of the manager to enact direct strategies to deal with the conflict in an open and fair manner. Although dominating conflict style is often practiced within the impartial approach, the collaborative conflict style with an employee is often viewed as the most effective strategy in dealing with individualistic workplace conflicts. Collaborative conflict style evokes the highest employee satisfaction and promotes positive quality of working relationships between managers and subordinates (Rahim & Buntzman, 1990). Collaborative conflict style refers to taking time to understand the needs and goals of both conflict parties and attempting to devise constructive, synergistic solutions to meet the goals of both disputants. Although collaborative dialogue style is the most effective conflict style in resolving workplace issues, not many managers and employees are well trained in using such dialogue style (see Chapter 6 for a detailed discussion). Compromising conflict style can be the next effective conflict mode because it allows the parties to meet some of the needs of both individuals while giving up pieces of their original plans. Dominating and avoiding conflict styles, however, from the impartial approach perspective, are often viewed as the least effective strategies in operating in an individualistic, small power distance work environment.

Status-Achievement Approach

The status-achievement approach represents the desire for a status position, with everyone having the opportunity to achieve such status. The status-achievement approach reflects an individualistic, large power distance orientation to managerial communication. Managers with a status-achievement approach tend to see themselves as independent and at a different status level than others (Triandis, 1995a). Two values that pervade this approach are freedom and earned inequality. Countries that predominantly reflect the status-achievement approach include Latin European nations (e.g., France and Italy) and to a lesser degree the United States and Great Britain.

The United States and Great Britain are classified between the impartial approach and status-achievement approach because they display characteristics of each approach. In the United States, during personal interactions, individuals are expected to verbally communicate in ways that reflect the same status. However, middle- and upper-class U.S. Americans (and Britons) want to stand out from others (e.g., by driving expensive cars and having the corner office). They emphasize the position that one can earn through hard work and that status should be displayed effectively.

The status-achievement manager is concerned with maintaining and recognizing one's status in addition to developing a unique way of dealing with employees. With this approach, the manager pays attention to various status cues that are available. At the same time, status-achievement managers also express their own feelings and ideas. The status-achievement manager communicates differently with a same-rank coworker (e.g., another manager) than with an employee. If conflict arises between a manager and an employee, the manager expects the subordinate to accommodate the manager's wishes. In France, for example, workers often complain about their bosses but do not try to change them because "they are the boss." The general perspective toward conflict is to achieve your individual goals, even at the expense of someone else's goals. Aggression or ambition is a hallmark of the status-achievement approach, compared with the assertiveness of the impartial approach. Impartial-approach managers tend to be more compromising with subordinates and work toward a mutually acceptable solution, unlike status-achievement managers. Subordinates, working under the status-achievement supervisors, often view authoritative, status-ambitious managers as abusing power from the top (Brislin, 1993; Hofstede, 1991).

To explore the status-achievement approach, we return to the earlier example of the manager addressing a conflict between two employees. In this scenario, the manager likely confronts the issue directly. It is expected that the individuals will express opinions and ideas clearly. Rather than objectively weigh the facts, the manager may look to see which employee has more status (through longer tenure or more responsibilities) and rule in favor of this employee. Alternatively, the manager may simply resolve the problem for the employees rather than encouraging them to develop a solution on their own. The effectiveness of the status-achievement approach lies in the ability of the manager to deal with issues in an efficient and decisive manner. Wasting time dealing with a conflict can be viewed as incompetence on the manager's part. Therefore, dominating or controlling style is viewed as a more effective strategy in the status-achievement approach than the impartial approach. Although collaborative conflict style can be effective, it can also be viewed as a weakness on the part of the manager. Finally, avoiding conflict style, under the status-achievement approach, is perceived as a weak strategy that would be ineffective altogether in dealing with individualistic, large power distance workplace conflicts.

Benevolent Approach

The benevolent approach is another common approach encountered around the world (Hofstede, 1991). Managers employing the benevolent approach tend to see themselves as interdependent and at a different status level than others (Triandis, 1995a). That is, these managers think of themselves as people with connections to others and as members of a hierarchical network. Two values that pervade this approach are inequality and obligation to others. Countries that predominantly reflect the benevolent approach include most Latin and South American nations (e.g., Mexico, Venezuela, Brazil, Chile), most Asian nations (e.g., India, Japan, China, South Korea), most Arabic nations (e.g., Egypt, Saudi Arabia, Jordan) and most African nations (e.g., Nigeria, Uganda).

Managers from a collectivistic, large power distance workplace are expected to use a style that is nurturing and mentoring and that demonstrates a high concern for interpersonal relationships. Employees who desire a benevolent leader want a manager to treat them like a member of the family (Brislin, 1993). When dealing with low-grade conflict, managers are supposed to consider the personal relationships and try to smooth over the conflict and maintain interpersonal harmony in the workplace . In contrast to the impartial manager, the benevolent manager practices particularism by treating members of ingroups better than members of outgroups (Hofstede, 1991). Furthermore, messages are not directly expressed; rather, they are implied through subtle nonverbal cues in a high-context manner (Hall, 1976). Both superiors and subordinates need to be able to effectively read into another's nonverbal and paralinguistic cues to interpret the verbal message accurately. Because of their low-status positions, subordinates are expected to anticipate the needs and wishes of their superiors. In addition, subordinates also expect the managers to serve as "protectors" or mentors of their career paths. They expect their managers to tell them clearly what to do in terms of their job responsibilities and they shun any open feedback system to their bosses. They respect the authority of their manager because of implied status power, network connection, and expert knowledge in a variety of work situations. The benevolent style is consistent with an other-face orientation in that individuals must be very aware of what the other is communicating and must consider the effects of their behavior on others (Ting-Toomey, 1994c).

In the example of a manager intervening in a conflict between two coworkers, the benevolent manager does not bring the disputants together to air out the issues. The manager talks with each of the disputants separately, being careful not to directly challenge the face of either party. The goal is to smooth over the issues to preserve relational harmony. The manager does not encourage direct discussion of the issue and does not ask the parties to solve the problem. Rather, the manager is supposed to make a decision about how to resolve the issues. The manager takes into consideration relational issues, as well as the objective facts of the case, and makes a decision that is in the best interest of relational and workplace harmony (Gao & Ting-Toomey, 1998; La Resche, 1992). The effectiveness of the benevolent approach lies in the ability to preserve the face of the other person and to be able to adequately interpret nonverbal cues. An effective supervisor is able to deal with conflicts before they escalate. In fact, the manager often addresses an issue (e.g., by sensing the tense, nonverbal atmosphere) without having it brought directly to his or her attention. Thus, from the benevolent approach, accommodating and avoiding are two effective conflict styles to deal with collectivistic, large power distance workplace conflicts. Furthermore, collaborative conflict style can also be effective if a conflict has escalated in the organization.

There is a striking difference between Latin American and Asian benevolent approaches in the use of restrained communication. For example, Chinese prefer a conflict style characterized by emotional restraint and self-discipline in the workplace. Similarly, for Japanese, it is better to smooth over or avoid a conflict relationship than to be open and candid in their work situation. The Brazilian style, in contrast, tends to be more expressive than the Japanese style (Graham, 1985). Brazilians touch and gaze frequently during business negotiations and believe that being emotionally expressive and dramatic develops strong interpersonal bonds (Graham, 1985). Cuban Americans tend to use humor or *choteo* and an exaggerated self-criticism style—styles that often involve dramatizations to bring their points across. These interaction styles are an attempt to modify stressful situations through jokes or satirical expressions or gestures (Fabelo-Alcover & Sowers, 1998). As can be seen by these examples, the benevolent approach encompasses a broad range of interaction styles and can often create unintentional clashes and frictions in the global workplace environment.

Communal Approach

The communal approach is the least common of the approaches. Managers with the communal approach tend to see themselves as interdependent and at the same level as others (Triandis, 1995a). That is, these managers think of themselves as people closely connected to others and as similar to other people in terms of status. The values embodied in this approach are a close connection to others and equality. Costa Rica is the only country found to fit this approach (Hofstede, 1991). However, two groups also fit this perspective: the kibbutz and organizations built on feminist principles. A kibbutz is a communal settlement in Israel that emphasizes socialistic ideology and collectivistic values (Erez & Somech, 1996). Principles of kibbutz include communal (rather than hierarchical) decision making, equal distribution of rewards (rather than status-based rewards), direct democracy so that everyone has a say, and rotating leadership. Similarly, feminist principles include integrative, holistic decision making, connectedness of individuals to their emotions, and cooperative talk and behavior (Buzzanell, 1994).

Although there is limited research on conflict styles from the communal approach, it is clear that managers are expected to emphasize communal goals during conflict and to resist using power to resolve conflict. Managers and employees are considered equals who are expected to be open and expressive during conflict and work together to develop mutually acceptable decisions. When conflict arises, all parties meet and discuss a variety of issues. They are not expected to focus on just the conflict at hand but may discuss other relevant issues including feelings. Thus, the communal approach is characterized by a high level of other- and self-face orientation, in which all decisions are made considering how they affect others and how they affect one's feelings.

Returning to the example in which the manager intervenes in a conflict between two coworkers, the communal approach could involve an open meeting for all concerned parties (including other coworkers who may be affected by the conflict). The purpose of the meeting is to air out feelings and to understand how each party's communicative behavior affected the others. Finding a solution is secondary to the issue of understanding how everyone is feeling (the solution often comes naturally from this discussion) and experiencing the conflict process. A great deal of emphasis is placed on trying to search for the root causes of the problem so that the key issues can be addressed. The manager is a subjective participant who also expresses her or his feelings and viewpoints. A solution is sought that maintains the relationships and addresses core issues. One interesting note is that there may not even be a manager in a communal organization: All parties may be equal. The effectiveness of the communal approach is measured by the ability of all parties to express their feelings and collectively reach a decision. Thus, collaboration would be the most effective strategy, whereas dominating or forcing would be seen as extremely ineffective. Avoiding and accommodating styles may be effective in certain situations, but the first choice would be collaborative dialogue.

CONFLICTS IN MULTINATIONAL ORGANIZATIONS

The multinational organization is becoming increasingly prevalent given the globalization of the economy. A multinational organization is one that has significant operations in more than one country. It has a home base in one country but may have manufacturing bases in other countries and service bases in countries where its products are sold. Multinational organizations are a fertile breeding ground for frictions, misunderstandings, and conflicts between culturally diverse managers and employees. Like any relationship between a manager and an employee, an international relationship is potentially filled with conflicts. Managers and employees often disagree about issues such as pay, performance evaluations, working overtime, and organizational commitment. However, an international interaction between a manager and an employee has the added difficulty of cultural and communication style differences.

When a company from the United States, for example, opens a plant in Mexico, existing managers are sent to make the business operational. They bring with them certain expectations about how to run a business and how to communicate. These expectations may not mesh with the expectations of the employees. The differences in styles and expectations can lead to misunderstandings that can develop into large conflicts. Cultural differences are easier to negotiate when there are commonalties between the cultures. For example, businesspeople from two cultures with the impartial approach would not have as much difficulty communicating with each other as they would interacting with a benevolent-approach person.

We examine the potential difficulties between the impartial and benevolent approaches, between the status-achievement and communal approaches, and the difficulties between cultures classified within the benevolent approach in the following examples.

Conflict Interaction Example 1

Juan is a manager of a Mexican firm located in the United States, close to the border of the United States and Mexico. Bill is a U.S. American who works for Juan. Juan asks about a new hire that Bill was overseeing.

Juan: So, have we hired someone for the new position?

Bill: I'm just finishing up the job posting and we should be able to start interviewing next week.

Juan: Do you know anyone that would fit well here?

Bill: (puzzled) No one comes to mind.

Juan: Well, how about your cousin John or your good friend Antonio?

Bill: Antonio has a job, but I don't think that hiring John would be a good idea. It would look like we are playing favorites.

Juan: Don't worry about it. Just make sure that you hire somebody that fits in well here. I think John would fit in well. He gets along with everyone in our department.

Bill: (confused) OK.

In this situation, Juan is being a benevolent boss. He is taking care of his workers by trying to hire someone who will maintain the good relationships in the workplace. He assumes that a relative or good friend will mesh well and help to maintain harmony. Bill disagrees because he sees this as nepotism. Because he disagrees, he directly confronts Juan about the idea, assuming that a discussion of procedures will take place. However, Juan diffuses the issue by informing Bill that he should hire someone that fits in well. He does not directly confront Bill. He probably dislikes Bill's direct approach and the challenge to his authority. By diffusing the conflict, he helps to save Bill's face because Bill will not have to embarrass himself by continuing to fight with the boss. Bill is puzzled because he assumes that the issue should be discussed clearly and assumes that whoever has the best idea will prevail. He likely does not recognize the face threat he gave by challenging Juan's authority. Furthermore, Bill is puzzled because the notion of hiring a relative is frowned upon in the United States. In all cultures, social networks help people to find jobs. Hiring a relative in the United States, however, is considered nepotism. In Mexico, the social networks from which to hire often include the family members of the boss and other employees. Hiring relatives is a way to support the collective unit of the family, and it also helps to maintain cohesion in the workplace.

Conflict Interaction Example 2

In the second example, Tim is a manager working for a large multinational company in India. He just moved from the United States, where he prided himself as an open, fair manager who always demanded the highest-quality work from his employees. Pratibha is Indian and has worked at the company for a few years. She is well respected by her colleagues and managers for being a hard worker. She works on a project that is directed by Tim.

> *Tim:*   Pratibha, Ajay [another project director] just received a quick deadline for editing these project reports. Can you help to work on these reports for the next week?
> *Pratibha:*   Certainly. I will have them done on Monday.

Monday comes and the reports are ready. However, Pratibha worked many hours of overtime because the computers went down. A week later, the following conversation takes place.

> *Tim:*   Ajay was so happy with your work that he asked if you could help with another report. I said that I would check with you. Can you help him out?
> *Pratibha:* Yes. Are our own reports due in two weeks as well?
> *Tim:*   Yes. Make sure to give our projects top priority.
> *Pratibha:*   OK.

The deadline comes and Pratibha is able to finish both projects. She worked many overtime hours without saying anything. Again, the computers went down, but she made sure to complete the projects. The next day, Tim approaches Pratibha with more work.

Tim: Because you did such a great job on the last reports, Ajay and I would like you to handle the reports from now on. Great job. The next ones are due in two weeks.

Pratibha: OK.

The next day, Pratibha hands in her resignation.

Tim: Why are you quitting? We need you. You do great work!

Pratibha: I worked many hours of overtime to complete the projects and yet I received no recognition. I feel very unappreciated for doing work outside of my job duties.

Tim: But, I asked you if it was OK and you said yes.

In this exchange, Tim is using the impartial approach to ask for his employee's opinion about the work involved. He was direct with Pratibha and expected her to let him know if what he requested was inappropriate. In addition, he expected Pratibha to inform him of any problems in completing the work. Because she said nothing, he assumed everything was satisfactory. He thought that he was helping her to succeed by giving her challenging assignments that would get her recognized. In contrast, Pratibha was not able to say no to her boss. She was clearly bothered by the request but assumed that the boss would know best. Furthermore, she would expect him to be involved in all of the details of the plant. If the computers went down, he should know about it and extend the deadlines. Finally, he should explain the degree to which her job duties have changed. In this manner, Tim did not support Pratibha's face. A simple compliment was not enough.

Conflict Interaction Example 3

In the third example, Claude is the organizational development manager of a French company located in the United States. Claude represents the status-achievement approach, whereas Valerie represents the communal approach. Valerie works for the organizational development team. Claude introduces a new plan for improving morale at the company.

Claude: (finishing) The theory of the idea makes perfect sense, thus increasing morale. Our supervisor will be very pleased.

Valerie: That's a very interesting theory, Claude, but what are some of the implications for the workers themselves? I think we should talk to the employees.

Claude: Why do we need to talk with the employees? The proposal will work for the company by improving productivity. Everyone will benefit.

Valerie: I just think it's a mistake to implement a procedure without understanding how all of those involved will feel about the new plan. They probably will like it, but it's still important to talk to them.

Claude: Nonsense. The idea is brilliant. It's backed up by research, and the employees will care only if it works or not. We will implement next week.

Valerie: I want to . . .

Claude: (interrupting) Let's move on to other business.

Claude is using his status-achievement approach by explaining that the idea has backing and that it will please the supervisors. Valerie seeks a communal approach by talking with all parties involved. The directness of this approach likely does not offend Claude. He would expect to be confronted if she had a good reason to object. However, he does not see the workers' feelings as a valid objection. Valerie is thinking more holistically in this situation. She wants to make sure all parties are involved. Both parties likely perceive that their face is being threatened because their ideas are not being validated. However, Claude has power (and he believes truth) so he is able to force his opinions. Valerie likely feels invalidated because her ideas are not given merit.

Conflict Interaction Example 4

In the final example, Hiroshi is a manager of a Japanese multinational firm in Mexico. Wintilo is an employee who works in Hiroshi's division. Their working relationship has been very good for the most part. Hiroshi appreciates Wintilo's hard work, and Wintilo appreciates the open and supportive management style of Hiroshi. The only area of conflict is over time. Wintilo often is 15 to 20 minutes late for work, and Hiroshi expects punctuality in his employees. Wintilo's tardiness has been continuing for months, and Hiroshi has tried to avoid the problem. He occasionally drops hints such as looking at his watch when Wintilo comes in the door. Wintilo has noticed the hints but has not been too worried about being on time. He figures that the extra work that he does during the day more than makes up for his tardiness. Hiroshi decides to talk about the issue one day.

Hiroshi: Wintilo, I want to let you know that you and your group are doing very good work here.

Wintilo: Thank you.

Hiroshi: Our division has been complimented many times by my superiors and our group is an important reason for that.

Wintilo: We have tried very hard to meet the company's goals.

Hiroshi: We do have one problem that I am hoping you can help me with. We do have a problem with tardiness in some of the employees. It is very important that we are on time so that we can have our status meetings right away. When one person is late, it interferes with the other employees' performance, and that may affect the overall performance of the division and potentially cost the division important benefits.

Wintilo: (feeling guilty) I understand. However, we can make up for the tardiness by working harder through the day. Please make sure that you recognize these extra efforts. Tardiness doesn't mean someone is a bad worker.

Hiroshi: Certainly we do. And you are right, but we can accomplish so much more without being tardy.

Hiroshi's approach consists of not confronting Wintilo directly. That is, he explains that the team may be suffering because of tardiness in general. In this manner, Hiroshi is trying to save face for Wintilo by not saying that he is acting inappropriately. Furthermore, Hiroshi appeals to the collectivistic face of Wintilo by explaining the consequences of tardiness for other employees and not just the company. Wintilo appreciates Hiroshi's indirectness because he is not being embarrassed. Wintilo disagrees with the policy because the work still gets done.

One difference between Japanese and Mexican cultures is the use of time in work situations. Japan tends to use monochronic time at work, whereas Mexico tends to use polychronic time. Wintilo also feels more comfortable directly confronting Hiroshi about the policy. Both Mexicans and Japanese try to avoid conflict if possible, but Mexicans are more likely than Japanese to use confrontation as a conflict resolution strategy.

These examples illustrate how cultural differences in communication styles can lead to difficulties and misunderstandings between managers and employees. We can see that contrasting organizational approaches lead to different viewpoints about appropriate work procedures and different modes of handling the conflict.

Therefore, the different approaches first lead to the conflict, and then the style differences can exacerbate the conflict. If these conflicts were to continue, we likely would see them worsen because each party would continue to use a conflict style that upsets the other. These problems can be alleviated with an understanding about how face issues affect conflict between managers and employees from different cultures. The key is to understand which face concerns are important as well as how individuals use communicative behaviors to support and uphold each other's face.

CULTURALLY DIVERSE ORGANIZATIONS IN THE UNITED STATES

If you live in the United States, you do not have to leave the country to interact with a person who is from a different culture. As we noted in the first chapter, demographic changes are leading to an increase in the diversity of the United States. Unfortunately, the different ethnic groups in the United States do not always get along well together. The history of ethnic relations in the United States is one of prejudice, discrimination, and oppression by the majority (i.e., European Americans) over the minority (e.g., African Americans, Asian Americans, Latino Americans, and Native Americans) (Daly, 1998).

Thus, power imbalance is an important factor shaping ethnic relations. Power imbalance, along with value pattern differences, has a major impact on the conflicts that occur between managers and employees of different ethnic groups in U.S. organizations. In this section, we describe the existing climate of the U.S. workforce, including issues of prejudice and discrimination, and then illustrate some conflict style differences in handling disputes.

Workplace Prejudice and Discrimination

Many people talk about the climate of ethnic relations and say, "Things are getting better." Whether this is true or not, prejudice and discrimination are still a part of the fabric of U.S. organizations. Statistics illustrate that European Americans (especially men) are overrepresented at the managerial level, whereas ethnic minorities are underrepresented (i.e., the glass ceiling effect) (Cox, 1994). Of the Fortune 500 companies in 1990, only 3 had a CEO who was not white. Of all female managers, 97% are European American. Native Americans own about 21,000 businesses in the United

States compared with 422,000 by Latinos, 424,000 by African Americans, and 2.6 million by women (Daniels et al., 1997). Ethnic minorities make up 20% of the workforce but hold less than 3% of senior management positions. This imbalance causes the structural inequality that pervades the U.S. workforce.

Inequalities do not necessarily permeate all organizations. When discussing cultural diversity, we generally see three types of organizations: monolithic, plural, and multicultural (Cox, 1991). The *monolithic* organization is predominantly composed of members from the majority group. Members of ethnic minorities, if any are employed, are generally restricted to the lower levels of the hierarchy. The organizational culture of monolithic organizations has an unfavorable attitude toward diversity. Employees are expected to assimilate into the workplace, and there is little tolerance for differences in procedures and behaviors. As a result, prejudice and discrimination are commonplace. The *plural* organization has employees who represent the larger society. However, most ethnic minorities are still located at the lower levels. Those employees from ethnic minority groups that have made it to the managerial ranks tend to not be informally integrated. That is, they do not have many personal connections to people in power. The organizational culture has a neutral attitude toward diversity. Employees of the plural organization, however, are also expected to assimilate, but there is some tolerance for deviations if they increase productivity. Prejudice and discrimination are still frequent, although there is some willingness to talk about and address problems.

The *multicultural* organization has a representative population, and majority and minority members are distributed throughout the levels of the organization. Ethnic minority managers are integrated informally as well. Diversity is viewed as a strength for the multicultural organization, and employees are encouraged to behave in culturally sensitive ways. Prejudice and discrimination are rare, but when such issues surface, there is an openness to confront problems and find solutions.

Unfortunately, most organizations in the United States fall into the monolithic category. Ethnic minorities in monolithic and plural organizations face prejudice and discrimination on a frequent basis. Many stories are published about the experiences of ethnic minorities in these organizations. One type of prejudice is overt and blatant racism. For example, one manager said to two other European American managers, but in a voice loud enough to be heard by two African American employees, that instead of celebrating Martin Luther King, Jr. Day, they should celebrate James Earl Ray Day (Daniels et al., 1997). Overt racism has a major effect on those who experience it. More often, prejudice and discrimination tends to be covert and subtle because it is not politically correct to be overtly racist (Pettigrew & Martin, 1992). Note the following example of this subtle prejudice: "I've been told very nicely, 'Gee you're Puerto Rican? You don't look Puerto Rican.' And my answer to that is 'What do Puerto Ricans look like?' "(Ferdman, 1995, p. 43).

The implication is that the person is not like most Puerto Ricans and that in itself is a compliment. The person making this type of comment may not even be aware of this prejudice. We have heard stories from students talking about foreign-born colleagues ("They don't speak very well and don't know how to teach very well" or "I wonder if they were an Affirmative Action hire."). People make these statements and often assume that they are not displaying prejudice. They often do not realize that they are creating a climate in which ethnic minorities feel uncomfortable because their every move is under microscopic examination.

The result of prejudice and discrimination is to feel threatened. In some cases, such as those with overt racism, the threat results in a fear for one's physical safety. If the threat is not to one's safety, it is certainly to one's identity or face. One response to the threat is to adopt behaviors that are different from one's cultural norms in order to fit in better. Latin American managers have been found to behave differently at work and at home in order to succeed (Ferdman, 1995; Ferdman & Cortes, 1992). This response is an accommodation to the larger organization, but it serves to hurt an individual's face because that person cannot be himself or herself. An excellent illustration of this feeling is by an African American man who worked in corporate America.

I worked in corporate America for a while, and now when I see guys walking down the street in a suit and tie and I'm like "phew." I bet he can't wait to go home and be a Black man again. Because you're not allowed to be Black in corporate America. Walk through some halls with some pride and you're going to scare some people. Show that you have some intelligence, you scare people. You've got to shuffle. It's a 1993 shuffle, but it's still a shuffle. (Wah, 1995)

Ethnic minorities conform to dominant group expectations. In the United States, this power imbalance reflects the adjustment made to European American standards rather than the other way around.

Another response is to seek and preserve ethnic identity. Minority group members are usually more aware of, and concerned with, preserving ethnic identity than majority group members (Cox, 1994). Often, majority group members will not understand the need for the positive affirmation that minority group members feel and may be annoyed by such efforts to differentiate themselves from the organization. Those who seek to preserve their ethnic identity at work, rather than use assimilation behavior, try to fight stereotypes as presented by others. This behavior is a defense mechanism that attempts to present a positive identity for one's ethnic group (Tajfel & Turner, 1986).

Our brief review of prejudice and discrimination by no means covers this topic to its full extent. Our purpose is to show that prejudice and discrimination are factors that frame the issue of race in the U.S. workplace. Thus, conflict is influenced by the power relationships of the parties involved. These power relationships are difficult to understand at times. For example, some European Americans feel that diversity programs give unfair advantage to ethnic minorities. There is no advantage from a societal level, but the individual (especially if this person has not had economic or position power) feels these effects. Ethnic relations, prejudice, and discrimination are difficult issues to discuss because of the sensitivity of the topics, which results because we do not know how to support each other's face during discussions of these issues. It is important to keep in mind the larger power dynamics of the United States when interacting with ethnically diverse others. (We have more suggestions at the end of this chapter.) With these power dynamics in mind, we now discuss style differences in resolving conflict.

Conflict Interaction Styles

In addition to power relationships, there appear to be some differences in conflict management behavior among ethnic groups in the United States. According to research (Cox, 1994; Ferdman & Cortes, 1992), African Americans, Asian Americans, and Latino Americans tend to use the benevolent approach (i.e., collectivistic-large power distance) in management practice because of their cultural roots in nations that generally adopt the benevolent approach. In comparison, European Americans tend to emphasize the impartial approach (i.e., individualistic-small power distance) because of their cultural roots in Europe, as well as being the dominant group in the United States. To some extent, these tendencies are true, but the mainstream U.S. culture and its history of prejudice and discrimination have to a certain degree altered these patterns.

We describe the conflict style pattern of five larger ethnic groups in the United States: African American, Asian American, European American, Latino American, and Native American. Our discussion provides a broad picture (see Chapter 2 for more detailed information). It is important to remember that each ethnic group is extremely rich and diverse. For example, Latinos include individuals whose roots are in many different Spanish-speaking nations, such as Cuba, Mexico, and Puerto Rico. Each group has differences and nuances that make it distinct from other backgrounds.

The conflict style pattern of Asian Americans is consistent with the benevolent approach of most Asian countries, whereas the European American pattern is consistent with the impartial approach of the United States. African Americans and Latin Americans deviate from the expectations slightly. African Americans have a strong collectivistic sense emphasizing the importance of family (Hecht et al., 1993). However, they also value the importance of uniqueness and individuality. These combinations would categorize the culture as a combination of communal and impartial approaches. The African American style of conflict resolution tends to be high-key, animated, interpersonal, and emotionally engaging (Kochman, 1981). The animated approach reflects self-pride and individuality and contrasts the linear-logic approach of European Americans who tend to be assertive, yet detached and low-key. The Latin American style at work also appears to match the combination of the communal and impartial approach. Tactfulness and consideration of others' feelings are considered to be important norms in interpersonal confrontation situations (Casas & Pytluk, 1995; Garcia, 1996). Furthermore, it is important to develop and maintain harmonious interpersonal relationships (Ferdman & Cortes, 1992). Large power distance, however, does not reflect either the African American or Latin American conflict approaches in the workplace, especially when people from these groups are confronted with unfair workplace treatments. One speculation is that these groups have faced prejudice and discrimination for many years and therefore they are very sensitive to power imbalance relationships. Although this is true of Asian Americans as well, Asian Americans (especially in the context of Asian immigrants) tend to observe the hierarchical structure of the workplace more so than their European American counterparts.

The Native American style matches most closely with the benevolent management approach (although there are strong communal aspects as well). For example, Native Americans place the utmost importance on interpersonal relationships. The key value is to live in harmony with others. Thus, conflict is often avoided (Rogers & Steinfatt, 1999). If conflict does arise, however, it is resolved with the other parties and the relationship in mind. Relationships begin with the immediate family but also include obligations to clan relatives through both the mother and father (Yazzie, 1995). Conflict participants view themselves as being on two different points of a circle. Rather than trying to defeat the other person, Native

Americans deal with the conflict by learning from the other party as they move along the circle. If individuals cannot resolve the conflict on their own, they seek a leader, such as an elder, who can provide wisdom, listening, and a balanced viewpoint through spiritual guidance, something that is a part of the fabric in their daily lives. The elder thus helps the parties resolve the conflict and preserve the relationship (Yazzie, 1995). However, it is important to note that there are 505 federally recognized tribes with 252 different languages. Because each tribe has varying traditions, beliefs, and approaches, the term *Native American* is a broad-based one.

Domestic Workplace Conflict Examples

We now look at an example of a conflict between an African American manager (Malik) and a Navajo employee (Celina). Celina recently began working for the company after spending most of her life on the reservation. Celina has come to Malik's office for a performance review. She has just completed an important project that landed the company a major account.

Malik: Overall, Celina your work has been wonderful. You did a great job on the Reynolds' account.

Celina: (looking at the floor) Thanks.

Malik: And your work in general has been outstanding. I'm submitting an "exceeds" rating for your review.

Celina: (still looking down) Thank you.

Malik: I do have one area for your improvement. There are some slight problems with communication difficulties that the Reynolds' people commented on.

Celina: (Silent)

Malik: (slightly irritated and raising his voice). It's about your style. You are often silent and don't respond quickly to others' comments. Also, you don't look people in the eye. Just like you are doing now.

Celina: (looks up slightly) I'll try to do better in the future.

Malik: Again, you are doing great work and people really like you. I just think that if you improve your communication, you'll be able to move up in the company.

Celina: (looking at him directly) Thank you.

In this situation, the conflict centers on what is an appropriate communicative style. Malik thinks that Celina needs to be more assertive and animated, whereas Celina is using a cultural pattern of limited direct contact (including limited eye contact because direct eye contact is disrespectful), modesty, and being soft-spoken. She also views silence as important to demonstrate respect for the other. Malik genuinely appreciates her work, and he does not want her to have any problems advancing because of a minor communication style difference. Thus, he provides very specific and direct feedback. He does not want her to be punished for not improving. Malik is being other-face oriented by showing concern for her. Celina is likely appreciative of the feedback but may be taken aback by the directness of the comments.

One caveat to this situation is that this pattern of behavior portrays a Navajo who has had relatively little interaction with people outside of her own reservation. Many Native Americans have grown up on reservations and pueblos and therefore display communication patterns consistent with traditional Native American values. However, many Native Americans have interacted frequently with other U.S. Americans. These individuals often maintain strong ties to their tribes but are also able to adapt their behavior to other situations. This scenario illustrates that it is important not to use broad stereotypes to interpret behavior. Individuals of all cultural groups have a variety of experiences that influence their communicative behavior.

The stresses of identity struggle, power imbalance, and racism converge in the following story. After graduating from Howard University, Debbie Holton, an African American, was hired to work as a reporter-editor for a major publishing company at a branch office in Washington, D.C. Here are several excerpts from her personal reflections (Holton, 1998):

At my first-year review, he [my white supervisor] told me that the quality of my work was good, that I adhered to the codes of the company well, but that I had a problem with time. I was late too often (didn't matter that I came in with other reporters), and I wasn't "blending." Wasn't blending. I was the only Black, one of the few women who worked at that level as a reporter-editor. The walls throughout were stark white. The desks, low without cubicles or partitions, also were white. My desk in front, in full view, was by the door. The blend for me would mean becoming what I obviously was not. To blend meant less Black, more White. . . . During the remaining years, I practiced the lessons learned from literature of social change. I found my way. I made one. Wanting to keep my job (I needed it), I conceived my own way of blending. Integration being the expectation, I quickly learned that integration was a one-way street; integration was tolerable if it meant that the minority become more like the majority. . . .

Meanwhile, I continued to refine my mask. During this time, I found myself needing to have my wisdom teeth removed. I went to a major university dental school because of its reputation. . . . An unfortunate accident occurred during surgery. A mallet to break the wisdom teeth slipped and broke my front teeth instead. . . . Because part of my mask at work required that I let go of my own sense of personal pain and suffering, I went back to work the day after the accident. With my mouth swollen on both sides, my front tooth missing, and in excruciating pain, I went to work. I went because I was afraid that they would think of me, in spite of my professionalism and reliability, as shiftless, lazy, and irresponsible after all. After all that I had done to try to erase the stereotype from their collective expectations, this was what I know to be true. When I arrived, it was clear to all that I was in pain. I said nothing. Like a "good darky woman," I put the "boss men" and how they thought about me before my self-worth and self-esteem. . . . *Where was I under the mask? What had I become—a spook, a shadow of myself? . . .*

Eventually, I was able to leave [the job] with dignity; I was offered another job and took it. It was then that I learned about the office "hot seat." For *3 years,* I had sat by the door in the desk that all the other reporters occupied during their *3-month probation* periods. The hot seat was part of the office ritual designed to see whether reporters could take the pressure and the heat. (pp. 280-282)

The personal sacrifices, pains, and emotional struggles in claiming a "space" in the majority culture often create tremendous stress and oppression in minority group members' work experiences. These excerpts reflect the sense of powerlessness, invisibility, identity frustrations, racism, and the fear of being negatively stereotyped by a minority group member in an organization. The examples also reflect the human struggle for self-pride, dignity, and competent face in a "blend" and "blended" workplace environment. The themes of fitting in versus opting out, adapting versus selling out, speaking up versus dumbing down, and visibility versus invisibility permeate the work experience of many minority members, causing a struggle between their daily internal chaos and external stressors. The above illustrations also resonate with many ideas presented in current research, as well as minorities' experiences working in a majority culture (Cox, 1994).

In this section, we have tried to illustrate how power dynamics and conflict style differences interact as a package to influence intercultural conflict between managers and employees of different ethnicities in the United States. Power dynamics must be considered to understand face issues and conflict approaches by majorities and minorities in the workplace. Power affects how we react, what is socially acceptable, who has to adapt, and how we resolve conflict. In the final section, we offer some general suggestions for managing these types of conflict.

INTERCULTURAL CONFLICT BETWEEN MANAGERS AND EMPLOYEES: PRACTICAL GUIDELINES

This chapter described four approaches to conflict management: impartial, status-achievement, benevolent, and communal. We described these approaches and the face issues associated with these approaches in conflicts between managers and employees. We then illustrated some of the difficulties that can result from style differences in international organizations. Finally, we looked at the unique context of culturally diverse organizations. A critical issue in this situation is the power dynamics between ethnic groups in the United States. We conclude this chapter by offering suggestions for resolving conflicts when the manager and employee come from different cultural backgrounds.

Suggestions for Managers

Understand power differences in the organization. Managers have more power than employees regardless of cultural background. However, cultural power can be just as important as positional power. Cultural power refers to the degree to which the organization and society support or oppress cultural difference. As we reviewed earlier, organizations can be monolithic, plural, or multicultural. A manager who works in a monolithic or plural organization needs to be particularly aware of cultural power. In these types of organizations, it is easy for managers to impose their will (or the organization's will) on employees, compelling culturally different employees to give up their own identity or style for that of the organization. This demand clearly threatens the face or identity dignity of the culturally different employee because it says that the employee's way of experiencing is not appropriate or welcome. Furthermore, and perhaps most importantly, not every employee is expected to change. Only those who do not fit the organization's normative values or profiles (i.e., the culturally different) are expected to change.

Culturally sensitive managers who are aware of the power imbalance issue can be a bridge for the employees in the organization. They can help to socialize the employees about constructive power and empowering moves, and at the same time, provide a safety net for the employees as they learn the system. It is important for managers to understand how difficult it is for culturally different employees to come to work and give up a part of themselves every day. It is simple for a manager to negate the feelings of the culturally different employees by saying, "Everybody who wants to can get ahead at this company. We all stand on our own ground." In reality, corporate ground is typically constructed on the platform of the power-dominant, European American male members. When managers make statements like this, they are demonstrating insensitivity to the power imbalances that occur between cultural/ethnic groups.

Effective managers, furthermore, can help by being a bridge between cultural majority and minority members. They can role-model appropriate behavior by investing in cultural diversity and using cultural diversity as a strength. They can champion cultural diversity issues in the company by treating diversity as a competitive business advantage. They can take the initiative to inquire about the cultural customs and style preferences of their employees in a culture-sensitive manner. They can pay extra attention to any signals that can be construed as exclusionary or prejudiced practices in the workplace. They can promote global and cultural diversity training in their workforce. Effective managers can help to create a work climate that is open, inclusive, and valuing of diversity. By doing so, competent managers help to create a vibrant atmosphere to achieve the benefits of diversity, such as improved morale, creativity, and synergistic problem solving.

Provide mentoring to culturally different employees. Consistent with the previous points, culturally different employees need mentoring in the organization. This is not to say that people from the same cultural background of the majority do not need guidance. Because it generally is easier to advise those people who are similar to us, however, culturally different employees do not often get the same level of mentoring. Guidance should include a variety of elements. First, employees need to learn their jobs and the duties of their jobs. Second, employees need to learn informal networks—whom to contact, whom to avoid, when to contact, when to speak up, and so forth. Third, employees need to be integrated into the informal networks (e.g., introducing the employee to other managers). This list is just a beginning. The important issue is to get culturally different people involved in all aspects of the organization so that they have opportunities to advance and succeed. Furthermore, it is important for managers to recognize their own oversights when providing mentoring to culturally different employees.

Suggestions for Employees

Recognize the authority of the manager. In every manager-employee relationship, conflict will occur. You may not be completely happy with your boss, and you may want to confront your boss. However, there are effective and ineffective ways to challenge. Employees need to realize that the manager does have power and to recognize this authority (although you may not agree with it).

A few proper and improper ways of confronting your manager (based on the culture-based situational model) need to be considered. First, do not confront your boss in public. This behavior is seen as a major face threat and damages the manager's credibility. Your supervisor is not likely to be pleased and will take steps to restore lost credibility. It is better to talk with your boss in private to protect the manager from a public face threat. Second, do not break the chain of command (at least initially). When you go above your boss's head, you are telling others that your manager cannot handle the problem. It is better to directly confront the boss with the problem (in private) and provide the opportunity to resolve the problem. In this manner, you again do not threaten the face of your manager, and in fact, you may solve the problem. Both of these approaches assume that the boss is reasonable and able to see things from a different perspective. In general, it is best to start from this position, allowing both you and the other person the opportunity to adapt and change. If you assume the worst of your boss from the beginning, the worst may happen. Usually, if you threaten your boss's face and your boss spends time trying to restore it, then you hinder the effective resolution of conflicts. By not threatening your boss's face, you are likely to facilitate more effective conflict management.

There are times when the boss is the problem and you cannot trust this person (e.g., you feel your boss is discriminatory or prejudiced). At these times, it is important to have some substantiation to your complaints. Gather evidence of the problems. Write down specific details and events and try to get other coworkers to corroborate your stories. Once you have enough evidence and documentation, going above the boss may be the best alternative. Again, we recommend directly confronting the manager first before seeing your manager's supervisor. We also recognize that direct confrontation does not always help.

Attempt proactive dialogue.   The final suggestion for employees is to attempt proactive dialogue. The best way to deal with intercultural conflict is to stop it from escalating in the first place. Issues regarding cultural and power differences can prove difficult. These are hard to discuss because people are very sensitive about racism, prejudice, and discrimination. However, discussion is easier if it occurs before a full-blown conflict arises. Numerous ways to communicate about intercultural issues include (a) convening monthly meetings to talk about cultural and diversity issues, (b) forming alliances with different diversity groups to explore common interests and common concerns, (c) approaching your supervisor to share intercultural knowledge and serving as active change agent in your organization, (d) approaching culturally different colleagues to inquire about their background in a culture-sensitive manner, and (e) promoting important cultural/ethnic events and celebrations to showcase the richness and cultural complexity of individuals within ethnic groups and across a diverse range of cultures.

Some people worry that talking about these problems will "open a can of worms" and create problems when none existed. To avoid this outcome, the key is to ensure that people enter the discussion with cultural/ethnic sensitivity and respect. Everyone will not agree with everyone's ideas. That is normal. It is important, however, for each party to be heard and to feel understood. The goal is to create a level of trust and safety within the organization so that as vital intercultural matters arise, issues can be dealt with in a win-win fashion that supports the face or dignity of everyone involved. Managers and employees can also work actively on common interests and common ground and realize that all individuals, regardless of culture or race, have the same human needs for respect, inclusion, and genuine connection. In the next chapter, we discuss some specific skills to create respectful attitudes and inclusive communication.

6

MANAGING
INTERCULTURAL
CONFLICT
COMPETENTLY

This chapter highlights some of the skills that all of us can practice in managing everyday culture-based intimate conflicts, group conflicts, and organizational conflicts. Intercultural conflict competence refers to a process of integrating knowledge, mindfulness, and constructive conflict skills in managing group membership differences on a cultural level. To engage in optimal conflict competence, we have to acquire in-depth knowledge, heightened mindfulness, and constructive conflict skills—and apply them ethically in a diverse range of intercultural situations. This concluding chapter is developed in three parts: knowledge categories, mindfulness, and conflict skills. Of the three dimensions of managing intercultural differences, knowledge is a critical theme that underscores the other two facets of intercultural conflict competence.

KNOWLEDGE DIMENSION

Without culture-sensitive *knowledge,* disputants cannot learn to uncover the implicit ethnocentric lenses they use to evaluate behaviors in an intercultural conflict situation. Without knowledge, people cannot have an accurate perspective or reframe their interpretation of a conflict situation from the other's culture standpoint. Knowledge here refers to developing in-depth understanding of important intercultural communication concepts that can help to manage culture-based conflict competently.

The chapters in this book offer the following knowledge classifications: (a) a set of guiding assumptions about intercultural conflict (see Chapter 1), (b) a culture-based situational model to explain the multifaceted nature of an intercultural conflict (see Chapter 2), (c) managing personal relationship conflict satisfactorily (see Chapter 3), (d) managing intercultural team conflict productively (see Chapter 4), (e) managing conflict effectively in multicultural organizations (see Chapter 5), and finally, (f) practical and constructive intercultural conflict competence skills (this chapter).

Overall, the knowledge blocks in this book focus on how individualists (independent selves) and collectivists (interdependent selves) and members of small and large power distance cultures encounter culture clashes, misunderstandings, and conflicts because of cultural value differences. Throughout this book, we emphasize the importance of paying close attention to situational features, such as ethnocentrism and prejudice, and perceived goal-salient issues that influence how different cultural members handle a conflict. Synthesizing some of the ideas in previous chapters, we contend that independent-self individualists tend to operate from the outcome-oriented model, which emphasizes the following conflict assumptions:

1. Conflict is perceived as closely related to the outcomes that are salient to the respective individual conflict parties in a given conflict situation.

2. Communication in the conflict process is viewed as dissatisfying when the conflict parties are not willing to deal with the conflict openly and honestly.

3. Conversely, communication in the conflict process is viewed as satisfying when the conflict parties are willing to confront the issues openly and disclose their feelings directly in a leveling manner.

4. The conflict outcome is perceived as unproductive when no tangible goals are reached or no plan of action is developed.

5. The conflict outcome is perceived as productive when tangible solutions are reached and an action plan is drawn.

6. Effective and appropriate management of conflict means individual goals are addressed and differences are being dealt with openly and fairly in the situational context.

Alternatively, interdependent-self collectivists tend to follow the conflict assumptions of a process-oriented model:

1. Conflict is weighed against the face-threat incurred in the conflict negotiation process; it is also being interpreted in the web of ingroup/outgroup relationships.

2. Communication in the conflict process is perceived as threatening when the parties push for substantive issue discussion before proper facework management.

3. Communication in the conflict interaction is viewed as satisfying when the parties engage in *mutual* face-giving behavior and attend to both conflict verbal messages and nonverbal nuances.

4. The conflict process or outcome is perceived as unproductive when face issues are not addressed adequately and relational/ingroup feelings are not attended to sensitively.

5. The conflict process or outcome is defined as productive when both conflict parties can claim win-win results on the facework front in addition to substantive agreement.

6. Appropriate and effective management of conflict means that the mutual faces of the conflict parties are saved or even upgraded in the interaction and they have dealt with the conflict episode adaptively in conjunction with substantive gains or losses.

Thus, whereas individualists are concerned with conflict problem solving and closure, collectivists are concerned with facework and process management issues. The outcome and process orientations are also influenced by power distance. In small power distance cultures, individuals should learn to employ self-empowering moves and use assertive techniques to manage the conflict constructively. In large power distance cultures, individuals should learn to use their personal and social networks appropriately to manage the conflict productively. However, in any given conflict situation for any particular culture, there remain some individuals who may choose an outcome or process conflict orientation because of distinctive personal attributes, situational factors, organizational culture practice, practical constraints, and time pressure.

Individualism-collectivism and power distance serve as primary influences on cultural members' conflict behaviors. The culture-based situational model (see Chapter 2) helps to explain the complexity of intercultural conflict by identifying the various layers involved in these entangled struggles. The model serves as a useful compass to guide the analysis of your own conflicts in a wide variety of contexts. More important, we want to emphasize the significance of the situational features (e.g., conflict intensity) that serve as the links that mediate between the primary orientation factors (e.g., values patterns, conflict norms, face concerns) on the one hand, and the conflict process factors (e.g., conflict styles, emotional expressions) on the other. The situational features of ingroup-outgroup boundaries, relationship parameters, conflict goal assessments, conflict intensity, and scarce resources converge and influence our conflict choices and actions. By probing deeper into the various situational and relationship features that affect an intercultural conflict process, we develop a more comprehensive analysis of the systems complexity in an intercultural conflict episode.

The knowledge that we acquire about the other conflict parties, our willingness to be mindful of our own and the others' conflict behaviors, and the skills that we use to manage the conflict adaptively will dramatically influence the outcome dimension of the conflict. Many historical factors (e.g., ethnic group history), socioeconomic factors, political factors, religious factors, and specific family socialization factors enter into various kinds of conflict. For the purpose of this book, we identify in our model the most salient conflict components that we believe have a strong impact on face-to-face intercultural conflict interaction. As insiders of the conflict, you may want to add additional factors to the conflict model to make the model more useful for your own reflection and analysis.

In translating knowledge into competent conflict practice, we must constantly double-check our own assumptions and reactive emotions that we bring into a conflict situation. We need to practice mindful thinking to be committed to managing the conflict constructively and satisfactorily.

MINDFULNESS DIMENSION

To be a mindful interpreter of intercultural conflict, one must develop a holistic view of the critical factors that frame the antecedent, process, and outcome components of a conflict episode. Mindfulness means attending to one's internal assumptions, cognitions, and emotions and, at the same time, becoming attuned to the other's conflict assumptions, cognitions, and emotions (Ting-Toomey, 1999). Mindful reflexivity requires us to tune in to our own cultural and personal habitual assumptions in scanning a conflict interaction scene (Thich, 1991, 1998).

Beyond mindful reflexivity, we also need to be open to novel or unfamiliar behavior. To be mindful of intercultural differences, we have to learn to see the unfamiliar behavior from a nonjudgmental perspective. In the context of intercultural conflict, we have to deal with our own vulnerable emotions regarding face-threatening behaviors and, at the same time, we have to be responsive to new conflict interaction scripts. We also need to develop multiple lenses for understanding the cultural-level and situational-level factors that shape the escalating conflict episode. Integrating new ideas or expanding a variety of perspectives into one's value system requires mental flexibility. Mental flexibility requires one to rethink assumptions about oneself and the world. Such rethinking may cause identity dissonance or confusion, but inevitably, also personal, relational, familial, and organizational development.

To act mindfully, we should learn to (a) see behavior or information presented in the conflict situation as novel or fresh, (b) view a conflict situation from several vantage points or perspectives, (c) attend to the conflict context and the person in whom we are perceiving the behavior, and (d) create new categories through which this new conflict behavior may be understood (Langer, 1989, 1997). In addition, we need to learn to shift perspective and base our understanding from the other's cultural frame of reference. This practice of analytical empathy enables disputants to see both differences and similarities between each other's cultural and personal perspectives. Analytical empathy is a systematic way of repositioning ourselves to see and to experience conflict events from the other conflict party's view and to gain alternative insights in approaching the problem (Rothman, 1997).

On a general level, we cannot learn to be suddenly mindful during a conflict episode. Mindfulness is a daily practice to learn how to be more in tune with our own emotions, experiences, and senses in our everyday interactions and also extending that attunement to others whom we know. A mindful conflict perspective fosters collaborative dialogue and collaborative listening. Through collaborative dialogue, conflict parties try to create multiple options for constructive conflict resolution and reconciliation. Through partnership dialogue, disputants (or with third-party help) learn to develop a facilitation process that pools divergent and creative insights and solutions together. A mindful conflict interpreter is also a creative problem solver. In the creativity literature, for example, researchers (e.g., Csikszentmihalyi, 1996; Gardner, 1995; Sternberg, 1999) have found certain tendencies in creative individuals:

1. They cultivate curiosity and interest in their immediate surroundings.
2. They look at problems from as many viewpoints as possible and are open to novelty.
3. They are alert to complexity and distinction within groups or cultures.
4. They are sensitive to different situational uniqueness.
5. They orient themselves to the present with focused five senses.
6. They cultivate "flow" or enjoyment in their everyday interaction with others.
7. They practice divergent thinking or sideways learning.

Sideways learning involves attending to multiple ways of seeing and experiencing. It also involves creating more distinctions and categories in our interpretations and analysis of a conflict situation (Langer, 1997). Thus, whereas a routine thinker practices mindless conflict behaviors, a creative thinker practices mindful conflict behavior and adaptive action. Mindfulness is the mediating step linking knowledge with skillful practice. In the next section, we discuss a set of constructive communication skills for managing intercultural conflicts competently.

CONSTRUCTIVE CONFLICT SKILLS DIMENSION

Constructive conflict management skills refer to our operational abilities to manage an intercultural conflict situation appropriately, effectively, satisfactorily, and productively (see Chapter 2). Constructive conflict communicators use culture-sensitive interaction skills to manage the process of conflict adaptively and reach important goals for all parties amicably. In contrast, destructive conflict management occurs when the conflict parties continuously engage in inflexible thinking and inflexible conflict patterns, which in turn lock them into prolonged cycles of defensiveness, impasse, and frustration. Many conflict skills are useful in enhancing inter-cultural interaction competence. We discuss 10 core constructive conflict skills that are critical in any intercultural conflict situation: mindful observation, mindful listening, mindful reframing, identity validation, facework management, productive power balancing, collaborative dialogue, problem-solving skills, transcendent dis-course, and interaction adaptability.

Mindful Observation

Mindful observation involves an O-D-I-S (observe, describe, in-terpret, and suspend evaluation) analysis concerning cultural style differences that create culture clashes. Rather than engaging in snapshot, negative evaluations, O-D-I-S analysis is a slowing-down process that involves learning to *observe* attentively the verbal *and* nonverbal signals that are being exchanged in the conflict process. After attentive observation, we should then try to *describe* mentally and in behaviorally specific terms (e.g., "She is not maintaining eye contact with me when speaking to me.") what is going on in the conflict interaction. Next, we should generate *multiple interpreta-tions* (e.g., "Maybe from her cultural framework, eye contact avoidance is a respectful behavior; from my cultural perspective, this is considered a disrespectful sign.") to make sense of the behav-ior we are observing and describing.

Finally, we may decide to respect the differences and *suspend* our ethnocentric evaluation. We may also decide to engage in open-ended evaluation (e.g., "I understand that eye contact avoidance may be a cultural habit of this person, but I still don't like it because I feel uncomfortable in such interaction.") by acknowledging our discomfort with unfamiliar behaviors. By engaging in an internal dialogue, we can monitor our ethnocentric emotions judiciously. We may also want to meet with a wide variety of people (and in a wide range of contexts) from this cultural group to check if eye contact avoidance is a cultural or individual habit. We may also decide to approach the person or a third party (with low-/high-context styles in mind) to metacommunicate about such differences. Metacommunication refers to the way we interact with each other in a conflict episode and processing the styles that we use in a conflict scene. The tone of voice (e.g., sincere inquiry vs. evaluative questioning) behind the use of metacommunication will determine whether we can clarify our cultural styles productively or unproductively. Mindful observation skills need to go hand-in-hand with mindful listening behaviors.

Mindful Listening

Acquiring new information in a conflict negotiation process means both conflict parties have to learn to listen mindfully to each other even when disagreeing. In a conflict episode, the disputants have to try hard to listen with focused attentiveness to the cultural and personal assumptions that are being expressed in the conflict interaction. They have to learn to listen responsively or *ting* (the Chinese word for listening means attending delicately with our ears, eyes, and a focused heart) to the sounds, tones, gestures, movements, nonverbal nuances, pauses, and silence in a given conflict situation.

By listening mindfully, disputants can learn to create new categories for interpreting the unfolding conflict sequences. Creating new categories in conflicts means learning to apply culture-sensitive concepts such as ingroup or outgroup interaction styles for making sense of conflict variation behaviors. We can also practice mindful listening by engaging in paraphrasing and perception checking statements. *Paraphrasing skill* refers to two characteristics: (a) verbally summarizing the content meaning of the speaker's message in your own words and (b) nonverbally echoing your interpretation of the emotional meaning of the speaker's message. The verbal summary, or restatement, should reflect your tentative understanding of the speaker's content meaning, such as, "It sounds to me that ..." and "In other words, you're saying that ..." You can also try to paraphrase the emotional meaning of the speaker's message by echoing your understanding of the affective tone that underlies the speaker's message. In dealing with high-context members, your paraphrasing statements should consist of deferential, qualifying phrases such as "I may be wrong, but what I'm hearing is that . . ." or "Please correct me if I misinterpret what you've said. It sounded to me that . . ." In interacting with low-context members, your paraphrasing statements can be more direct and to the point than with high-context members.

Moving beyond paraphrasing, perception-checking statements are designed to help us ensure we are interpreting the speaker's nonverbal and verbal behavior accurately during an escalating conflict episode. Perception-checking statements usually end with a clarifying question-type format. It is a double-checking questioning skill that should be used judiciously and in a culture-sensitive manner. It can be used when we are unsure whether we are reading the meaning of the nonverbal or verbal message accurately. Culture-sensitive perception-checking statements involve both direct (for low-context individuals) or indirect (for high-context individuals) perceptual eyewitness statements and perceptual verification questions. For example, a high-context perceptual statement can be, "From your puzzled facial expression, maybe I'm not making myself very clear. I apologize for that confusion. When I mentioned that I need the report by early next week, I meant the latest by Tuesday at 5:00 P.M. Do you have any questions about the deadline? [pause]" Perception checking is part of mindful observation and mindful listening skills. It should be used cautiously, especially in accordance with the particular topic, relationship, timing, and the situational context.

Mindful listening essentially involves a fundamental shift of conflict perspective. It means taking into account not only how things look from one's own conflict perspective, but how they look and feel from the other conflict partner's perspective. Through mindful listening, we can also learn to be more reflective about our own patterns of conflict approaches and also be more aware of our partner's conflict orientations.

Mindful Reframing

Mindful reframing means creating alternative contexts to frame your understanding of the conflict behavior. Just as the frame may change your appreciation of a painting, creating a new context to understand the conflict behavior may redefine your interpretation and reaction to the behavior or conflict event. Reframing is a critical conflict management skill because how you frame the conflict event may change how you respond to it. Reframing during a conflict episode can take place at multiple levels. We can reframe on the cultural inquiry level and the personal inquiry level. We can also reframe the different types of conflict goals that are involved in the conflict situation.

Cultural dimensions of reframing or inquiry concerning the other conflict team can include the following questions:

1. What are their cultural identity tendencies—individualistic based or group based?
2. What are their power value tendencies—horizontal based or vertical based?
3. What are their facework assumptions—I-identity or we-identity face model?
4. What are their preferred conflict styles—direct, low-context or indirect, high-context?
5. How do they view ingroup-outgroup relationships?
6. What are their collective and individual conflict goals and needs?

Personal dimensions of reframing or introspective perspective taking can include the following questions:

1. What activates their personal motivations—independent-self or interdependent-self motivations—and what is the extent of discrepancy between the personal-self and the cultural-self motivations?

2. How would they like to be respected—on an equal basis or a deferential basis?
3. What would it take to satisfy their face needs—autonomy face, approval face, and/or competence face?
4. What are their expectations in entering this relationship or working on this multicultural team?
5. What are their individual experiences in working with culturally different others?
6. What are the unique attributes, dreams, talents, or desires that the two teams share that actually move beyond the cultural membership differences?

By mentally walking through some of the above questions, we can reframe with a heightened sense of cultural and personal empathy. We can also reframe the content conflict goal issues—perhaps, from a win-lose frame to a win-win frame. In addition, we can also reframe relationship and identity conflict goals from a competitive or passive-aggressive frame to a collaborative frame. Finally, we can also learn to shift the destructive conflict metaphors that we hold about conflicts to more constructive, solution-generating ones.

Identity Validation

Through mindfulness, we can also pay close attention to the speech patterns and the nonverbal actions that we use in engaging people in the conflict scene. Ethnic-sensitive identity validation skills include addressing people by their preferred titles, labels, names, and identities. Addressing people by their desired titles or identities conveys to others our recognition of their existence and the validity of their experiences. For example, individuals sometimes may identify strongly with their ethnic-based memberships and sometimes their person-based identities. By being sensitive to people's self-images in particular situations and according due respect to their desired identities, we confirm their self-worth. Calling others what they want to be called and recognizing group memberships that are important to them are part of supporting their self-images.

In addition, using inclusive language (e.g., "We, although different") rather than exclusive language (e.g., "You people") and using situational language rather than polarized language are part of other-identity consideration skills. *Inclusive language* means we are mindful at all times of our use of verbal messages when we converse with both ingroup and outgroup members in a team setting. We should cross-check our own verbal habits and ensure that we are directing our comments to both ingroup and outgroup members on an equitable basis. Inclusive language usage also entails inclusive nonverbal behavior (e.g., eye contact is evenly spread out to both ingroup and outgroup members and not just to ingroup members).

Situational language means that when we observe outgroup members' behavior, we are willing to take ethnic and situational features into account for understanding outgroup members' behavior. We honor the identities of outgroup members by acknowledging vital group membership differences that outgroup members deem important. At the same time, we should not overexaggerate group membership differences (especially based on rigidly held stereotypes) at the expense of finding common ground and a common solution. We convey our respect to outgroup members by acknowledging their viewpoint.

Finally, a mindful communication strategy that helps to validate different identities is *resisting privileged discourse* (Fine, 1991). The first step in resisting privileged discourse is to forge an assumption of difference, recognizing multiple discourses and interpretations of reality, and resisting dominant-group views. One of the key ideas of resisting privileged discourse is to assume that people are different and not homogeneous. This assumption encourages people to look for alternative hypotheses and explanations and to accept different behaviors as normal. Furthermore, resisting privileged discourse means challenging stereotypical and dominant views. Question someone's assumption of another group or use balancing statements: For example, "My coworker speaks English

with an accent, *and* she is one of our most productive employees."
"I've learned to really listen to Carlos. His views and experiences
are very different from mine, and I often learn from him." "Hmmm,
I just don't agree with your statement at all concerning 'All Chinese
are always late.' That's hasn't been my experience at all. And your
'All Chinese' statement consists of a category of 1.2 billion people."
These types of constructive strategies—actively sharing a counter-
example to balance the prejudiced picture, pointing out the positive
aspects of diversity, and politely yet firmly disagreeing with a racist
statement or stereotypical blanket statement—can help resist privileged discourse.

Thus, we confirm and disconfirm dissimilar others by the words
we choose to address them and by the attitude behind the words we
use to refer to them. Sometimes we may want to downplay group-
based identities because members who belong to dissimilar groups
do not identify strongly with their groups. However, we may also
be interacting with dissimilar individuals who value their cultural
or ethnic group memberships enormously. To communicate sensitively with others, we must pay close attention to their preferences
of identity affiliation in particular conflict situations.

Facework Management

Facework management skills are consistent with identity validation skills because they help to validate the conflict party's social
self-esteem and social self-worth issues. Facework skills address the
fundamental issues of preserving or protecting our own communication identity during a conflict episode and at the same time allow
us to deal with the communication identity of the other conflict
party. All human beings like to be respected and be approved of,
especially during vulnerable conflict situations. How diverse individuals protect and maintain self-face needs, however, and at the
same time monitor, threaten, or learn to honor the face needs of the
other conflict party very likely differ from one culture to the next,
and differ from a particular conflict scene to the next.

On a general level, both individualists and collectivists need to learn to save face strategically and give face appropriately to each other during a conflict episode. Self-oriented face-saving behaviors are attempts to regain or defend communication images after threats to face or face loss. Other-oriented face-giving behaviors are attempts to support others' face claims and work with them to prevent further face loss or help them to restore face constructively. *Giving face* means not humiliating others, especially one's conflict opponents, in public.

For individualists having conflicts with collectivists, this means acknowledging collectivists' ingroup conflict concerns and obligations. It means learning to mindfully listen and hold an other-orientation perspective in the conflict process. It means learning to apologize when you are part of the conflict problem. It means giving credit to the teamwork or family members that frame the collectivists' action or accomplishment. For collectivists having conflicts with individualists, giving face means honoring others by sharing your voice (or opinions) actively with other conflict parties in a candid manner. It means engaging in explicit verbal acknowledgment and feedback during a conflict negotiation process. It means recognizing the individual names, faces, abilities, and skills of members of the other team and complimenting the unique contributions of each individual member.

Similarly, individuals from different power distances need to learn to give face in a different manner. Small power distance individuals need to understand the importance of status for maintaining face for large power distance individuals. They may want to use face-honoring speech, such as acknowledging titles during interaction, remaining poised under all circumstances, and using higher-status individuals to help resolve workplace conflict with peers. Large power distance individuals, on the other hand, may want to use self-restraint in using their status or power base to resolve the problem. They may have to use more proactive conflict strategies such as active consultation and fact-finding processes, joint problem solving, and productive power balancing techniques to resolve the conflict issue with small power distance individuals. For large power distance individuals, mindful curbing of status difference will help to "level the playing field" and allow for the other party to maintain face or restore face loss.

Productive Power Balancing

Power refers to the degree of perceived or actual influence person A has over person B. From a systems analytical perspective, the degree of influence person A has over person B (and vice versa) is related directly to the nature of the relationship between person A and person B (Emerson, 1962). Power is a relational property: Person A has power over person B to the extent that B is dependent on A for goal attainment of any kind (and vice versa). The degree of dependence of person B on person A is a function of (a) the perceived importance of the goals the other can influence and (b) the availability of other alternatives for person B to achieve her or his needs or goals (Wilmot & Hocker, 1998).

Several constructive conflict skills can be used by both parties to balance their power bases in the relationship. If you perceive yourself in the dependent and hence less powerful position (on either the cultural level or relational level, or both), you can:

1. Cultivate and develop a wealth of power currencies: Learn a new language, master a new computer program, develop your network contacts, hone your communication and leadership skills, take an assertiveness training class, develop your exclusive knowledge in a special domain.
2. Reframe the importance of the goals in the conflict situation: By de-emphasizing the importance of your wants and needs in the particular conflict goal (e.g., relational intimacy), you lessen your dependence on the other conflict party.
3. Reassess your relational resources: You may lack tangible power currencies (e.g., money, a house, a corner office), but you may hold rich socioemotional currencies (e.g., in satisfying the other party's dependent needs for attention, affection, inclusion, or support).

4. Cultivate and diversify your alternatives and opportunities: broaden your social circle, work with different teams, take some risks on different assignments, volunteer for overseas assignments, meet new culturally diverse individuals—by expanding your own horizon and life experiences, you also lessen your dependence on the other conflict party.

If you perceive yourself as having too much power in the conflict relationship and you would like to share power constructively, here are some of the things you can do:

1. Practice mindful self-restraint in activating your power currencies—learn to develop trust and learn to delegate responsibilities evenly to members of diverse cultural and ethnic groups.
2. Actively solicit feedback from less-powerful individuals—take the proactive step to approach them rather than wait for them to come to you and assume responsibility to mentor them and to share in their success.
3. Acknowledge your interdependence with each other—recognize that they hold valuable intangible resources (cultural level, relational level, skills level, contact level, etc.) and make your compliments explicit through culture-sensitive words and actions.
4. Look out for constructive opportunities and challenges for the less powerful individuals—offer them encouragement, enhance their self-esteem and self-confidence level, put them in leadership situations in which they have a good chance to succeed.

People (consciously or unconsciously) choose how to use power—positively or negatively. Power can be positive when we choose a partnership power perspective and deal with conflicts effectively and improve relationships constructively. Power can be productively shared when both sides genuinely listen to the other side's concerns, needs, expectations, and wishes. Power, however, can be abused when one side consistently imposes his or her power (or viewpoint) on the other side through coercion, intimidation tactics, or overt threats. In sharing power constructively, conflict individuals or teams can also learn to practice collaborative dialogue.

Collaborative Dialogue

Collaborative dialogue attempts to discover common ground, share power productively, and assumes that each cultural team has a piece of the bigger picture. On the other hand, a mindless monologue approach pushes for egocentric to ethnocentric goals exclusively (see Table 6.1).

In heated conflicts, we often escalate the interaction by using a monologue rather than a dialogue approach. The characteristics of a monologue approach are (a) the exclusive use of an ethnocentric lens in evaluating a conflict, (b) emphasizing conflict positional differences, (c) using unilateral coercive power to intimidate or dominate, (d) monopolizing conflict goals, (e) employing a singular procedure in resolving the conflict, and (f) a strong win-lose to lose-lose orientation. On the other hand, the characteristics of a dialogue approach are (a) the willingness to use an ethnorelative lens (i.e., using multiple cultural perspectives) to interpret a conflict situation (Bennett, 1993), (b) emphasizing conflict common interests, (c) a willingness to share power productively, (d) employing integrative conflict goals, (e) creating multiple conflict resolution paths, and (f) viewing conflict as a win-win, collaborative dance.

In collaborative dialogue exchange, individuals orient themselves fully in the present. They are inwardly reflexive and outwardly reflective of identity-, relational-, and content-based conflict issues. They use all the previously mentioned skills in this chapter such as mindful observation, listening, and reframing in engaging themselves in constructing the collaborative dialogue process. In the entry phase of collaborative dialogue, a dialogue process assumes that, "Each person within a dialogue is different; each one speaks a different language. Each one prefers a different 'system paradigm.' Each one has a different story and way to make meaning. Listening carefully to each person and speaking uniquely

Table 6.1 Intercultural Conflict Management: Two Approaches

A Monologue Approach	A Dialogue Approach
Ethnocentric Lens	Ethnorelative Lens
Selective Seeing	Mindful Observation
Selective Hearing	Mindful Listening
Defensive Judgment	Mindful Reframing
Impositional Self-Interest	Invitational Inquiry
Coercive Power	Shared Power
Self-Face Assertion Only	Mutual-Face Giving
Emphasize Positional Difference	Emphasize Common Interests
Fixed Objectives	Creative Options
Win-Lose to Lose-Lose Outcome	Win-Win Synergistic Outcome

to him or her matters enormously when creating the initial setting for a dialogue" (Isaacs, 1999, p. 293; see also Yankelovich, 1999).

In practicing collaborative dialogue on the stylistic level with collectivists, individualists may want to (a) practice patience and nonverbal attentiveness in surfacing (i.e., eliciting) collectivists' personal stories, feelings, interests, goals, and wants; (b) use vocal segregates or back-channeling cues such as "uhm, uhm," or "uh-huh" to signal listening mindfulness; (c) be open to the expressions of proverbs, metaphors, analogies, spiral-logic examples, and understatements; (d) use self-effacing questions to encourage the others to coach you or show you the way; (e) address the conflict problem to general team members rather than singling out one person; (f) accept longer turn-taking pauses and reflective silences; (g) use appropriate head nods to indicate identity affirmation; and (h) listen to the identity and relational meanings that underscore the conflict content messages.

In collaborative dialogue sessions with individualists, collectivists may want to (a) practice verbal expressiveness in soliciting individualists' personal interests, goals, desires, and wants; (b) use direct verbal responses to indicate agreements, negotiable points, and disagreements; (c) articulate clearly the reasons behind the disagreement from either an inductive mode (i.e., from specific reasons to general conclusions when dealing with, say, U.S. Americans) or a deductive logical mode (i.e., from a general framework to specific reasons, for example, when dealing with Western Europeans); (d) use direct, specific questions to cross-check facts, interests, and unclear goals; (e) target the questions to a specific individual; (f) learn to engage in overlap talks and faster turn-taking verbal behavior; and (g) use verbal paraphrasing and perception-checking statements to summarize what you have heard in your own words to prevent misunderstanding.

Collaborative dialogue, in a long-term negotiation session, aims to unfold common identity-need issues such as safety, security, connection, inclusion, respect, approval, competence, creativity, and meaning. The more we learn to display a genuine, inquiring attitude, the more we may uncover deep-level common interests and common ground in the conflict dialogue process.

Problem-Solving Skills

After identifying and understanding the different angles on all conflict issues, the two cultural teams can then use the following substantive problem-solving sequence to attempt to resolve the conflict: differentiation, mutual problem description, and integration (Papa & Papa, 1997).

The *differentiation* phase refers to the important stage of setting the scene in which conflict problems arise. It aims to clarify the contrasting conflict positions and goals, and pursue the underlying reasons that underscore the positional differences. It involves the exchange of individual conflict perspectives and surfacing the conflict perceptions and intentions that underlie the problematic conflict behaviors. The *mutual problem description* phase refers to the stage when the key conflict problem is described in specific, mutually understandable terms. Each party tries to identify the conflict roadblocks that stop effective conflict resolution. Conflict parties describe for each other the conflict situation and its related dilemmas and pressure points. Individuals refrain from any evaluative comments or intrusive interruptions. Individuals also focus on possible resolution outcomes rather than on assigning blame.

Finally, the *integration* phase includes (a) displaying cooperative, mutual-interest intentions through culture-sensitive interaction acknowledgment and supportive, face-honoring messages; (b) generating creative and inclusive solutions through a wide range of cultural modes such as traditional dramas, storytelling, cultural metaphors, pictures, visualization journey, sculpting techniques (i.e., using people as symbolic living sculptures to role-play the solutions), and Western-style brainstorming; (c) evaluating the positive and negative aspects of each solution and making sure that all cultural members are committed and involved in the creating and selection process; (d) combining the best of different solutions that members of both cultural teams help to blend together; (e) selecting the best synergistic solutions that are applicable (i.e., desirable and feasible) to both cultural teams; and (f) establishing a monitoring system (e.g., a timeline and criteria for successful implementation) to determine if the solution or action plan is culturally viable. Through working together in the collaborative dialogue process, mutual respect is forged, commitment to the new solution is developed, and trust has been enhanced.

Transcendent Discourse

Unfortunately, not all conflicts can be resolved. At times, intercultural conflicts that involve power and identity issues can result in moral conflicts (Littlejohn, 1995). Moral conflict involves "disputes over the proper course of action based on deeply held assumptions about reality" (Littlejohn, 1995, p. 101). Moral conflicts involve identity issues because the conflict parties have deeply held assumptions, which form a core part of their beings. Power issues are involved because changing one's position often is perceived as giving in or deferring to the other party, which involves a loss of face.

Littlejohn (1995) suggests that the goal for handling moral differences is not to resolve the differences, but to provide healthy ways in which they can be expressed, to allow all voices to be heard with respect, and to avoid the negative patterns often associated with a moral clash. He suggests transcendent discourse to accomplish these goals. Transcendent discourse has five qualities: (a) it educates; (b) it is creative; (c) it is comparative; (d) it is dialogic; and (e) it is critical.

Transcendent discourse educates because it seeks out underlying assumptions about the conflict and not just basic goals and interests. Transcendence is creative because it allows parties to reframe the conflict and bring out new ways of thinking about the conflict. Transcendence is comparative because, through reframing, it allows conflict parties to make a perceptual shift that does not privilege one particular view. Transcendence is dialogic because it discusses, not dominates, and expresses, not hides, differences. Finally, transcendence is critical because it aims to explore the power and limits of moral orders in an evenhanded manner.

Transcendent discourse focuses on the process of conflict management, not conflict outcomes. Moral conflicts often do not have a perceived middle ground, and thus, there will never be a satisfactory outcome to the conflict for at least one of the parties. By focusing on the process, transcendent discourse is a tool that allows individuals the opportunity to be heard and therefore maintain face.

Interaction Adaptability

All the skills already mentioned cannot be applied prescriptively. Depending on the context, the conflict issue, the people, relationship, resources, and timing, no conflict resolution can rely on collaborative dialogue or mindful reframing alone. Even in the best of negotiations, there will be a mixed pattern of competitive and collaborative messages. The key in any constructive conflict management is to be flexible and adaptable and not be locked into one set of behavioral or thinking patterns.

Interaction adaptability is one of the key skills in intercultural conflict competence. Interaction or communication adaptability refers to our ability to change our conflict goals and behaviors to meet the specific needs of the situation (Duran, 1985). It signals our mindful awareness of the other person's perspectives, interests, goals, or all three, and our willingness to modify our own interests

.s to adapt to the conflict situation. Adaptability can also im-
cognitive, affective, and behavioral flexibility in dealing with
.1e intercultural conflict episode. By mindfully observing what is
going on in the intercultural conflict situation, both parties may
modify their nonverbal and verbal behavior to achieve a more syn-
chronized interaction process. In modifying or tailoring our behavioral styles, polarized views on the conflict content problem may
also be depolarized or "softened."

We have identified ten constructive conflict skills in this chapter,
namely, mindful observation, mindful listening, mindful reframing,
identity validation, facework management, productive power balancing, collaborative dialogue, problem-solving skills, transcendent discourse, and interaction adaptability. The objective in practicing all these skills in competent conflict management is to display
basic human respect even if we are disagreeing. We believe that human respect is a fundamental starting point for any productive,
transcultural dialogue to take place.

CONCLUSIONS

In sum, constructive intercultural conflict management requires us
to communicate appropriately and effectively in different intercultural situations. This approach necessitates creativity, adaptability, and flexibility. Effective conflict management requires us to
be knowledgeable and respectful of different worldviews and to use
multiple approaches in dealing with a conflict situation. It requires
us to be sensitive to the differences and similarities between individualistic-small power distance and collectivistic-large power distance cultures. It demands that we be aware of our own ethnocentric
biases and cultural-based attributions when making snapshot evaluations of other people's conflict management approaches.

Effective conflict negotiation promotes flexible, adaptive behaviors by focusing on managing the antecedent, process, and outcome
components of an intercultural conflict episode. Although the study
of intercultural conflict is a complex phenomenon, understanding

conflict from a culture-based situational model serves as a beginning step in explaining conflict from a conjoint cultural-situational variability angle. To engage in optimal conflict competence, we need to be mindful of our habitual conflict scripts, thinking patterns, affective states, language usage, and nonverbal rhythms that we bring into an intercultural conflict situation. At the same time, we should also be willing to commit ourselves to consider the perspective of our conflict partners to experience their dilemma. In competent conflict management, we aim to rebuild broken relationships, expand the diversity of conflict management approaches, and heal hurts, wounds, and resentments. In the process of transforming our own approach in dealing with everyday intercultural conflicts, hopefully we can develop a more inclusive way of looking at the multicultural world.

APPENDIX

Measures of Face Concerns and Facework Behaviors in Four National Cultures

Over the years, there have been numerous studies examining facework and conflict styles across cultures. Many of these studies (e.g., Cocroft & Ting-Toomey, 1994; Oetzel, 1998a, 1998b; Ting-Toomey et al., 1991, 2000; Trubisky et al., 1991) have used the face-negotiation theory (Ting-Toomey, 1988), which provided a strong foundation to the culture-based situational conflict model we presented in Chapter 2. One limitation of prior research using face-negotiation theory is that face concerns were often not measured directly. Rather, they were assumed to be the link between cultural variability and conflict styles (for an updated measure on cross-ethnic conflict styles, see Ting-Toomey et al., 2000). An exception to this limitation is Ting-Toomey et al.'s (1991) study, which did measure self- and other-face. However, the measure used (Baxter, 1984) focused only on a narrow range of face concerns. We felt that measures or survey instruments of face concerns and facework patterns should include a wider range of cross-cultural face concerns and facework styles. Therefore, we sought to create original measures that can be used by researchers interested in face concerns.

In this section, we describe a large, cross-cultural study of face concerns and facework behaviors in four nations: China, Germany, Japan, and the United States. The data from this study were used to confirm the validity of several research measures of face concerns and facework behaviors. These measures also have applications for intercultural trainers and teachers of intercultural communication and conflict. We begin by describing the data collection procedures and then discuss the results of the factor analyses.

DATA COLLECTION PROCEDURES

Participants

There were 912 participants who responded to the questionnaire used in the current study. The participants reported about a recent conflict they had with another party. A few of these participants were excluded from analysis because they were not from the national cultures under investigation (n = 20). There were 238 Chinese, 226 Germans, 214 Japanese, and 210 U.S. Americans. The respondents were students recruited from a medium-sized engineering university in China, a small technical university in Germany, a large university in Japan, and a large university in the southwestern United States. The average age of the participants was 21.54 (SD = 3.76).

In the Chinese sample, 63% were female and 37% male. The average age was 19.82 (SD = 1.12). There were 57 who reported a conflict with an equal status and close person, 62 who reported a conflict with an equal status and distant person, 61 who reported a conflict with a higher status and close person, and 58 who reported a conflict with a higher status and distant person. In the German sample, 55% were female and 45% male. The average age was 23.50 (SD = 2.95). There were 61 in the equal/close, 52 in the equal/distant, 65 in the higher/close, and 48 in the higher/distant cells. In the

Japanese sample, 62% were female and 38% were male. The average age was 19.96 (SD = 1.97). There were 56 in the equal/close, 53 in the equal/distant, 53 in the higher/close, and 52 in the higher/distant cells. In the U.S. American sample, 63% were female, 35% were male, and 2% were unreported data. The ethnic backgrounds included 46% European Americans, 24% Latin Americans, 10% of mixed ancestry, 9% Asian Americans, 3% Native Americans, 2% African Americans, and 4% unreported data. The average age was 23.55 (SD = 5.58). There were 59 in the equal/close, 47 in the equal/distant, 50 in the higher/close, and 54 in the higher/distant cells.

Instrument

A questionnaire format was used to investigate several objectives (including identifying categories of face concerns and facework behaviors). The respondents were asked to recall a conflict with a person who fit a set of criteria. All respondents were asked to recall someone of same-sex and same ethnic/cultural group. Two variables were manipulated in the questionnaire—status and level of intimacy. For status, participants were asked to recall a conflict with someone who is equal status or higher status. For level of intimacy, the respondents were asked to recall a conflict with someone to whom they were very close or not very close. National culture was measured with a single item (i.e., what is your country of permanent residence).

Self-construal was measured with 20 items from Gudykunst et al.'s (1996) instrument. Ten items measured independent self-construal, and 10 items measured interdependent self-construal. The validity of the self-construal scales is based on findings that the independence items correlate with individualistic values, whereas the interdependence items correlate with collectivistic values. In addition, the scales have been found to be reliable with Cronbach alphas ranging from .73 to .85 across four cultures (Gudykunst et al., 1996). Face concerns were measured with 34 items written specifically for this study. The items were designed to measure self-, other-, and mutual-face concerns. Facework behaviors were measured with 87 items written for this study or modified from other instruments (Ting-Toomey et al., 2000). The items were designed to capture more fully the 13 facework categories discovered in a previous study (Oetzel et al., in press). The 13 categories and brief descriptions are

1. *third party*—seeking an outside party to help resolve the conflict;
2. *apologizing* for behavior;
3. *expressing* how one is feeling;
4. *defending*—standing up for one's opinions and persuading others to accept these opinions;
5. *private discussion*—avoiding a public confrontation;
6. *giving in*—accommodating the other's wishes;
7. *remaining calm* during the conflict;
8. *integrating*—behaviors used to join together perspectives of the parties;
9. *pretending* that the conflict does not exist;
10. *consider the other*—listening to the other person to demonstrate respect for him or her;
11. direct/passive *aggression*;
12. *avoiding* the person or the issue;
13. *compromising* points in order to resolve the issue.

All of the items (except national culture) were measured with a five-point Likert-type scale ranging from five (strongly agree) to one (strongly disagree). A team of researchers from different cultures collaborated to create the measures of face concerns and facework behaviors. The team consisted of a Chinese who now lives in the United States, one Japanese who lives in the United States, one Japanese who is studying in the United States, and one European American.

Procedures

The questionnaire asked the participants to recall a conflict in one of the four situations. Conflict was defined for the participants as any intense disagreement between two parties that involves incompatible goals, needs, or viewpoints. The participants were asked to remember a particular conflict and respond to a series of items about the conflict. The questionnaire was laid out in the following format: (a) self-construal items, (b) face concern items, (c) face behavior items, (d) items describing the conflict, (e) power distance items (for another purpose), and (f) demographic information.

The questionnaire was written in English. Then, the English questionnaire was translated and retranslated into Chinese, Japanese, and German to ensure conceptual equivalence. All participants completed the questionnaire in their native language. Participants were recruited through undergraduate courses and many were given extra credit for participating. The questionnaire was self-administered and required approximately 30 minutes to complete. Participants completed the questionnaire on their own time and returned it to the researchers.

RESULTS OF PANCULTURE FACTOR ANALYSES

The data were submitted to several factor analyses in order to understand the structure and confirm the validity of the measures. We completed separate factor analyses for face concerns and facework behaviors. We used the following procedures for each of the factor analyses. First, all data were standardized within culture. Second, the data for face concerns and facework behaviors were submitted to a principal components factor analysis with equamax rotation because of the expected correlation among factors. Third, the criteria for interpreting factors were (a) the primary loading had to be at least .5, (b) the secondary loading had to be at least .2 less than the primary loading, and (c) a factor needed to have at least three items with sufficient reliability (at least .60 Cronbach's alpha).

The first factor analysis was for face concerns. Three factors accounting for 42.8% of the variance were discovered. The first factor was composed of 11 items, accounted for 17.48% of the variance, and had an eigenvalue of 9.13. The items focus predominately on the concern for the other person's poise, pride, face, and credibility. The factor was labeled *other-face concern* ($\alpha = .87$). The second factor consisted of four items, accounted for 13.26% of the variance, and had an eigenvalue of 3.73. The items focus on a concern for the relationship and having peace in the interaction. This factor was labeled *mutual-face concern* ($\alpha = .77$). The third factor was composed of seven items, accounted for 12.06% of the variance, and had an eigenvalue of 1.70. The items measure the concern for an individual's own image, dignity, and poise. This factor was labeled *self-face concern* ($\alpha = .80$). Table A.1 at the end of this appendix displays the factor loadings for each of the items.

The *second factor analysis* was for facework behaviors. Eleven factors accounting for 46.38% of the variance were discovered. Table A.2 at the end of this appendix displays the factor loadings for the specific items. The first factor consisted of nine items, accounted for 5.64% of the variance, and had an eigenvalue of 11.67. The items measure the degree to which a person tries to insult, hurt, or ridicule another person. The factor was labeled *aggression* ($\alpha = .89$). The second factor consisted of eight items, accounted for 5.38% of the variance, and had an eigenvalue of 8.21. The items focus on behaviors that attempt to resolve a conflict through compromising or integrating viewpoints. The factor was labeled *problem-solve* ($\alpha = .89$). The third factor consisted of eight items, accounted for 4.71% of the variance, and had an eigenvalue of 7.37. These items focus on "standing one's ground" and trying to persuade the other person to change his or her mind. *Defend* was the label for this factor ($\alpha = .82$).

The fourth factor had six items, accounted for 4.50% of the variance, and had an eigenvalue of 3.35. The items measure the degree of sensitivity, attentiveness, and listening shown toward the other person. We labeled this factor *respect* ($\alpha = .79$). The fifth factor was composed of five items, accounted for 4.32% of the variance, and had an eigenvalue of 2.48. The items focus on apologizing for behavior during the conflict, and thus we labeled it *apologize* ($\alpha = .82$). The sixth factor consisted of five items, accounted for 3.98% of the variance, and had an eigenvalue of 2.15. The items focus on the downplaying the conflict and acting as if the conflict does not exist. The label for this factor is *pretend* ($\alpha = .75$).

The seventh factor had five items, accounted for 3.96% of the variance, and had an eigenvalue of 1.89. The items emphasize the desire to have another person intervene in the conflict. Hence, we labeled it *third party* ($\alpha = .81$). The eighth factor consisted of four items, accounted for 3.73% of the variance, and had an eigenvalue of 1.76. The items measure the amount of direct expression of feelings during the conflict. The factor was labeled *express* ($\alpha = .70$). The ninth factor consisted of five items, accounted for 3.53% of the variance, and had an eigenvalue of 1.56. The items focus on trying to maintain composure during conflict and not getting angry. We labeled this factor *remain calm* ($\alpha = .68$).

The tenth factor had five items, accounted for 3.32% of the variance, and had an eigenvalue of 1.46. The items emphasize the desire to avoid an argument in public. We labeled the factor *private discussion* ($\alpha = .64$). The eleventh factor consisted of three items, accounted for 3.29% of the variance, and had an eigenvalue of 1.38. The items measure accommodating or giving in during the conflict. The factor was labeled *give in* ($\alpha = .69$).

The results of the panculture factor analysis demonstrate that face concerns and facework behaviors can be measured consistently across the four cultures of study. The items for face concerns measure three distinct factors: self-, other-, and mutual-face. These are consistent with expectations of prior theoretical research (Ting-Toomey & Kurogi, 1998). Each of these measures, furthermore, had good reliabilities for each of the four cultures of study. Thus, this instrument is useful for researchers and facilitators interested in measuring the level of face concerns. The items for facework behaviors measure 11 distinct factors. This discovery is important because it demonstrates a wide variety of behaviors that were used to manage face during conflict. Most prior research has examined a limited range of facework behavior. The majority of the facework dimensions had good reliabilities. However, more collaborative research effort on a global level is needed to test the cross-cultural validity of the facework measurements. Future researchers may want to test these newly developed facework measures in a diverse range of problematic facework situations, and within a diverse range of ethnic communities and cultures.

Table A.1 Pancultural Factor Loadings for Face Concerns

Items	Other-Face	Mutual-Face	Self-Face
3. I was concerned with respectful treatment for both of us.	.20	.65*	.10
7. Relationship harmony was important to me.	.41	.61*	.02
8. I was concerned with maintaining the poise of the other person.	.57*	.37	−.02
9. Maintaining humbleness to preserve the relationship was important to me.	.59*	.25	−.04
10. I was concerned with not bringing shame to myself.	.12	.06	.64*
11. Helping to maintain the other person's pride was important to me.	.65*	.28	.02
12. I was concerned with protecting my self-image.	.14	−.05	.63*
13. My concern was to act humble in order to make the other person feel good.	.59*	.14	.03
16. My concern was to help the other person maintain his/her dignity.	.57*	.29	.12
18. I didn't want to embarrass myself in front of the other person.	.09	.10	.64*
20. Maintaining peace in our interaction was important to me.	.34	.60*	.01
22. I wanted to maintain my dignity in front of the other person.	−.06	.23	.66*
23. A peaceful resolution to the conflict was important to me.	.22	.67*	.08
25. My primary concern was helping the other person to save face.	.74*	.05	.01
26. Preserving our mutual self-images was important to me.	.57*	.20	.25
28. Saving both of our faces was important to me.	.61*	.10	.25

(continued)

Table A.1 Continued

Items	Other-Face	Mutual-Face	Self-Face
29. I was concerned with maintaining my own poise.	.08	.03	.58*
30. I was concerned with helping the other person maintain his/her credibility.	.58*	.28	.05
31. My primary concern was protecting both of our feelings.	.54*	.26	.09
32. I was concerned with not appearing weak in front of the other person.	.05	−.04	.66*
33. I was concerned with helping the other person to preserve his/her self-image.	.64*	.16	.15
34. I was concerned with protecting my personal pride.	.02	−.02	.78*

*Items used to define factor.

Table A.2 Pancultural Factor Loadings for Facework Behaviors

Items						Factor					
	1	2	3	4	5	6	7	8	9	10	11
1. I tried to maintain my composure.	.06	-.09	.02	.13	-.05	-.09	-.03	-.05	.61*	.14	.07
2. I apologized for my behavior.	.03	.05	-.14	.10	.70*	-.04	.05	-.06	.14	.11	.11
4. I showed sensitivity in respecting the other person's feelings.	-.07	.22	-.26	.50*	.22	.02	-.05	.01	.22	.14	.12
7. I didn't argue with the other person in public.	-.12	-.02	-.10	-.07	.06	-.09	-.08	-.09	.24	.58*	.16
8. I tried to ask a third party to make a suggestion about how to settle the dispute.	.01	.05	-.10	.07	.02	-.11	.63*	-.11	.08	.10	.04
10. I acted like I wasn't upset.	.08	.02	-.03	-.02	.07	.32	.04	-.14	.55*	-.07	.02
11. I said bad things about the person behind his/her back.	.59*	-.03	-.06	-.06	-.10	.05	.14	-.07	.22	-.14	-.08
12. I tried to verbally insult him/her.	.73*	-.04	.17	-.13	.03	.07	.10	.01	-.06	-.07	-.03
13. I tried to be firm in my demands and didn't give in.	.21	-.16	.53*	.08	-.11	-.03	-.01	.09	-.06	.05	-.28
15. I tried to meet the other person halfway.	.04	.59*	-.09	.05	.14	-.01	.08	.04	.10	.11	.22
18. I worked with the other to find a mutually acceptable solution.	-.02	.57*	.01	.25	.13	-.07	.12	.17	.08	.15	-.01

(continued)

Table A.2 Continued

Items	Factor										
	1	2	3	4	5	6	7	8	9	10	11
20. I tried to use "give and take" so that a compromise could be made.	.07	.62*	-.02	.04	.24	.04	.07	-.02	.07	.17	.20
21. I tried to ridicule the other person.	.67*	-.07	.22	-.11	.05	.13	.06	.04	-.08	-.04	-.03
24. I tried to damage the other person's reputation behind his/her back.	.74*	.03	.03	-.04	.05	.04	.18	-.16	-.04	-.05	.01
25. I gave in in order to end the conflict.	.08	.10	-.14	-.11	.15	.16	.04	-.11	.07	-.04	.52*
26. I tried to give the person wrong information so he/she would get into trouble.	.57*	.11	.16	.17	.16	.11	.12	-.20	-.17	.04	-.06
28. I proposed a middle ground for breaking the deadlock.	-.04	.64*	.03	.18	.08	-.02	.14	-.03	.08	.23	.34
30. I tried to persuade the other person to accept my viewpoint.	-.03	.08	.58*	.04	.04	-.05	.16	.07	-.09	.05	.13
31. I tried to involve a third party to discuss the problem.	.10	.09	.14	-.08	.06	-.04	.77*	-.06	.03	-.06	.08
32. I waited until we were by ourselves to talk about the problem.	-.03	.15	-.03	.09	.07	-.09	.03	.02	.08	.66*	-.07
33. I tried to compromise with the other person.	-.06	.60*	-.13	.05	.20	-.06	.09	.02	.11	.24	.26
34. I tried not to get overtly angry.	-.15	.08	-.09	.06	.13	.17	.04	-.01	.60*	.04	.07

Item											
35. I asked for forgiveness for my actions.	-.02	.07	-.07	.10	.77*	-.04	.11	.02	.09	.07	.12
36. I apologized even though I didn't do anything wrong.	.11	.08	.06	.08	.58*	.13	.10	-.05	-.01	.14	.15
39. I tried to hurt the other person indirectly.	.63*	-.05	.12	-.12	-.05	.05	.15	-.04	-.07	-.02	.10
40. I tried to listen well to work on our problems.	-.10	.12	.02	.53*	.11	-.13	.08	.14	.19	.19	.16
42. I listened to the other person to show respect.	-.12	-.02	.03	.56*	.06	-.13	.06	-.02	.19	.14	.31
43. I used nasty words to put down the other person.	.69*	-.02	.20	-.14	.04	.12	.10	.06	-.20	-.04	.12
44. I pretended not to be hurt.	.09	-.09	-.04	-.15	.04	.52*	-.08	-.03	.28	.04	.17
45. I suggested that we should go to a place where we could be alone to discuss the problem.	.09	.24	.03	.03	.22	.06	.16	.14	-.04	.54*	.02
46. I was direct in expressing my feelings.	.09	.12	.17	.04	.12	-.10	-.04	.61*	-.12	-.01	-.10
47. I admitted I made a mistake and apologized.	.02	.16	-.08	.12	.69*	.02	.10	.02	.01	.10	.25
48. I tried to remain calm.	-.17	.05	.03	.10	-.05	.15	.05	-.08	.67*	.03	-.02
49. I tried to ask another person to help negotiate an agreement with the other person.	.12	.11	.10	-.07	.13	.04	.79*	.03	.06	-.02	.03

(continued)

Table A.2 Continued

Items		*Factor*									
	1	2	3	4	5	6	7	8	9	10	11
51. I tried to ignore the conflict and behaved as if nothing happened.	.04	-.01	-.04	-.09	-.05	.68*	.05	-.12	.10	-.08	.21
53. I called the other person mean names.	.70*	-.03	.21	-.14	.09	.12	.15	-.07	-.17	-.02	.06
55. I tried to persuade the other person that my way was the best way.	.16	.10	.63*	-.03	-.05	.06	.09	.04	.09	-.07	-.03
56. I tried not to get upset when we discussed the problem.	-.13	.10	.06	.11	.04	.12	.06	.03	.59*	.11	.14
57. I tried to combine both of our viewpoints in our discussion.	-.17	.57*	.01	.33	.08	-.04	.12	.04	.14	.18	.09
59. I tried to find a middle course to resolve the situation.	-.03	.64*	.08	.22	.09	.05	.16	-.06	.07	.18	.22
60. I gave in to the other person's wishes.	.08	.09	-.09	.12	.28	.19	.10	-.17	.09	.03	.65*
61. I tried to keep our discussion private.	.10	.02	-.06	.13	.08	.23	.03	-.09	.05	.63*	.09
62. I tried to talk with the other person through an outside party.	.19	.05	-.04	.09	.06	.23	.63*	-.10	-.07	.14	-.03
63. I tried to pretend that the conflict didn't happen.	.06	-.10	-.06	.09	.09	.70*	.03	-.21	.13	.15	.15
65. I tried to express my feelings in a straightforward manner.	.03	.09	.30	.06	.08	-.12	-.02	.61*	-.06	-.02	-.17
66. I apologized for what was happening.	-.09	.06	.02	.12	.78*	.06	.10	-.02	-.03	.06	.24

67. I tried to be considerate to show respect for the other person.	-.23	.18	.05	.63*	.20	.03	-.02	-.07	.09	.13	.11
68. I expressed myself in a somewhat vague manner.	.10	.12	.15	.06	.20	.19	-.01	-.57*	-.03	-.08	-.09
69. I yelled at the other person to be disrespectful.	.57*	-.05	.26	-.16	.06	.13	.09	.11	-.33	-.05	.13
70. I tried to defend my position.	.06	-.03	.56*	-.07	-.21	-.13	.04	.15	.06	-.04	.06
71. I agreed with the other person to end the conflict.	-.05	.14	-.05	.13	.23	.13	.09	-.10	-.03	-.03	.58*
72. I tried not to discuss the problem in front of others.	-.07	.09	.06	.06	.03	.13	-.04	-.08	-.02	.60*	-.04
73. I tried to ask a third party to intervene to help us settle the problem.	.08	.03	.03	-.02	.09	.05	.82*	-.07	-.06	-.08	.04
74. I wanted to be open-minded to understand the other person's situation.	-.23	.21	-.08	.57*	.16	.01	.12	.12	.12	.10	.01
75. I insisted I was right.	.23	-.13	.66*	-.18	-.13	.02	.07	.13	-.09	-.11	-.05
76. I acted as if the conflict didn't exist.	.09	-.10	-.05	.08	-.03	.66*	.08	-.09	.13	.12	.15
77. I was attentive to the other person's feelings.	-.10	.08	-.12	.56*	.19	.09	.08	-.09	.09	.22	.07
78. I let the other person know clearly what I was thinking.	-.06	.04	.24	.16	-.02	-.07	.07	.64*	-.03	-.02	-.13
81. I dominated the argument until the other person understood my position.	.27	.01	.64*	-.02	.09	.13	.05	.08	-.04	-.03	-.13

(continued)

211

Table A.2 Continued

Items	Factor										
	2	2	3	4	5	6	7	8	9	10	11
82. I insisted my position be accepted during the conflict.	.14	-.02	.69*	.01	-03	.10	-.10	.10	-.25	-.14	-.22
83. I suggested solutions which combined both of our viewpoints.	.04	.56*	.04	.25	.08	.12	.14	.09	-.05	.13	.01
84. I tried to downplay the importance of the disagreement.	.09	.21	.16	-.05	.12	.51*	.11	-.10	-.08	-.03	.05
87. I stood firm in expressing my viewpoints to the other person.	.13	-.02	.59*	-.01	-05	-.10	.04	.30	-.05	-.02	-.20

* Items used to define factor.

REFERENCES

Adler, N. (1997). *International dimensions of organizational behavior* (3rd ed.). Cincinnati, OH: South-Western College Publishing.

Alderfer, C. P., & Smith, K. K. (1982). Studying intergroup relations imbedded in organizations. *Administrative Science Quarterly, 27*, 5-65.

Asante, M., & Asante, K. (Eds.). (1990). *African culture: The rhythms of unity.* Trenton, NJ: African World Press.

Bales, R. F. (1950). *Interaction process analysis: A method for the study of small groups.* Reading, MA: Addison-Wesley.

Barkema, H. G., & Vermeulen, F. (1997). What differences in the cultural backgrounds of partners are detrimental for international joint ventures. *Journal of International Business Studies, 28*, 845-864.

Barker, J. (1993). Tightening the iron cage: Concertive control in self-managing teams. *Administrative Science Quarterly, 38*, 408-437.

Barnlund, D. (1989). *Communicative styles of Japanese and Americans: Images and realities.* Belmont, CA: Wadsworth.

Bateson, G. (1972). *Steps to an ecology of mind.* New York: Ballantine.

Baxter, L. (1984). An investigation of compliance-gaining as politeness. *Human Communication Research, 10*, 427-457.

Bennett, M. (1993). Toward ethnorelativism: A developmental model of intercultural sensitivity. In R. M. Paige (Ed.), *Education for the intercultural experience* (pp. 21-71). Yarmouth, ME: Intercultural Press.

Berry, J. W., Kim, U., & Boski, P. (1987). Psychological acculturation of immigrants. In Y. Y. Kim & W. Gudykunst (Eds.), *Cross-cultural adaptation: Current approaches* (pp. 62-89). Newbury Park, CA: Sage.

Billingsley, A. (1992). *Climbing Jacob's ladder.* New York: Simon & Schuster.

Blake, R. R., & Mouton, J. S. (1964). *The managerial grid.* Houston, TX: Gulf Publishing.

Brilhart, J. K. (1978). *Effective group discussion* (3rd ed.). Dubuque, IA: William C. Brown.

Brislin, R. (1993). *Understanding culture's influence on behavior.* Fort Worth, TX: Harcourt Brace Jovanovich.

Brown, P., & Levinson, S. (1978). Universals in language usage: Politeness phenomenon. In E. Goody (Ed.), *Questions and politeness: Strategies in social interaction* (pp. 56-289). Cambridge, UK: Cambridge University Press.

Brown, P., & Levinson, S. (1987). *Politeness: Some universals in language usage.* Cambridge, UK: Cambridge University Press.

Burgoon, J., Buller, D., & Woodall, W. G. (1996). *Nonverbal communication: The unspoken dialogue* (2nd ed.). New York: McGraw-Hill.

Buzzanell, P. (1994). Gaining a voice: Feminist organizational communication theorizing. *Management Communication Quarterly, 7,* 339-383.

Casas, J. M., & Pytluk, S. (1995). Hispanic identity development. In J. Ponterotto, J. Casas, L. Suzuki, & C. Alexander (Eds.) *Handbook of multicultural counseling* (pp. 155-180). Thousand Oaks, CA: Sage.

Chen, G. M. (Ed.). (1997). Conflict resolution in Chinese [Special Issue]. *Intercultural Communication Studies, 8.*

Chua, E., & Gudykunst, W. B. (1987). Conflict resolution style in low- and high-context cultures. *Communication Research Reports, 4,* 32-37.

Clackworthy, D. (1996). Training Germans and Americans in conflict management. In M. Berger (Ed.), *Cross-cultural team building: Guidelines for more effective communication and negotiation* (pp. 91-100). London: McGraw-Hill.

Clarke, C., & Lipp, G. D. (1998). *Danger and opportunity: Resolving conflict in U.S.-based Japanese subsidiaries.* Yarmouth, ME: Intercultural Press.

Cocroft, B., & Ting-Toomey, S. (1994). Facework in Japan and the United States. *International Journal of Intercultural Relations, 18,* 469-506.

Collier, M. J. (1991). Conflict competence within African, Mexican, and Anglo-American friendships. In S. Ting-Toomey & F. Korzenny (Eds.), *Cross-cultural interpersonal communication* (pp. 132-154). Newbury Park, CA: Sage.

Condon, J. C. (1984). *With respect to the Japanese: A guide for Americans.* Yarmouth, ME: Intercultural Press.

Conrad, C. (1983). Power and performance as correlates of supervisors' choice of modes of managing conflict: A preliminary investigation. *Western Journal of Speech Communication, 47,* 218-228.

Conrad, C. (1991). Communication in conflict: Style-strategy relationships. *Communication Monographs, 58,* 135-155.

Cox, T. H., Jr. (1991). The multicultural organization. *Academy of Management Executive, 5*(2), 34-47.

Cox, T. H., Jr. (1994). *Cultural diversity in organizations: Theory, research, and practice.* San Francisco: Berrett-Koehler.

Cox, T. H., Jr., & Beale, R. L. (1997). *Developing competence to manage diversity: Readings, cases & activities.* San Francisco: Berrett-Koehler.

Cox, T. H., & Blake, S. (1991). Managing cultural diversity: Implications for organizational competitiveness. *Academy of Management Executive, 5*(3), 45-56.

Cox, T. H., Lobel, S. A., & McLeod, P. L. (1991). Effects of ethnic group cultural differences on cooperative and competitive behavior on a group task. *Academy of Management Journal, 34,* 827-847.

Crohn, J. (1995). *Mixed matches: How to create successful interracial, interethnic, and interfaith relationships.* New York: Fawcett Columbine/Ballantine.

Csikszentmihalyi, M. (1996). *Creativity: Flow and the psychology of discovery and invention.* New York: HarperCollins.

Cupach, W. R., & Canary, D. J. (Eds.). (1997). *Competence in interpersonal conflict.* New York: McGraw-Hill.

Cupach, W. R., & Metts, S. (1994). *Facework.* Thousand Oaks, CA: Sage.

Cushner, K., & Brislin, R. W. (1996). *Intercultural interactions: A practical guide* (2nd ed.). Thousand Oaks, CA: Sage.

Dace, K. (1990). *The conflict-group decision-making link: An exploratory study.* Unpublished doctoral dissertation, University of Iowa, Iowa City.

Dahl, R. (1957). The concept of power. *Behavioral Science, 2,* 201-215.

Daly, A. (Ed.). (1998). *Workplace diversity: Issues and perspectives.* Washington, DC: National Association of Social Workers Press.

Daniels, T. D., Spiker, B. K., & Papa, M. J. (1997). *Perspectives on organizational communication* (4th ed.). Madison, WI: Brown & Benchmark.

Deutsch, M. (1969). Conflicts: Productive and destructive. *Journal of Social Issues, 25,* 7-41.

Donohue, W., & Bresnahan, M. I. (1994). Communication issues in mediating cultural conflict. In J. P. Folger & T. S. Jones (Eds.), *New directions in mediation: Communication research and perspectives* (pp. 135-158). Thousand Oaks, CA: Sage.

Duran, R. (1985). Communicative ability: A measure of social communicative competence. *Communication Quarterly, 31,* 320-326.

Earley, P. C. (1997). *Face, harmony, and social support: An analysis of organizational behavior across cultures.* New York: Oxford University Press.

Ellis, D. G., & Fisher, B. A. (1994). *Small group decision making: Communication and group processes* (4th ed.). New York: McGraw-Hill.

Emerson, R. M. (1962). Power-dependence relations. *American Sociological Review, 27,* 31-41.

Erez, M., & Somech, A. (1996). Is group productivity loss the rule or the exception? Effects of culture and group-based motivation. *Academy of Management Journal, 39,* 1513-1537.

Espinoza, J. A., & Garza, R. T. (1985). Social group salience and intergroup cooperation. *Journal of Experimental Social Psychology, 21,* 380-392.

Fabelo-Alcover, H., & Sowers, K. M. (1998). Latino diversity in communication in the workplace. In A. Daly (Ed.), *Workplace diversity: Issues and perspectives* (pp. 215-227). Washington, DC: National Association of Social Workers Press.

Fairhurst, G. T., Green, S. G., & Snavely, B. K. (1984). Face support in controlling poor performance. *Human Communication Research, 11,* 272-295.

Falk, G. (1982). An empirical study measuring conflict in problem-solving groups which are assigned different decision rules. *Human Relations, 35,* 1123-1138.

Faure, G. O. (1995). Conflict formulation: Going beyond culture-bound views of conflict. In B. Bunker, J. Rubin, & associates (Eds.), *Conflict, cooperation and justice* (pp. 39-57). San Francisco: Jossey-Bass.

Ferdman, B. M. (1995). Cultural identity and diversity in organizations: Bridging the gap between group differences and individual uniqueness. In M. M. Chemers, S. Oskamp, & M. A. Costanzo (Eds.), *Diversity in organizations: New perspectives for a changing workplace* (pp. 37-60). Thousand Oaks, CA: Sage.

Ferdman, B. M., & Cortes, A. C. (1992). Culture and identity among Hispanic managers in an Anglo business. In S. Knouse, P. Rosenfeld, & A. Culbertson (Eds.), *Hispanics in the workplace* (pp. 246-277). Newbury Park, CA: Sage.

Fine, M. (1991). New voices in the workplace: Research directions in multi-cultural communication. *Journal of Business Communication, 23,* 259-275.

Fisher, R., & Brown, S. (1988). *Getting together: Building relationships as we negotiate.* New York: Penguin.

Fitch, K. (1998). *Speaking relationally: Culture, communication, and inter-personal communication.* New York: Guilford.

Folger, J., Poole, M. S., & Stutman, R. (2000). *Working through conflict: Strategies for relationships, groups, and organizations* (4th ed.). New York: Addison Wesley Longman.

Frankenberg, R. (1993). *White women, race matters: The social construction of whiteness.* Minneapolis: University of Minnesota Press.

Gao, G., & Ting-Toomey, S. (1998). *Communicating effectively with the Chinese.* Thousand Oaks, CA: Sage.

Garcia, W. R. (1996). *Respeto:* A Mexican base for interpersonal relationships. In W. Gudykunst, S. Ting-Toomey, & T. Nishida (Eds.), *Communication in personal relationships across cultures* (pp. 137-155). Thousand Oaks, CA: Sage.

Gardner, H. (1995). *Leading minds: Anatomy of leadership.* New York: Basic Books.

Garza, R. T., & Santos, S. J. (1991). Ingroup/outgroup balance and interdependent interethnic behavior. *Journal of Experimental Social Psychology, 27,* 124-137.

Goffman, E. (1959). *The presentation of self in everyday life.* Garden City, NY: Anchor/Doubleday.

Gottman, J. (1999). *The marriage clinic: A scientifically-based marital therapy.* New York: Norton.

Gottman, J., & Silver, N. (1999). *The seven principles for making marriage work.* New York: Crown.

Graham, J. L. (1985). The influence of culture on the process of business negotiations: An exploratory study. *Journal of International Business, 16,* 81-96.

Gudykunst, W. B. (1995). Anxiety/uncertainty management (AUM) theory. In R. L. Wiseman (Ed.), *Intercultural communication theory* (pp. 8-58). Thousand Oaks, CA: Sage.

Gudykunst, W. (1998). *Bridging differences* (3rd ed.). Thousand Oaks, CA: Sage.

Gudykunst, W. B., Matsumoto, Y., Ting-Toomey, S., Nishida, T., Kim, K. S., & Heyman, S. (1996). The influence of cultural individualism-collectivism, self construals, and individual values on communication styles across cultures. *Human Communication Research, 22,* 510-543.

Gudykunst, W. B., & Ting-Toomey, S. (1988). *Culture and interpersonal communication.* Newbury Park, CA: Sage.

Hackman, J. R. (1990). *Groups that work and those that don't.* San Francisco: Jossey-Bass.

Hall, E. T. (1976). *Beyond culture.* Garden City, NY: Doubleday.

Hall, E. T., & Hall, M. (1987). *Hidden differences: Doing business with the Japanese.* Garden City, NY: Anchor /Doubleday.

Healey, J. F. (1997). *Race, ethnicity, and gender in the United States: Inequality, group conflict, and power.* Thousand Oaks, CA: Pine Forge.

Healey, J., & Bell, R. (1990). Assessing alternative responses to conflict in friendship. In D. Cahn (Ed.), *Intimates in conflict: A communication perspective* (pp. 25-48). Hillsdale, NJ: Lawrence Erlbaum.

Hecht, M., Collier, M. J., & Ribeau, S. (1993). *African American communication: Ethnic identity and cultural interpretation.* Newbury Park, CA: Sage.

Herring, R. D. (1997). *Counseling diverse ethnic youth.* Fort Worth, TX: Harcourt Brace.

Hirokawa, R. Y., & Rost, K. M. (1992). Effective group decision-making in organizations: A field test of vigilant interaction theory. *Management Communication Quarterly, 5,* 267-288.

Hirokawa, R. Y., & Salazar, A. J. (1991, October). *The necessity of chimera hunting: Why group communication scholars should maintain a "bottom-line" focus in group decision-making research.* Paper presented at the annual meeting of the Speech Communication Association, Atlanta, GA.

Hofstede, G. (1991). *Culture and organizations: Software of the mind.* London: McGraw-Hill.

Holton, D. W. (1998). Unsettling that delicate balance: Reflections on experiential subtleties. In M. Hecht (Ed.), *Communicating prejudice* (pp. 272-284). Thousand Oaks, CA: Sage.

Hu, H. C. (1944). The Chinese concept of "face." *American Anthropologist, 46,* 45-64.

Isaacs, W. (1999). *Dialogue and the art of thinking together.* New York: Currency/ Doubleday.

Janis, I. L. (1982). *Victims of groupthink* (2nd ed.). Boston: Houghton Mifflin.

Johnson, M. (1991). Commitment to personal relationships. In W. Jones & D. Perlman (Eds.), *Advances in personal relationship* (Vol. 3, pp. 117-143). London: Kingsley.

Jones, J. M. (1997). *Prejudice and racism* (2nd ed.). New York: McGraw-Hill.

Judy, R., & D'Amico, C. (1997). *Work force 2020: Work and workers in the 21st century.* Indianapolis, IN: Hudson Institute.

Kanter, R. M. (1977). *Men and women of the corporation.* New York: Harper.

Kashima, Y., & Triandis, H. C. (1986). The self-serving bias in attribution as a coping strategy: A cross-cultural study. *Journal of Cross-Cultural Psychology, 17,* 83-97.

Katriel, T. (1986). *Talking straight: Dugri speech in Israeli Sabra culture.* Cambridge, UK: Cambridge University Press.

Kidwell, R. E., & Bennett, N. (1993). Employee propensity to withhold effort: A conceptual model to intersect three avenues of research. *Academy of Management Review, 18,* 429-456.

Kirchmeyer, C., & Cohen, A. (1992). Multicultural groups: Their performance and reactions with constructive conflict. *Group and Organization Management, 17,* 153-170.

Kochman, T. (1981). *Black and white styles in conflict.* Chicago: University of Chicago Press.

Kochman, T. (1990). Force fields in black and white communication. In D. Carbaugh (Ed.), *Cultural communication and intercultural contact* (pp. 193-217). Hillsdale, NJ: Lawrence Erlbaum.

Kolb, D. M. (1989). Labor mediators, managers, and ombudsmen: Roles mediators play in different contexts. In K. Kressel & D. Pruitt (Eds.), *Mediation research: The process and effectiveness of third-party intervention* (pp. 91-114). San Francisco: Jossey-Bass.

Langer, E. (1989). *Mindfulness.* Reading, MA: Addison-Wesley.

Langer, E. (1997). *The power of mindful learning.* Reading, MA: Addison-Wesley.

La Resche, D. (1992). Comparison of the American mediation process with a Korean-American harmony restoration process. *Mediation Quarterly, 9,* 323-339.

Larkey, L. K. (1996). Toward a theory of communicative interactions in culturally diverse groups. *Academy of Management Review, 21,* 463-491.

Larson, C. E., & LaFasto, F. M. J. (1989). *Teamwork: What must go right/what can go wrong.* Newbury Park, CA: Sage.

Lederach, J. P. (1997). *Building peace: Sustainable reconciliation in divided societies.* Washington, DC: U.S. Institute of Peace.

Leung, K., & Bond, M. (1984). The impact of cultural collectivism on reward allocation. *Journal of Personality and Social Psychology, 47,* 793-804.

Leung, K., & Iwawaki, S. (1988). Cultural collectivism and distributive behavior. *Journal of Cross-Cultural Psychology, 19,* 35-49.

Lewicki, R. J., & Bunker, B. B. (1995). Trust in relationships: A model of development and decline. In B. Bunker, J. Rubin, & associates (Eds.), *Conflict, cooperation and justice* (pp. 39-57). San Francisco: Jossey-Bass.

Lim, T.-S., & Bowers, J. (1991). Face-work: Solidarity, approbation, and tact. *Human Communication Research, 17,* 415-450.

Lim, T.-S., & Choi, S. (1996). Interpersonal relationships in Korea. In W. B. Gudykunst, S. Ting-Toomey, & T. Nishida (Eds.), *Communication in personal relationships across cultures* (pp. 122-136). Thousand Oaks, CA: Sage.

Littlejohn, S. (1995). Moral conflict in organizations. In A. M. Nicotera (Ed.), *Conflict in organizations: Communicative processes* (pp. 101-125). Albany: State University of New York Press.

Loden, M. (1996). *Implementing diversity.* New York: McGraw-Hill.

Loden, M., & Rosener, J. (1991). *Workforce America! Managing employee diversity as a vital resource.* Homewood, IL: Business One-Irwin.

Loving V. Commonwealth of Virginia, 388 U.S. 1 (1967).

Lulofs, R., & Cahn, D. (2000). *Conflict: From theory to practice* (2nd ed.). Boston: Allyn & Bacon.

Maltz, D., & Borker, R. (1982). A cultural approach to male-female communication. In J. Gumperz (Ed.), *Language and social identity.* Cambridge, UK: Cambridge University Press.

Markus, H. R., & Kitayama, S. (1991). Culture and self: Implication for cognition, emotion, and motivation. *Psychological Review, 98,* 224-253.

McGrath, J. E. (1984). *Groups: Interaction and performance.* Englewood Cliffs, NJ: Prentice-Hall.

McIntosh, P. (1995). White privilege: Unpacking the invisible backpack. In A. Kasselman, L. D. McNair, & N. Schneidewind (Eds.), *Women, images, and realities: A multicultural anthology* (pp. 5-8). Mountain View, CA: Mayfield.

McLeod, P. L., Lobel, S. A., & Cox, T. H. (1996). Ethnic diversity and creativity in small groups. *Small Group Research, 27,* 248-264.

McNamara, R. P., Tempenis, M., & Walton, B. (1999). *Crossing the line: Interracial couples in the South.* Westport, CT: Praeger.

Merritt, A. C., & Helmreich, R. L. (1996). Human factors on the flight deck: The influence of national culture. *Journal of Cross-Cultural Psychology, 27,* 5-24.

Mesquita, B., & Frijida, N. (1992). Cultural variations in emotions: A review. *Psychological Bulletin, 112,* 179-204.

Miller, G. R., & Steinberg, M. (1975). *Between people: A new analysis of interpersonal communication.* Chicago: Science Research Associates.

Morisaki, S., & Gudykunst, W. B. (1994). Face in Japan and the United States. In S. Ting-Toomey (Ed.), *The challenge of facework* (pp. 47-94). Albany: State University of New York Press.

Morley, D. M., & Shockley-Zalabak, P. (1986). Conflict avoiders and compromisers: Toward an understanding of their organizational communication style. *Group and Organizational Behavior, 11,* 387-402.

Nadler, L. B., Keeshan-Nadler, M., & Broome, B. J. (1985). Culture and the management of conflict situations. In W. Gudykunst, L. Stewart, & S. Ting-Toomey (Eds.), *Communication, culture, and organizational processes* (pp. 87-113). Beverly Hills, CA: Sage.

Nemeth, C. J. (1992). Minority dissent as a stimulant to group performance. In S. Worchel, W. Wood, & J. A. Simpson (Eds.), *Group process and productivity* (pp. 95-111). Newbury Park, CA: Sage.

Oetzel, J. G. (1995). Intercultural small groups: An effective decision-making theory. In R. L. Wiseman (Ed.), *Intercultural communication theory* (pp. 247-270). Thousand Oaks, CA: Sage.

Oetzel, J. G. (1998a). Culturally homogeneous and heterogeneous groups: Explaining communication processes through individualism-collectivism and self-construal. *International Journal of Intercultural Relations, 22,* 135-161.

Oetzel, J. G. (1998b). The effects of self-construals and ethnicity on self-reported conflict styles. *Communication Reports, 11,* 133-144.

Oetzel, J. G. (1998c). Explaining individual communication processes in homogeneous and heterogeneous groups through individualism-collectivism and self-construal. *Human Communication Research, 25,* 202-224.

Oetzel, J. G. (1999). The influence of situational features on perceived conflict styles and self-construals in small groups. *International Journal of Intercultural Relations, 23,* 679-695.

Oetzel, J. G. (2001). Self-construals, communication processes, and group outcomes in homogeneous and heterogeneous groups. *Small Group Research, 32,* 19-54.

Oetzel, J. G., & Bolton-Oetzel, K. (1997). Exploring the relationship between self-construal and dimensions of group effectiveness. *Management Communication Quarterly, 10,* 289-315.

Oetzel, J. G., Ting-Toomey, S., Masumoto, T., Yokochi, Y., & Takai, J. (in press). Developing a cross-cultural typology of facework behaviors in interpersonal conflicts. *Communication Quarterly.*

Olsen, M. (1978). *The process of social organizing* (2nd ed.). New York: Holt, Rinehart & Winston.

Orbe, M. (1998). *Constructing co-culture theory: An explication of cultures, power, and communication.* Thousand Oaks, CA: Sage.

Papa, M., & Papa, W. (1997). Competence in organizational conflicts. In W. Cupach & D. Canary (Eds.), *Competence in interpersonal conflict* (pp. 148-173). New York: McGraw-Hill.

Pelled, L. H., Eisenhardt, K. M., & Xin, K. R. (1999). Exploring the black box: An analysis of work group diversity, conflict, and performance. *Administrative Science Quarterly, 44,* 1-28.

Pettigrew, T. F., & Martin, J. (1992). Organizational inclusion of minority groups: A social psychological analysis. In J. P. Van Oudenhoven & T. M. Willemsen (Eds.), *Ethnic minorities: Social psychological perspectives* (pp. 169-200). Berwyn, PA: Swets North America.

Phinney, J., & Chavira, V. (1995). Parental ethnic socialization and adolescent outcomes in ethnic minority families. *Journal of Research on Adolescence, 5,* 31-54.

Pood, E. A. (1980). Functions of communication: An experimental study in group conflict situations. *Small Group Behavior, 11,* 76-87.

Putnam, L. L., & Poole, M. S. (1987). Conflict and negotiation. In F. M. Jablin, L. L. Putnam, K. H. Roberts, & L. W. Porter (Eds.), *Handbook of organizational communication* (pp. 549-599). Newbury Park, CA: Sage.

Putnam, L. L., & Stohl, C. (1990). Bona fide groups: A reconceptualization of group in context. *Communication Studies, 41,* 248-265.

Putnam, L., & Wilson, C. E. (1982). Communicative strategies in organizational conflicts: Reliability and validity of a measurement scale. In M. Burgoon (Ed.), *Communication Yearbook 6* (pp. 629-652). Beverly Hills, CA: Sage.

Rahim, M. A. (1983). A measure of styles of handling interpersonal conflict. *Academy of Management Journal, 26,* 368-376.

Rahim, M. A. (1992). *Managing conflict in organizations* (2nd ed.). Westport, CT: Praeger.

Rahim, M. A., & Buntzman, G. (1990). Supervisory power bases, styles of handling conflict with subordinates, and subordinate compliance and satisfaction. *Journal of Psychology, 123,* 195-210.

Rogan, R. G., & Hammer, M. R. (1994). Crisis negotiations: A preliminary investigation of facework in naturalistic conflict discourse. *Journal of Applied Communication Research, 22,* 216-231.

Rogers, E. M., & Steinfatt, T. M. (1999). *Intercultural communication.* Prospect Heights, IL: Waveland.

Rosen, R., Digh, P., Singer, M., & Phillips, C. (2000). *Global literarcies: Lessons on business leadership and national cultures.* New York: Simon & Schuster.

Rosenblatt, P., Karis, T., & Powell, R. (1995). *Multiracial couples: Black and White voices.* Thousand Oaks, CA: Sage.

Rothman, J. (1997). *Resolving identity-based conflict in nations, organizations, and communities.* San Francisco: Jossey-Bass.

Rubin, J. Z., & Levinger, G. (1995). Levels of analysis: In search of generalizable knowledge. In B. Bunker, J. Rubin, & associates (Eds.), *Conflict, cooperation and justice* (pp. 13-38). San Francisco: Jossey-Bass.

Rusbult, C. E. (1987). Responses to dissatisfaction in close relationships: The exit-voice-loyalty-neglect model. In D. Perlman & S. Duck (Eds.), *Intimate relationships: Development, dynamics, and deterioration* (pp. 209-337). Newbury Park, CA: Sage.

Russell, J. (1991). Culture and the categorization of emotions. *Psychological Bulletin, 110,* 426-450.

Salacuse, J. W. (1993). Implications for practitioners. In G. Faure & J. Rubin (Eds.), *Culture and negotiation* (pp. 199-208). Newbury Park, CA: Sage.

Shively, L. A. (1999, July 30). Making tribal stew. *Albuquerque Journal,* pp. E14-E15.

Siegman, A. W. (1994). Cardiovascular consequences of expressing and repressing anger. In A. W. Siegman & T. W. Smith (Eds.), *Anger, hostility, and the heart* (pp. 173-197). Hillsdale, NJ: Lawrence Erlbaum.

Sillars, A. (1980). The sequential and distributional structure of conflict interactions as a function of attributions concerning the locus of responsibility and strategy of conflicts. In D. Nimmo (Ed.), *Communication yearbook 4* (pp. 217-235). New Brunswick, NJ: Transaction Books.

Smith, P. B., Dugan, S., Peterson, M. F., & Leung, K. (1998). Individualism, collectivism and the handling of disagreement: A 23 country study. *International Journal of Intercultural Relations, 22,* 351-367.

Socha, T. (1997). Group communication across the life span. In L. R. Frey & J. K. Barge (Eds.), *Managing group life: Communicating in decision-making groups* (pp. 3-28). Boston: Houghton Mifflin.

Sternberg, R. J. (Ed.). (1999). *Handbook for creativity.* Cambridge, UK: Cambridge University Press.

Sternberg, R. J., & Lubart, T. I. (1995). *Defying the crowd: Cultivating creativity in a culture of conformity.* New York: Free Press.

Sue, D. W., & Sue, D. (1999). *Counseling the culturally different: Theory and practice* (3rd ed.). New York: John Wiley.

Tajfel, H. (Ed.). (1978). *Differentiation between social groups: Studies in the social psychology of intergroup relations.* New York: Academic Press.

Tajfel, H., & Turner, J. (1986). The social identity theory of intergroup behavior. In S. Worchel & W. Austin (Eds.), *The social psychology of intergroup relations* (2nd ed., pp. 7-24). Chicago: Nelson-Hall.

Tannen, D. (1990). *You just don't understand: Women and men in conversation.* New York: William Morrow.

Tannen, D. (1994). *Talking from 9 to 5.* New York: William Morrow.

Thich, N. H. (1991). *Peace is every step: The path of mindfulness in everyday life.* New York: Bantam.

Thich, N. H. (1998). *The heart of the Buddha's teaching.* Berkeley, CA: Parallex.

Thomas, K. W., & Kilmann, R. H. (1974). *Thomas-Kilmann conflict MODE instrument.* New York: XICOM, Tuxedo.

Thomas, R. R. (1990, March-April). From affirmative action to affirming diversity. *Harvard Business Review, 68,* 107-117.

Ting-Toomey, S. (1983). An analysis of verbal communication patterns in high and low marital adjustment groups. *Human Communication Research, 9,* 306-319.

Ting-Toomey, S. (1985). Toward a theory of conflict and culture. In W. Gudykunst, L. Stewart, & S. Ting-Toomey (Eds.), *Communication, culture, and organizational processes* (pp. 71-86). Beverly Hills, CA: Sage.

Ting-Toomey, S. (1986). Conflict communication styles in Black and White subjective cultures. In Y. Y. Kim (Ed.), *Interethnic communication: Current research* (pp. 75-95). Newbury Park, CA: Sage.

Ting-Toomey, S. (1988). Intercultural conflict styles: A face-negotiation theory. In Y. Kim & W. Gudykunst (Eds.), *Theories in intercultural communication* (pp. 213-235). Newbury Park, CA: Sage.

Ting-Toomey, S. (1991). Intimacy expressions in three cultures: France, Japan, and the United States. *International Journal of Intercultural Relations, 15,* 29-46.

Ting-Toomey, S. (1993). Communicative resourcefulness: An identity negotiation perspective. In R. Wiseman & J. Koester (Eds.), *Intercultural communication competence* (pp. 72-111). Newbury Park, CA: Sage.

Ting-Toomey, S. (Ed.). (1994a). *The challenge of facework: Cross-cultural and interpersonal issues.* Albany: State University of New York Press.

Ting-Toomey, S. (1994b). Managing conflict in intimate intercultural relationships. In D. Cahn (Ed.), *Intimate conflict in personal relationships* (pp. 120-147). Hillsdale, NJ: Lawrence Erlbaum.

Ting-Toomey, S. (1994c). Managing intercultural conflicts effectively. In L. Samovar & R. Porter (Eds.), *Intercultural communication: A reader* (7th ed., pp. 360-372). Belmont, CA: Wadsworth.

Ting-Toomey, S. (1997). Intercultural conflict competence. In W. R. Cupach & D. J. Canary (Eds.), *Competence in interpersonal conflict* (pp. 120-147). New York: McGraw-Hill.

Ting-Toomey, S. (1999). *Communicating across cultures.* New York: Guilford.

Ting-Toomey, S., & Cole, M. (1990). Intergroup diplomatic communication: A face-negotiation perspective. In P. Korzenny & S. Ting-Toomey (Eds.), *Communicating for peace: Diplomacy and negotiation* (pp. 77-95). Newbury Park, CA: Sage.

Ting-Toomey, S., Gao, G., Trubisky, P., Yang, Z., Kim, H. S., Lin, S.-L., & Nishida, T. (1991). Culture, face maintenance, and styles of handling interpersonal conflict: A study in five cultures. *International Journal of Conflict Management, 2,* 275-296.

Ting-Toomey, S., & Kurogi, A. (1998). Facework competence in intercultural conflict: An updated face-negotiation theory. *International Journal of Intercultural Relations, 22,* 187-225.

Ting-Toomey, S., Oetzel, J. G., & Yee-Jung, K. (in press). Self-construal types and conflict management styles. *Communication Reports.*

Ting-Toomey, S., Yee-Jung, K., Shapiro, R., Garcia, W., Wright, T., & Oetzel, J. G. (2000). Cultural/ethnic identity salience and conflict styles in four U.S. ethnic groups. *International Journal of Intercultural Relations, 24,* 47-81.

Training and Development. (1999, November). Training & Development annual trend reports: Trendz. *Training & Development, 53,* No. 1, pp. 22-43.

Triandis, H. C. (1994). *Culture and social behavior.* New York: McGraw-Hill.

Triandis, H. C. (1995a). *Individualism and collectivism.* Boulder, CO: Westview.

Triandis, H. C. (1995b). A theoretical framework for the study of diversity. In M. M. Chemers, S. Oskamp, & M. A. Costanzo (Eds.), *Diversity in organizations: New perspectives for a changing workplace* (pp. 11-36). Thousand Oaks, CA: Sage.

Trubisky, P., Ting-Toomey, S., & Lin, S.-L. (1991). The influence of individualism-collectivism and self-monitoring on conflict styles. *International Journal of Intercultural Relations, 15,* 65-84.

Tubbs, S. L., & Moss, S. (1994). *Human communication* (7th ed.). New York: McGraw-Hill.

Turner, J. C. (1975). Social comparison and social identity: Some prospects for intergroup behaviour. *European Journal of Social Psychology, 5,* 5-34.

Turner, J. C. (1987). *Rediscovering the social group.* Oxford, UK: Blackwell.

Vangelisti, A. L. (1994). Messages that hurt. In W. Cupach & B. Spitzberg (Eds.), *The dark side of interpersonal communication* (pp. 53-82). Hillsdale, NJ: Lawrence Erlbaum.

Wah, L. M. (Producer and Director). (1995). *The color of fear* [film]. (Available from Stir-Fry Seminars and Consulting, 3345 Grand Avenue, Suite 3, Oakland, CA 94610)

Watson, W. E., Kumar, K., & Michaelson, L. K. (1993). Cultural diversity's impact on interaction process and performance: Comparing homogeneous and diverse task groups. *Academy of Management Journal, 36,* 590-602.

Watson, W. E., & Michaelson, L. K. (1988). Group interaction behaviors that affect group performance on an intellective task. *Group & Organizational Studies, 13,* 495-516.

Watzlawick, P., Beavin, J., & Jackson, D. (1967). *The pragmatics of human communication.* New York: Norton.

Wehrly, B., Kenney, K. R., & Kenney, M. E. (1999). *Counseling multiracial families.* Thousand Oaks, CA: Sage.

Wheatley, M. (1999). *Leadership and the new science* (2nd ed.). San Francisco: Berrett-Koehler.

Wilmot, W., & Hocker, J. (1998). *Interpersonal conflict* (5th ed.). Boston: McGraw-Hill.

Wilson, G. L., & Hanna, M. S. (1993). *Groups in context: Leadership and participation in small groups* (3rd ed.). New York: McGraw-Hill.

Wood, J. (1997). *Gendered lives: Communication, gender, and culture* (2nd ed.). Belmont, CA: Wadsworth.

Yankelovich, D. (1999). *The magic of dialogue: Transforming conflict into cooperation.* New York: Simon & Schuster.

Yazzie. (1995, Spring). Traditional Navajo dispute resolution in the Navajo Peacemaker Court. *NIDR Forum,* 5-16.

INDEX

ABOUT THE AUTHORS

Stella Ting-Toomey, Ph.D., is Professor of Speech Communication at California State University at Fullerton. She is the author and editor of 12 books, most recently *Communicating Across Cultures* (1999) and *Communicating Effectively With the Chinese* (coauthored, 1998). She teaches courses in interpersonal conflict management, intercultural communication theory, and intercultural communication training. She is the creator of conflict face-negotiation theory. Her research interests focus on testing and refining the conflict face-negotiation theory and the cultural/ethnic identity-negotiation theory. She has held major leadership roles in international communication associations and has served on numerous editorial boards. She is an experienced trainer in the area of transcultural competence issues and has lectured widely throughout the United States, Asia, and Europe on the theme of mindful conflict management.

John G. Oetzel, Ph.D., is Assistant Professor at the University of New Mexico. He teaches courses in intercultural, group, and organizational communication, as well as research methods in the Department of Communication and Journalism. His research interests focus on investigating communication in culturally diverse groups and organizations and understanding how to effectively manage conflict in these contexts. His work has appeared in journals such as *Human Communication Research, Management Communication Quarterly, Small Group Research, Communication Reports,* and the *International Journal of Intercultural Relations.*